Welcome the Traveler Home

Welcome the Traveler Home

JIM GARLAND'S STORY OF THE KENTUCKY MOUNTAINS

Edited by Julia S. Ardery

Garland, Jim, and Julia S. Ardery. Welcome the Traveler Home: Jim Garland's Story of the Kentucky Mountains. Lexington, KY: U of Kentucky, 1983. Print.

THE UNIVERSITY PRESS OF KENTUCKY

Copyright © 1983 by The University Press of Kentucky

Scholarly publisher for the Commonwealth serving Berea College, Centre College of Kentucky, Eastern Kentucky University, The Filson Club, Georgetown College, Kentucky Historical Society, Kentucky State University, Morehead State University, Murray State University, Northern Kentucky University, Transylvania University, University of Kentucky, University of Louisville, and Western Kentucky University.

Editorial and Sales Offices: Lexington, Kentucky 40506-0024

Library of Congress Cataloging in Publication Data

Garland, Jim, 1905-1978.
   Welcome the traveler home.

   Bibliography: p.
   Discography: p.
   Includes index.
    1. Mountain life—Kentucky. 2. Kentucky—Social life and customs. 3. Garland, Jim, 1905-1978. I. Ardery, Julia S., 1953-   . II. Title.
F456.G28   1982   976.9'00943   80-50564
ISBN 0-8131-1432-2

Contents

Foreword by Thomas N. Bethell   vii
Editor's Introduction   xxxi

Introduction   1
1. The Wilderness   3
2. The Logger's Away, The Miller's at Home   9
3. Bad Blood   17
4. Meat Skins   23
5. The Feast   35
6. The Legendary Bad John Garland   42
7. Here We Come A'Roving   50
8. Woman's Work   61
9. Cocks, Hounds, Foxes, Kick-outs   69
10. Holiness People   80
11. Shooting from the Solid   88
12. Sparks and Dust   102
13. Out-scab the Scabs, 1923-1924   111
14. Hard Times at Coleman's Mine, 1924-1928   122
15. Bloody Harlan   133
16. Grabbing at Straws: The National Miners Union   143
17. Won't the Bosses Be Surprised   154
18. In the Footsteps of Harry Simms   166
19. Reading between the Lines   175
20. I Don't Want Your Millions, Mister   189

Bibliography   203
Discography   209
Index   225

Illustrations follow page 128

Foreword

These are the stories of a traveling man. He came into the world in 1905 at a place called Fourmile in the mountains of southeastern Kentucky, a quiet place in a quiet time poised on the edge of permanent disruption. Great changes were just beginning to sweep across the mountains. They caught him up and carried him along, whether he wanted to go or not, and in that sense he was a traveler despite himself. But he wanted to know where he was headed, and he thought he had a right to have some say about it. He was his own guide across time and geography, and he managed to keep track, in his head, of where he was, what he saw, what he heard, what he came to believe, what he chose finally to remember.

Jim Garland was not a historian, and this is not, strictly speaking, history. It is a book filled with folklore and music, but he did not make a full-time career either as a folklorist or as a musician. He was not a sociologist or an anthropologist, nor in any other way officially accredited to study the human condition, and there is in this book no single thread or thesis that would pass any of the tests of academia. But that is part of the special quality of this book. He brings his own credentials.

This is a personal record, then. But it is not so much an autobiography as it is a recalling of the people and events and ideas that made an impact on Jim Garland one way or another, helping him to construct an understanding of the world into which he happened to be thrown by accident of birth. He lived through times that deserve hurlyburly adjectives — *roiled, convulsive, tumultuous*. From first-hand experience he knew about hunger, violent death and injury in the mines, strikes, blacklists, murderous gun thugs, clandestine meetings, fear, Red-baiting, desperate poverty, the Great Depression in all its infamy. He speaks here not as a scholar but as a survivor. Others can write of these same times with much greater omniscience, with olympian detachment or with passionate outpourings of theory buttressed by long hours in the library. This is a different kind of record entirely.

It is the testament of a working man — a man whose immediate first priority was to endure, and after that to feed himself and his wife and children, every day, three times a day if possible, and after that (and only then) to reflect upon what it all might mean. It is a working man's recollection of the best and worst of his times, an eyewitness account filtered through memory — his own and others — and compiled in bits and pieces, fits and starts, when time and circumstances allowed. As such it is not always a complete record, not always consistent, sometimes confusing, occasionally contradictory.

Jim Garland lived in a world he wanted to change. He tried hard. With hindsight it is possible to see that he succeeded to some extent — certainly less than he hoped to, but probably more than he ever knew. He wanted to know. He wanted desperately to know what was happening to his world while he was still part of it and wrestling with it. He wanted to know why it offered so much resistance to improvement; he wanted to find the handles. He was raised up thinking of himself as a free citizen in a free country, and when he found out at an early age that the facts were otherwise, he worked hard to figure out why that was, who was responsible, what could be done about them. In this he was not very different from millions of other working men and women then and now. What sets Jim Garland apart from most people is that he persisted, and that he got it all down on paper.

Toward the end of his life he was able to go back to look at where he had come from, to talk with some of the people who were still there — at least there in place if not in time. He could try, and did try, to corroborate his recollections (at the same time that he gave others a priceless opportunity to dust off their own). In this respect he was able to do something that most working people can never hope to do. But in every other respect this is a book that many other people have contributed to, and might have written themselves, if only they had found a way. So it is their book as well as his, and because of that it deserves a place of respect alongside the more conventional efforts to assess these same times — these extraordinary times through which Jim Garland traveled, watching, listening, and, most of all, participating.

As the Editor's Introduction explains, Jim did not intend this book to be an autobiography, but you need at least a rough sketch of his life in order to appreciate the range and scope he brings to bear on the writing of his book. The time and place of his birth have already been mentioned. Fourmile is in Bell County, in the tumbled foothills of the Cumberland Mountains, almost within sight of the bluegrass country but philosophically and historically not a part of that world.

"I am a true mountain person," Jim Garland declares in the first paragraphs of his narrative, and you should approach that deceptively simple statement with proper caution. Millions of words and almost as much film and television footage have contributed to the piling up of layer upon layer of misrepresentation about the people with whom Jim Garland claims general kinship. He has his own authoritative point of view, and you will find him, throughout this book, insisting on setting the record — as he understands it — straight.

His own record traces back to 1637, when Garlands coming from England arrived in Boston and then, over time, made their way southward, migrating across Virginia and on into the mountains. He is proud that they could survive quite well with "a pack mule, a hound dog, parched corn, salt, string, and fishhooks," and he writes of their world with admiration: it was hard but not unjust, rugged but not cruel. His ancestors were free to run their own lives and make their own decisions, not always in conformity with convention. A great-grandmother was a full-blooded Cherokee, and he had grandfathers on both sides of the Civil War.

It was in his father's time that the demands of industrial America began to overpower the delicate agrarian equilibrium within which the Garlands lived. Unwittingly they had already put their economic independence in jeopardy, because they tended to divide and subdivide their tillable land from generation to generation. When they could no longer count on the land for subsistence, they fell prey to economic forces they could not hope to control. Worse, they could not even hope to meet those forces with a united front — because, as Jim points out, the spirit of neighborliness in the mountains survived only "until there remained no more unclaimed farm land for people to take up." After that point had been passed, people tended to spend more and more of their time pursuing local jealousies, grievances, and feuds, all of which tended to distract their attention from an immediate and much greater threat.

In distant places like Philadelphia and Pittsburgh and New York, men who had never met the Garlands were making plans for them. Coal deposits, great in quantity and quality, lay beneath the mountains of Kentucky. Between 1870 and 1900 title to those deposits was aquired by men who could foresee a day when the steel mills and power plant boilers and locomotives of America would need every ton of black gold that the mines could disgorge.

Someone would have to mine it, of course. And because coal from southeastern Kentucky would have to compete for markets against coal from the mines of Illinois, Indiana, Ohio, Pennsylvania, and northern West Virginia, mine owners would have to produce Kentucky coal on the cheap. The competing coalfields were all closer to the major markets, and their reserves were so large that they could meet any possible demand for centuries to come without help from Kentucky. This was widely known at the time; in a rational, orderly world, the mines of Kentucky might never have been developed at all. But the men who owned the coal of Kentucky believed they could compete successfully, and there was a vicious kind of truth to that belief. They simply didn't intend to pay miners much for the honor of digging their coal. They would clear land on the hillsides and put up company houses because there were few existing towns; they would fill the company houses with mountaineers in need of work. They would pay those men a reasonable wage if the market permitted. But they did not intend to lie awake at night worrying about the financial well-being of their employees, any more than they would worry about the safety of the miners or about what should be done for miners too old or too battered to work any more.

The prevailing view of the day was that nobody *had* to be a miner, after all — it was a voluntary decision, and you made your choice and took the consequences. From its earliest days, the coal industry of southeastern Kentucky was something to avoid if you could. Most of the Garlands couldn't. They needed work. And the only work available — except for the hardscrabble hillside farms that could no longer reliably support large families — was in the mines.

Jim Garland's father tried, for a time, to avoid either of these alternatives by operating a general store. But when he allowed miners to buy on credit during a strike, he put the store at risk; when the strike collapsed, he went broke. After that, he worked intermittently in the mines, and was the first of the Garlands to experience the hazards that lay there with the coal: he was caught in a slate fall, and the accident left him blind for three years — probably the victim of a concussion or damaged nerves or some other relatively straightforward affliction that went undiagnosed and untreated, a common experience for miners. Jim's brothers were drawn into the mines, too, one after another — one at the age of fourteen, another at twelve, another at nine. And, one after another, they too suffered there: Jim saw his oldest brother, Bob, carried home a cripple; his brother Richard died under a two-ton fall of slate that broke his neck.

Jim wanted none of that. He made other plans for himself. After completing common school, he would go on to a church-run settlement school, and then away to college. He got off to a fast start, completing the eight grades of common school in four years. But then, in 1919, with his father ill, he had to help support the family — a family of fifteen — and that meant following his brothers. He went into the mines when he was thirteen years old and spent most of the next fourteen years making his living as a coaldigger, down on his knees in the low seams under the Cumberlands, in the mines known collectively as the Harlan coalfield.

The Garlands still prided themselves on their independent thinking, but his father had understood enough about the impersonal economic weight massed against them to join the United Mine Workers of America. The union had successfully organized many of the new southern mines around the turn of the century. The Harlan field was opened in 1910, at the beginning of a boom when it sometimes seemed as though the nation's industrial growth and demand for coal would be without limit. Riding the boom, coal operators were generally willing to deal with the UMW rather than risk the possibility of being shut down in a strike while competitors made off with hatfuls of cash. The operators had not yet learned how to stick together in defiance of the union's demands. During World War I, demand for steel surpassed all expectations. Harlan coal was ideal for coking, and the operators could, almost literally, name their own price. The UMW took the opportunity to demand higher wages and better working conditions and, when the operators balked, shut down the whole field for a time in 1917. The union and the operators were summoned to Washington by the Wilson administration and a contract was worked out in short order. Operators who might have been willing to fight to the death under other circumstances were desperate to get back into production; coal prices were tripling, and the potential profits were so mind-boggling that accommodation with the UMW was almost painless.

But no sooner had the armistice of 1918 been signed than everything changed. Operating at full capacity, the coal industry at the beginning of 1919 could produce nearly 30 percent more coal than the nation could consume under reduced peacetime demand. Moreover, the industry was still expanding rapidly, because thousands of new mines developed during the war were still coming into production. By 1920, the industry's total productive capacity was 11 percent higher than it had been the previous year, although demand was about that much lower. This trend continued, ominously, for years. Long after the war-profits game had ended, mine owners were still trying to get into it; production from the mines of Kentucky increased steadily until 1927, even though demand shrank, almost as steadily, throughout this entire period. Nothing dissuaded the mine owners, not even rapidly increasing competition from oil and natural gas. As a group, they seemed to operate on the assumption that if worse came to worst, they could pay their miners less and still get by.

Worse came to worst at just about the exact moment that Jim Garland first went down into the mines to make a living. The UMW that he joined was, in theory, the same union to which his father belonged, but in District 19 — the union's designation for the organized mines of Tennessee and southeastern Kentucky — it was verging on serious trouble. Mine operators no longer able to command high prices in secure markets were already looking for ways to cut production costs. This would be done, for the most part, at the expense of the UMW and its members, and it would be done with a savagery unsurpassed in the annals of American labor relations.

Some of the larger companies could cut costs by bringing in coal-cutting machines and other labor-saving machinery. Those companies might still pay reasonably adequate wages, but those wages were paid to fewer men. The cast-offs were, of course, expected to fend for themselves, even to the point of being driven from their homes — because those homes belonged to the company, and a man could live in a company house only so long as he was on the company's payroll. When he lost his job, he lost his home — and he had to move out of town, because the town belonged to the company too.

The smaller companies lacked either the capital or the foresight to mechanize. The great governing principle of supply and demand was, to them, as immaterial as theories of agronomy would be to a pig. They knew things were getting worse, but they thought that maybe after a while things would get better. Meanwhile it was only a matter of common sense to go ahead and develop new mines, because that was what they knew how to do, and they wanted to have the productive capacity ready as soon as market conditions improved. Thus they created an ever-expanding surplus, guaranteeing that there could be no demand for higher-priced coal. From a macro-economic perspective this was madness, but they lived in a world of micro-horizons. For them, the simplest expedient was to cut wages, contract or no contract. There were, of course, many men looking for work, so miners who were lucky enough to have jobs were under intense pressure to accept whatever wages the operators were willing to pay.

For a time the situation in the Harlan coalfields was full of apparent contradictions. The naked eye could clearly see evidence of a continuing boom. All through the 1920s, new mines were being opened up, new company houses built. See the long trains loaded with coal? They go out full, they come back empty. Every day, every night. Must be a market *somewhere*. Otherwise, why open all these mines? On the other hand, miners' wages were being cut every few months, mines sometimes worked only two or three days a week, and operators complained bitterly about the competition. It was feckless griping, of course; they were really complaining about themselves.

The Louisville & Nashville Railroad contributed greatly to the confusion for many years by offering the Harlan operators a favorable freight rate to the Great Lakes. This was not a matter of altruism. Coal constituted about 25 percent of the L&N's traffic. The railroad had a vested interest in getting Harlan coal to distant markets at a delivered cost that would permit competition against coal being mined much closer to those markets — coal which was carried on other railroads. The L&N subsidized its low coal rates by charging high rates to other customers shipping other kinds of freight. When the Interstate Commerce Commission barred this practice, the railroad was abruptly forced to raise its coal rates in 1929. This had the effect of suddenly putting even greater pressure on the smaller operators to cut their costs — just months before the stock market collapse of October 1929 threw the entire nation into economic chaos. When that happened, the demand for coal fell off so swiftly — about 30 percent in the course of a few months — that the entire industry suddenly found itself at the edge of ruin.

Jim Garland writes nostalgically of the days when miners and mine operators were on friendly terms with each other, and he draws a distinction, from memory, between amiable local operators and ruthless absentee barons. But in reality the distinction blurs. True, the local bosses were real people with real faces, and on good days you could joke with them, and they might even do you small favors from time to time, but the overriding fact is that all of the operators, great and small, contributed alike to the industry's troubles, falling into a trap that they had dug for themselves. And they had used tens of thousands of men like Jim Garland to do the digging. Call it greed, or shortsightedness, or free enterprise, or what you will: the inescapable fact is that the problems of the coal industry were widely foreseen and highly predictable. The industry operated like a man traveling around the world on a stolen credit card. It was obvious, for a long time, that sooner or later the law would catch up. When the law of supply and demand finally overtook the mine operators during the Depression, they tried, in desperation, to present the bill to the miners.

Jim Garland was one of those who refused to pay. "I'm not a brave man and never was," he said years later, "but if we had to wait for heroes to win our battles we'd never have won any." When the Depression began in earnest for the rest of the nation, he already knew what it was like. He was a veteran. He had been mining coal for more than a decade. In that time he served his union as a local officer and saw, close up, the UMW's inability to hold the gains that had been won in 1917. At the union's headquarters in Indianapolis, John L. Lewis might clearly discern the great principle that confronted the mine workers — when too many men want work at any price it is all too easy to break a strike — but Jim Garland had the perspective of an infantryman in the trenches, called out to make one suicidal charge after another. The union's strikes in the Harlan field during the 1920s were like that. The union lost all of them. Jim tired of hearing that the union would provide relief for strikers, only to learn later that no relief would be forthcoming. It made no difference to him that the union was under attack all over the country, was unable to collect dues from men working only a day or two a week or not at all, and could not possibly bear the costs of a genuine strike-relief effort that might last months or years. What he knew, and what thousands of other miners knew, was that the union had asked them to stand up and be counted, and that when they stood they found themselves standing alone, exposed, no sign of the union behind them.

Under the circumstances it is not surprising that men like Jim Garland finally turned elsewhere. Some simply gave up, deciding that there was no future in fighting. They took whatever the operators offered, and if nothing was offered, they went on relief or hopped a freight and went off in search of work somewhere else. Other men, driven to the point of desperation by the sight of their wives and children withering away on a diet of beans and bulldog gravy (flour, water, grease), chose to fight. It was not really a matter of choice; they simply could see no alternative. They found themselves in a war of survival, and they fought.

In this war, however, the other side had almost all the weapons. The Hoover administration rejected the idea that the federal government had any responsibility to citizens victimized by economic forces that had run amok. This meant that miners were at the mercy of state and local governments, and in 1931 those governments were controlled by the same men who controlled the mines. The mine owners had, in fact, a variety of weapons. They had machine guns, rifles, shotguns, and dynamite. They had money enough to pay mine guards and sheriff's deputies, men who knew how to use the guns and bombs. They controlled the courts. They could search houses without warrants and issue injunctions without cause. They could and did prosecute men for criminal syndicalism without ever troubling to define the term. And they could kill, if necessary, without much fear of the consequences. Jim Garland's war was, in short, one in which the odds of surviving, intact, were very poor.

Those odds were not markedly improved by the arrival on the scene of the National Miners Union — but at the time the NMU looked good to Jim Garland. In the remoteness of the coalfields it was not a matter of great concern to him that the NMU was under the control of the Communist party, and he could not have known much about its previous failed efforts to support strikes in other coalfields. What he knew was that the NMU was willing to send organizers to Harlan, that it was willing to provide lawyers for the defense of miners taken prisoner in the war and willing to operate soup kitchens to sustain unemployed, blacklisted strikers and their families.

Moreover, the NMU encouraged the miners' wives to participate in the strike by organizing auxiliaries — something the UMW had never done — and its publicists did a remarkably effective job of calling conditions in the coalfields to the attention of the public at large. The mine wars of the mountains were largely a matter of local concern until the NMU arrived; within a few months, magazine and newspaper readers from Massachusetts to California knew about "bloody Harlan," and even if the battlefield dispatches sometimes were distorted by revolutionary rhetoric, the stark facts were gripping enough. For many people they were unforgettable — absolute proof that the American laissez-faire economic system had gone berserk and would have to be transformed into something more humane if not replaced entirely.

The strike of 1931-32 failed by every objective standard. It ended with the United Mine Workers no longer on the scene at all and with the bloodied remains of the National Miners Union scattered, its most prominent organizer killed and martyred and some of its strongest supporters, like Jim Garland, no longer able to live in the coalfields at all. The story of that strike, of the circumstances leading up to it, its principal events, and its aftermath, is described further below, and it forms a large part of Jim Garland's narrative. Suffice to say here that it cannot be judged by objective standards alone; it had, as noted, a marked and lasting impact on public consciousness. It was certainly one of many events in the Depression that led directly to the election of Franklin Roosevelt and the construction of the New Deal, in the sense that it helped give impetus to the wide belief that government did indeed have a responsibility to care for the victims of the "business cycle," as *Fortune* delicately described the wreckage of Wall Street's collapse. When Roosevelt's director of relief, Harry Hopkins, proclaimed flatly that "hunger is not debatable," numberless people who remembered the news from Harlan could not fail to agree with him, and for years they voted their convictions. On the other hand, those who believed that the striking Harlan miners were the vanguard of the second American revolution were bitterly disappointed by the discovery that the revolution was not to be. And in the mountains the strike that began in desperate defiance ended, for some men, in the grave. So there is no way, really, to judge the failed NMU strike of 1931-32 by strictly "objective" standards. It makes better sense, for the moment, to look at the effect that the strike had on one of its leading participants.

The strike was certainly the single most important event in Jim Garland's life, an event for which he took some of the responsibility and for which he was willing to suffer the consequences, and an event that never really ended for him. It shaped his political beliefs. Somehow he came out of it with humor, with hope, and with very little bitterness. But it also complicated his life in ways he could never have anticipated. Afterward he was a mountain man who could not live in the mountains, an organizer of miners who would never again be able to work with them as one of them. Jim Garland could not live safely in Kentucky in the months immediately after the strike ended, and except for a brief time he never lived there again, but his life was so much a part of Kentucky that the years lived elsewhere seemed a little incomplete — sketchy, somehow, and even a little *jittery*. Perhaps intentionally, perhaps not, he writes of them that way.

The first months and years must have seemed particularly bizarre. For all practical purposes, he was a political exile in a nation that rejects the idea that it has any. He went to New York, for his own safety and because the party recognized that he would be a valuable fund-raiser. He could rent an apartment there, with the help of the party. He could go to Washington and appear before a Senate hearing on coalfield conditions. He and his half-sister, Aunt Molly Jackson, and his youngest sister Sarah Ogan Gunning could write and sing songs of protest, and young people in New York and at colleges all over the East would listen in fascination to the flat hard keening songs, the words direct and tough and the music borrowing heavily from its origins in church singing. And the songs, two of them in particular — *I Don't Want Your Millions, Mister* and *The Ballad of Harry Simms* — made Jim something of a celebrity. He would meet Woody Guthrie and Cisco Houston and Earl Robinson, Pete Seeger and Lee Hays and Leadbelly, and he would sing with them in Greenwich Village on Sundays at the headquarters of the Almanac Singers. He would even have his own radio program for a while, and he would perform at the 1939 World's Fair.

But at first he was not content to stay in New York. He wanted to go back to Kentucky, to work with the miners he had left behind, and he was unhappy when the party delayed letting him go because it valued him so much as a fundraiser in New York. Then, when he did go, he found that it was impossible to organize unemployed miners without reasonably adequate financial support, which the party promised but did not deliver. He tried then to get by on his own, working a little doghole mine that produced just enough coal to bring in just enough money to keep him and his wife and daughter just this side of malnutrition, but the mine caved in while Hazel was pregnant with their second child, and she and Jim decided it was time to go back to New York.

This time he stayed. It was not long before he grew bored with the Communist party. Its heavy emphasis on ponderous theory seemed, as he writes, "all feathers and no meat," and its meetings struck him as so much "yak-yak-yak." He shifted gears, becoming less of an organizer and more of a folk singer, participating in demonstrations but not leading them, talking to college students about the miners and their music; the next time he went to Kentucky, it was to record miners for the Library of Congress.

To survive in New York he took jobs that were vastly different from anything he had ever done in Kentucky. He worked for the Works Progress Administration (WPA), the New Deal jobs program, and to supplement his income he rented a pushcart and worked as a food vendor in Union Square. In the winter he sold hot chestnuts from a baby carriage rigged up with a charcoal burner — the kind of makeshift operation that many a self-sufficient Kentucky miner would admire. He worked as a janitor in a church and took a job helping to operate a broom factory that employed blind workers. And he sang songs of protest, his songs about miners and millionaires.

World War II took him farther away, to a job at a shipyard on the West Coast. Thousands of miles from Kentucky he found a degree of stability that had eluded him before. At the end of the war, knowing what was to come, he figured out a way to survive the inevitable layoff at the shipyard; using his past experience in New York, he opened a broom-and-mop manufacturing shop employing handicapped people. He doesn't dwell on this point in his narrative, but it is not surprising that Jim Garland ultimately found a way to make money without making it at the expense of other people. He operated his small factory for 21 years.

His music stayed with him wherever he went, whatever else he was doing. In the 1940s he and Hazel and their children and a friend who played fiddle began playing on Saturday nights for a club in Vancouver, Washington, a few miles away from his home in Washougal. They called themselves the Garland Orchestra, and when word got around that they were pretty good, they began getting invited to play for union locals. Sometimes they got paid, sometimes they didn't. Jim took it upon himself to do a little more organizing — this time a group of musicians called the 50/50 Club. Whenever they played for pay, they got 50 percent of the gate and the organization they played for kept the other half. It was a way to raise money, for organizations and candidates that Jim approved of. The music and the organizing persisted, together, although the sources of the music and the sources of Jim's political beliefs were a long way away.

During the last fifteen years of Jim Garland's life he was able to go home again, not quite literally but more in the sense of paying homage to where he had come from, and in letting other people know something of who he was and what he stood for. His songs of protest had been part of the political coming-of-age of young men and women in the 1930s; when he went to sing at the Newport Folk Festival in 1963 he became a part of the same process thirty years later. He sang the old songs and reminded people of Harry Simms, dead long before they had been born; he wrote new songs, sometimes deceptively good-humored, about the emerging civil rights battles of the 1960s —

They sell us the same colored hat —
Now what do you think about that?
   If so different we be
   In this land of the free
Why do they sell us the same colored hat?

He joined the "so-called retired," as he put it, in 1966, but he never retired in fact. He worked on his book. He sang on radio programs and in concerts, sometimes with his daughter Betty. He went to Kentucky for Folkways Records to record old friends and new acquaintances singing songs and telling stories. He visited with friends from the 1930s and sat up late into the night remembering how it was in the mine wars. He went to Washington twice to participate in folk festivals sponsored by the Smithsonian Institution. He never seemed to lecture people about remembering the 1930s, but he had no intention of letting them forget. He had helped to make history, and then he had gone on with the business of his own life, the business of making a living and raising a family — but he was still tied to the mountains, to the mine wars, to an old and honorable battle for fundamental principles, and most of all to the miners and organizers who gave a good account of themselves against terrible odds. Across the years he had done a good bit of traveling, and was proud of it, but really he had never left home.

Volumes could be written about the mine wars in which Jim Garland fought, without doing proper justice to the participants. The problem is with saying too much or too little. To say nothing at all would be to leave many readers of Jim's narrative in a state of befuddlement, because he is, like anyone dealing in recollections, not particularly concerned with chronology, and because he saw the battles from within the trenches. But his friend Harry Simms used to tell him that "everything has a material base," and the only way to get at an understanding of the material base beneath the great mine wars of the 1930s is to put them in context.

The general characteristics of the American coal industry in the years before the 1931 mine wars have been mentioned already, but the point bears emphasizing that although the Harlan coalfields exploded in political violence during the Depression, the pressure had been building for more than a decade. This was an industry with too many mines in production, too many men available for hire at whatever price an operator was willing to pay, and it was an industry with no capacity for self-regulation. Sooner or later something had to give.

At the top there were Morgans and Insulls and Mellons and Rockefellers, commanding vast coal holdings and unlimited resources for their development. Left to their own devices, the great barons would doubtless have moved swiftly to form a classic cartel capable of limiting production, forcing up prices, and divvying the cash. To some extent this was done in the anthracite fields of northeastern Pennsylvania, and sporadic efforts were made in that direction in the northern bituminous coalfields of western Pennsylvania, northern West Virginia, Ohio, Indiana, and Illinois. But even there the cartel structure could not be made to work efficiently, at least not for long, because the coal reserves of the United States were simply so vast that not even the great barons could get a lock on the supply. When they made compacts among themselves, someone else would spoil the fun by shipping coal from some other source at a lower price. The railroads in the early years of the century were still expanding and looking for new sources of freight; even more importantly, almost anybody could get into the coal-mining business. Lacking total control of reserves, the barons could not prevent numberless small entrepreneurs from opening mines, whenever and wherever the opportunity arose.

Well before the Louisville & Nashville Railroad ran its first tracks up into the remoteness of Harlan County in 1910, the coal industry was already showing unmistakable signs of developing more productive capacity than there was demand. Once created, this problem would be alleviated only by the demands of two world wars and, to a lesser extent, by the intervention of the federal government during the New Deal, and it would still be a key characteristic of the coal industry going into the last twenty years of this century. Along the way, it would precipitate a sickening series of rollercoaster boom-bust cycles, very nearly destroy the coal miners' principal union, and cause unspeakable personal tragedies for men, women, and children beyond the counting.

The opening of the Harlan coalfields was part and parcel of this irrationality. The impetus for development of this coal, locked up deep beneath mountains that might otherwise have remained in a state of rural semi-wilderness for decades, came primarily from three sources. Businessmen in Philadelphia who had acquired title to the coal between 1870 and 1900 looked at the profits being made by mine owners elsewhere and decided that they wanted a piece of the action (although, being upstanding Philadelphia businessmen, they certainly would not have put it that way). The L&N was expanding and looking for new sources of large-volume freight: coal was ideal. And, finally, tests of core-drilled Harlan coal showed that it would be excellent for coking, the process enabling blast furnaces to produce high-quality steel.

It was this third factor that swiftly attracted some of America's largest corporations to the Harlan field. They could obtain metallurgical-quality coal elsewhere, but Harlan offered them the opportunity to move in and lock up large supplies of it rather than relying on other producers. In short order, Wisconsin Steel (International Harvester), United States Steel, Peabody Coal Company, General Motors and Ford were all busily engaged in buying up tracts of coal and developing mines.

The L&N carried their coal, and it carried coal for the general Great Lakes market — coal going to the boilers of power plants, to produce heat and light for Chicago, Detroit, Duluth and the other lakeside cities and towns. Soon the mine operators began to experience chronic shortages of railroad hopper cars. Deliveries to large-volume customers — the utilities particularly — were erratic. In classic fashion, this problem was "solved" not by forcing the L&N to supply more cars but, typically, by Detroit-Edison coming down to Harlan to dig its own coal in its own mine and ship the coal in its own railroad cars. The so-called captive mines — those whose output did not enter the commercial market — were a noteworthy anomaly. Ostensibly they were developed to help stabilize supply; in fact they simply contributed to the excess capacity of the industry. By 1928 they would account for nearly half of the total output o the Harlan field.

The development of that field took place with extraordinary speed. There were three mines operating in Harlan County in 1911 with a combined output of about 18,000 tons. They employed 170 miners, more or less full-time. By the beginning of 1929 there were 60 mines operating in the county, production had reached nearly 15,000,000 tons, and more than 10,000 men were working in the mines. The total population of the county in that short span of time had gone from 10,000 to 64,000.

Much of this growth had taken place since the end of World War I — and this, too, was illogical, because the coal industry was already thoroughly overdeveloped in terms of its potential peacetime market. But in the 1920s the idea of economic planning was anathema everywhere in the United States. Certainly it was not considered a responsibility of the federal government. If the industry wanted to develop itself beyond all reason, why not?

There was, however, more to the growth of the industry than met the eye. It was not just a matter of unbridled free enterprise. In the northern coalfields, the United Mine Workers and the mine operators had for some time been moving toward a degree of accommodation with each other. When coal markets and prices moved generally upward in the immediate prewar and wartime years, the UMW succeeded in negotiating improved contracts — not everywhere in the north by any means, but generally. Then, after the war, with the market softening and prices wobbling, pressure began building to supply coal at lower prices. Locked into their contracts, the northern operators could not freely cut their costs by arbitrarily lowering the wages paid to their miners. But the union had a much more tenuous hold in the southern coalfields; the southern operators moved swiftly into the northern markets, and prepared to hold those markets by cutting production costs whenever necessary. The success with which they did it is probably best illustrated by statistics on coal shipments to the Great Lakes. Southern mines accounted for only 14 percent of all traffic to the lakes in 1909. By 1925, they accounted for 73 percent.

Those numbers reflect several things. They show, of course, that the center of the bituminous coal industry was shifting southward, very quickly. From another perspective, they show that it was a runaway industry. Northern mines could supply the lakes trade for centuries to come — but the southern operators were finding ways to do it at lower cost. In this respect the coal industry's experiences ran parallel to the abandonment of northern mills by the textile industry. Both operated on the premise that the nation offered an inexhaustible supply of labor, and that when labor costs stabilized in one area the obvious solution was to move to another.

And the numbers show, finally, that it behooved the miners to build themselves a first-class union; otherwise they would be divided and conquered. But a first-class union was beyond the reach of the miners in the 1920s. Throughout this period, the United Mine Workers was a house divided — ripped apart by internal struggles for power between John L. Lewis and his opponents, and weakened further every time it failed to hold a group of companies under contract. With the dues base of the union declining all through the 1920s, the union could not mount the kind of sustained relief effort without which strikes cannot be won. More fundamentally, the union confronted the terrible reality that there were too many men looking for jobs in the industry.

This had to do, of course, with the general contraction of the industry after the war. Pressure on the operators to lower the cost of production stimulated mechanization, and mechanization meant layoffs. Every week throughout the 1920s thousands of men were set adrift in a deepening sea of unemployment. The industry had jobs for nearly 640,000 men in almost 9,000 mines in 1920, and those mines were working 220 days a year, on the average. By 1929 the number of jobs had dropped to about 500,000 and the number of operating mines had fallen to about 6,000, working an average of 219 days a year. By 1932, in the bottom of the Great Depression, employment had dropped to 406,000 — the lowest level since 1904 — and the number of operating mines had dropped to about 5,400, working less than 150 days a year on the average. Nearly a quarter of a million mining jobs had simply disappeared. Those miners still clinging to their jobs were working one-third fewer days at hourly wages slashed to half — or less than half — their previous level. It was a rare miner who could dare to stand up to the boss about anything. Too many other men were out there in the shadows waiting for his job.

Even if the UMW had not been troubled by internal turmoil, it could hardly have hoped to prevail against such odds and in a climate of such widespread apprehension, uncertainty, and fear. The union tried and failed. John L. Lewis ordered industry-wide strikes three times in the 1920s, all of them desperate responses to unceasing pressure by the mine owners to cut wages. The first strike, in 1922, ended in a stalemate after 20 weeks, but Lewis declared it a victory because the union had not actually lost ground. The second strike, in 1924, was narrowly averted at the last minute, largely because there was a temporary increase in coal demand and the mine operators saw an opportunity to profit by it. But the third strike was a disaster. After negotiations for a new contract deadlocked early in 1927, Lewis felt that he had no alternative to calling the miners out, and a general industry-wide strike began in April. It lasted, technically, for 15 months, until Lewis cancelled the strike order in July 1928. But the notice from headquarters was a formality. Long before that, most mines were back in operation, working either with scab labor or with union men drawn back by the specter of starvation. Lewis told district officers to settle for the best terms they could get. Translated, this meant they were on their own, and the "best" terms were those the operators offered — those few operators who were still willing to work with the union at all. The union was, in fact, all but dead. About 70 percent of all bituminous coal production came from union mines in 1919; by 1930 the union could claim less than 20 percent, and that claim, as government statisticians demonstrated, was probably inflated.

In the coal camps of Kentucky the United Mine Workers had found especially tough going. To some extent this was their own fault: In his deployment of organizers, Lewis placed greater value on loyalty than on skill, and his man in District 19, Bill Turnblazer, was widely known for the zeal with which he avoided making personal appearances in Harlan. But the main reason that the union made such little headway was that the mine operators owned the entire territory, flat out.

About three-fourths of the miners in Harlan County lived in company towns. They lived there at the company's pleasure and could be turned out instantly at the company's whim. The operators knew how to deal with troublemakers. Violence was always possible but not always necessary. A miner could be fired for any reason or for no reason at all, and a man who lost his job for union activity had nowhere to turn. The blacklist was real and foolproof. Even if a job opened up somewhere nearby, you couldn't qualify for it unless you could produce a letter of recommendation from the superintendent of your last mine.

Company guards served as deputy sheriffs. Deputy sheriffs served as company thugs. The law and the company were indistinguishable. When the sheriff of Harlan County, the infamous John Henry Blair, acknowledged in 1932 that he had 180 deputies on his payroll — an amazing ratio of one deputy for every 60 miners in the county — it was learned that all but three of them were being paid not from county funds but by the coal companies. This was, perhaps, a technical distinction, since the county funds came solely — almost solely — from the operators. They paid for the law, the law was what they bought. The sheriff himself owned mines, as did the county judge and the prosecutor. Deputies were paid per arrest, and jurors were paid only for convictions. Miners, since they owned no property and paid no property taxes, were barred from jury duty; a miner on trial would not be judged by his peers. In the coal camps even the roads were private property, and a UMW organizer walking up the road could be arrested for trespassing. Men stopping to talk were subject to arrest for "banding and confederating." When a man failed to show up for work on Monday morning, a deputy would likely as not come banging into the bedroom to verify that the miner was sick. If he wanted to search the house for union literature, he needed no warrant because the house belonged to the company and he worked for the company. Some of the coal camps had their own private jails, and the jailer's stipend was determined by the number of prisoners. At least one camp was kept closed at all times by a padlocked cable stretched across the only access road. If you wanted to drive in or out, you had to get the key from the mine superintendent.

The totality with which the operators controlled life in the mountains defies exaggeration. They ran the schools — and the per-pupil expenditures of the coal-camp schools of Kentucky in 1932 stood at roughly one-fourth the statewide average, at a time when Kentucky ranked 44th among all the states. They operated the clinics and paid the doctors (deducting a fee from each miner's paycheck) — and infant mortality rates were three times the national average. They made the miner buy his tools from the company shop (and deducted a fee for sharpening his pick). They made him buy the explosives he needed to blast loose their coal (and deducted for the blasting powder). They made him buy his cap lamp (and deducted for the supply of carbide to light it). They made him buy his groceries at the company commissary (and charged 20 to 40 percent more than the independent stores where he was forbidden to trade). Anticipating the inevitable, they owned the cemeteries — and deducted a burial fee.

Early in 1931 the Harlan operators announced a 10 percent cut in wages. It was the fifth or sixth cut in the past couple of years and the operators apparently expected no special reaction to it. But they were cutting the wages of men who were already working only two or three days a week, men who often had no take-home pay at all after the deductions. Or a man might, after the deductions, collect three or four dollars from the paymaster. That was all the money he would have until the next pay period, two weeks away. Eggs were 25 cents a dozen, flour was 95 cents a sack, lard was 15 cents a pound, bacon was 40 cents a pound . . . and now the companies were cutting back another 10 percent. Miners who had all but abandoned any hope for the UMW began asking for help, one more time. "It was time to fight," a Harlan miner explained later, "while we still could fight."

On March 1, the UMW held a rally. More than 2,000 miners attended it, and when Philip Murray, then vice president of the union, asked them to sign up and pay a dollar in dues money, they did, in a rush. It was not a dollar well spent. The UMW was heavily bogged down in strikes and soon-to-be strikes elsewhere in the coalfields, it was fighting injunctions, it was perilously close to bankruptcy, and it had neither the wherewithal nor the will to take on the Harlan coal operators. In the wake of the rally, hundreds of miners who had been spotted there were summarily fired — Jim Garland among them. In the following weeks the firings continued. Partly they were in retaliation for union activity, but partly they were simply convenient; the entire industry was retrenching once again, buckling down for the worst year — in terms of total sales — since 1906 (1931 was a year when the average price for a ton of coal would be $1.54, compared to $3.75 in 1920).

The union held another rally, across the line in Tennessee, where a sympathetic congressman urged miners to join the union and Bill Turnblazer reportedly promised: "If you'll get us 10,000 dues-paying members, we'll give you the food and money for a strike." If the promise was actually made it could not possibly have been kept. But Harlan miners, desperate for help, kept joining up and urging their buddies to do the same, and the operators kept evicting them; there were scattered strikes at dozens of mines, a rally on the lawn of the courthouse; gun thugs rode through the coal camps at night, shooting up the shacks where the most active union men lived, stopping cars and seizing weapons and generally doing whatever they could to terrorize the miners back into submission.

But the miners were, some of them anyway, far beyond that point. They began looting the company stores — it was that or watch their children starve. They began shooting back at the deputies, and there were killings on both sides. And then on May 5 there was the bloody confrontation that later became known far and wide as the Battle of Evarts.

In Harlan County there were only five communities not owned by coal companies. Evarts, a few miles away from Peabody Coal Company's big Black Mountain Mine, was one of them. By the beginning of May it was a refugee center, filling up with thousands of blacklisted miners evicted from Kenvir, the Peabody camp, and other company towns. Rumors periodically flew through Evarts to the effect that John Henry Blair and his deputies were going to come in and clean out the town. It was not an unreasonable fear. Evarts was a hotbed of union activity, comparatively speaking. District 19 had failed to send any organizers into Harlan, but rank-and-file miners were organizing in Evarts on their own authority. They anticipated that they would be attacked sooner or later and they were prepared for it, as best they could be; everyone who owned a gun kept it loaded and close to hand, day and night.

On the morning of May 5 the superintendent of the Peabody mine sent a company truck past Evarts to Verda, another company camp, to pick up the household belongings of a miner named Roy Hughes and bring them back to Kenvir. Hughes had been hired to replace one of the blacklisted miners. He was going to do a little scabbing. It didn't sit well with the miners at Evarts.

They had taken to gathering in crowds at the railroad station, and there was a crowd of them watching when the truck went by and word went around about Hughes. Supposedly the men got to talking about how they might stop the truck when it came back. The L&N clerk in the depot overheard the talking and telephoned the Peabody superintendent to warn him. The superintendent got on the phone to John Henry Blair. In short order, arrangements had been made to send three carloads of deputies from the mine to Evarts, to meet the truck. At the same time, Blair would send some of his men from Harlan to Verda to try to intercept the truck before it left with Hughes's furniture. The men from Harlan would convoy the truck to Evarts, where they would meet the deputies coming from the mine. There was no way the rabblerousing union men at Evarts would stop that truck. The deputies were going to preserve law and order, regardless. That was the official explanation for sending so many of them to Evarts. It was the explanation given later in court, under oath, by the sheriff and the superintendent.

But the miners at Evarts had as much use for the official version as they had for the sheriff's oath. On the morning of May 5 they had ample cause to believe they were going to be attacked. Instead of waiting, they went up into the underbrush on the hillsides above the road from the mine, and when the three carloads of deputies slowed down to make a sharp turn, the miners opened fire. The deputies fired back, but for once they were outgunned. When the shooting stopped fifteen minutes later, three deputies and one miner were dead.

In the immediate aftermath of the battle, several things happened in Harlan County. Dozens of arrests were made in Evarts, effectively snuffing out the union activity there for the time being. Although it could be argued that the county had always been under martial law before, it certainly was now. Militiamen were sent in by the governor, ostensibly to restore order in an even-handed way — but mainly they seemed to augment the deputies, searching shacks and seizing weapons. Within a few weeks the United Mine Workers concluded that the situation in Harlan County was hopeless and abandoned the organizing effort, without troubling to tell any of the union's supporters that the decision had been made. When word got around, the general feeling was that it would be a long time, if ever, before anybody in Harlan County trusted John L. Lewis again — and there were some people there who never did, and some of them who still live there today speak of him with hatred that blooms fresh and green 50 years after the fact.

Into this maelstrom in the summer of 1931 another union appeared, to offer support for the striking miners. Its appearance on the scene was all that was necessary to create total chaos. The National Miners Union, despite its name, was not national in scope nor was it, strictly speaking, something created by miners, and it was not really a union in the sense that most American workers understood the term. The NMU was actually a creation of the Communist party, cobbled together in 1928 on orders from Moscow a few months after the Soviet overseers of the party had decided that there was no longer anything to be gained from trying to take over the American Federation of Labor. Boring from within — previously the official party policy — was out. Now the party would set up so-called dual unions, attempting to lure militant workers away from the impossibly conservative AFL unions (of which the United Mine Workers was one). By 1931 the Communists, despite the appalling economic conditions of the Depression, were doing poorly. The NMU was one of half a dozen party-sponsored unions in which, all told, perhaps 20,000 people had enlisted. It had gotten itself involved in three other coal strikes before moving into Harlan and had taken bad beatings in all of them. Its organizers were no longer welcome in Illinois, the Kanawha Valley of West Virginia, and the anthracite coalfields of Pennsylvania. But these places were far from Harlan. The mine wars of Kentucky offered another opportunity. The NMU appeared on the scene in June in the person of an organizer, Dan Slinger, traveling under the name of Dan Brooks. He was followed soon by a young woman, Jessie Wakefield, who came from New York as the representative of the International Labor Defense, one of the party's strike-support organizations.

With the benefit of fifty years of hindsight it is easy to say that the NMU effort was doomed from the start — and it clearly was — and that the NMU organizers and support people were either hopelessly naive or coldbloodedly manipulative. That is certainly the perspective adopted by historians who have written about the Harlan mine wars. But Jim Garland saw them differently, and through his eyes you may too. They may even remind you of other hopelessly naive people who went into places like Alabama and Mississippi some years ago in the name of civil rights. The NMU activists went into Kentucky in 1931 knowing full well that when they crossed the state line they would be completely without protection, in territory fully under the control of the mine owners and the gun thugs. Once there, they could not take a step without being watched. They could not make a telephone call without being overheard. They could not post a letter without assuming that it would be opened. There were places in the county where they could not safely go in broad daylight, and there was no place in the county where they could safely go at night. Still, they went — and for months they stayed and worked, and lived in shacks with miners and their families, and got shot at, and had their cars blown up in the night, and set up soup kitchens only to have *them* blown up, and set them up again, and got arrested without cause and jailed without being charged. Some were seized in the night and taken for rides by deputies who drove them to remote places and beat them senseless and left them to stumble back in the darkness to wherever they could find shelter. And one of them, a nineteen-year-old organizer named Harry Simms, a Jewish boy from a mill town in Massachusetts, was shot to death in cold blood in the twilight of a February day, a few weeks after the NMU had launched its abortive "general strike" on the first day of 1932.

Harry Simms, who became the NMU's most famous martyr and the subject of Jim Garland's most famous song, was the kind of outsider that the mine owners particularly and especially despised. They didn't have any reason to be afraid of him, exactly, any more than the authorities in Alabama had any real reason to be afraid of outsiders thirty years later, but there was something unspeakably arrogant about him. It wasn't his personality — he was remembered later as cheerful, quiet, good-humored, patient, a good listener — so much as it was the fact that he was there at all. People said he was particularly good at stirring up young people, the children of miners, to support the strike. He was good at organizing meetings, even when people were tired of meetings or afraid to go to them. When he talked to miners about political theory and economics, he did not condescend. Harry Simms was not his real name — his real name was Hirsh, and before going to Kentucky he had been organizing for the party in Tennessee under the name "Harris Gilbert" — but his identity seemed unimportant. He had been jailed for helping to organize a demonstration of unemployed workers in Connecticut in 1930, he had volunteered to organize miners in Kentucky; he believed in what he was doing, there was no bravado about it, and miners who had never before had any help at all from outsiders admired him greatly.

In point of fact the one thing that the NMU did well was to bring in outside help. In the fall of 1931 a party offshoot, the National Committee for the Defense of Political Prisoners, led by novelists Theodore Dreiser, John dos Passos, and others, traveled to Kentucky in a cloud of publicity and conducted hearings on conditions there. The mine wars of Harlan made the front pages and stayed there; the *New York Times* ran dozens of stories in the next few months. Writers, lawyers, churchmen and students began going to Kentucky to see for themselves. One such group, headed by the writer Waldo Frank, was headed for Kentucky early in February; Harry Simms and Jim Garland and some other NMU activists began traveling around Harlan and Bell counties, rounding up people to meet with Frank's committee. Simms and another organizer, Green Lawson, were walking along a railorad track a few miles from Pineville, the Bell County seat, when a handcar came along carrying two deputies. Simms and Lawson stepped out of the way. As the handcar went slowly past, one of the deputies stood up and took a shot at them — without first saying so much as a word. Simms fell by the track, a bullet in his abdomen.

He was bleeding badly. The gunmen went off in their handcar. It was a long time before Green Lawson and some miners who lived nearby could get Harry Simms to a hospital, carrying him there on another handcar, bumping painfully along the uneven tracks, and when they got there the hospital would not admit him at first because the doctors wanted someone to guarantee his bill. It made little difference whether they admitted him or not. He did not live many hours longer.

The death of Harry Simms gave the Communist party an opportunity to indulge in one of its favorite pastimes — the holding of a martyr's funeral in New York, the body lying in state at party headquarters attended by an honor guard of miners wearing their pit clothes and cap lamps. Jim Garland was one of them, very much a participant in the occasion, but Harry Simms had another meaning for him. "He was the bravest union man that I have ever seen," Jim wrote later in his song, and that was part of it, but there was more. There is an obvious risk of mawkishness here, but it ought to be pointed out that Harry Simms's courage was of a particular kind that the party did not choose to emphasize — because it did not want to publicize the fact that he was not a miner, and it did not boast of his being an outsider. In retrospect, however, what seems most memorable about Harry Simms is that he *was* an outsider who was willing to go to Kentucky and take whatever risks were waiting there in order to prove a point. The point was that the miners in their fight were no different from anyone else, and that it behooved anyone who cared at all about elemental justice to do what could be done to help them. That point may have been obscured by the Communist romanticist rhetoric of the day and it has certainly been overshadowed since by the almost universal distaste felt by most Americans — most miners included — for anything associated with the party. Maybe Jim Garland's book will help clear away some of the fog. The NMU certainly was not what the miners of Kentucky needed, and the rigid ideology of the Communist party cannot have been of any lasting value there — but people like Harry Simms did go, did take up the cause, did bring the writers and reporters in, and, at a critical time, stood by Jim Garland and others like him when nobody else would.

And in the final irony it was the Communist party that made the United Mine Workers look respectable by comparison, and helped the UMW in the early days of the Roosevelt administration to press for legislation giving workers the unrestricted right to organize and form unions without fear of reprisal. That legislation was incorporated in the National Industrial Recovery Act of 1933, and later in the National Labor Relations Act of 1935, and it was rightly described by John L. Lewis as a Magna Carta for workers. Using it as a shield, Lewis and the UMW recovered almost overnight and succeeded not only in organizing — rather, reorganizing — the coalfields but in branching out to organize millions of other workers in the Congress of Industrial Organizations (CIO).

That is another story — but it has a bearing on this one, and on Jim Garland's narrative. The coalfields of southeastern Kentucky, true to form, did not succumb to organization simply because Franklin D. Roosevelt, Congress, and John L. Lewis decreed that miners could join together freely to engage in collective bargaining. All through the 1930s the mine wars continued, and Harry Simms was by no means the last activist to lose his life in them. Kentucky did not pass a law controlling the power of sheriffs and gun thugs until 1938, and the union did not bring the mines of Harlan County under a binding contract until 1941. When the union fell on hard times again in the years after World War II, the mine operators of Harlan County were among the first to abrogate their contracts, and much of the coal that comes out of the Harlan coalfields today carries no union label. You could take that, perhaps, as evidence that Jim Garland ultimately failed in what he set out to do. But you could reach the same conclusion simply by looking anywhere in the country and noticing that injustices persist wherever you turn. In all his traveling Jim Garland did not change the world the way he hoped — not with his traveling, or his striking, or his speaking out, or his singing. But what if he had done none of those things?

Finally the great strength of this book is that it is the work of an ordinary man who, given the opportunity, would have lived an entirely ordinary life and died without troubling to make a record of it. He was not given that opportunity. He was given another kind of opportunity instead, made the most of it, made a record of it, and leaves that record to inform and inspire other men and women who, most certainly, will be called upon, in their own time and in their own way, to travel far from any place they ever expected to be.

THOMAS N. BETHELL

Editor's Introduction

In the winter of 1967, at his beach house on Washington's Pacific Coast, Jim Garland began to piece together and write down his version of Kentucky's mountain history. "It was a bad winter, snow on the ground and everything. I had begun to forget some of the things I thought were important. I felt these ought to be written down before nature stopped me from remembering." Garland's daughter Margaret Harrington remembers her father seated at a card table with a manual typewriter, his weak eyes five inches from the page. During that winter, Garland typed out in duplicate some 300 single-spaced pages, what accounts in large measure for the first twelve chapters of the edited manuscript.

That this material alone comprised Garland's original book evidences his major intention: to chart the waves of social upheaval across two hundred years in the mountains (white men's settlements, the building of an agrarian society, the subsequent concentration of land holdings, the influx of small-scale industrialists, the mountains' usurpation by an outside, money-minded technocracy) and to narrate a coeval family history, his own, showing how mountain people met these changes. Because Jim Garland's own life so obviously attests to the strength of mountaineer stock and so adamantly shows how mountain people, buttressed by the artistic, political, and religious traditions of their region, have been able to survive the challenges of history, it is puzzling that the original book does not contain more autobiographical material. When I met Jim in the summer of 1979, two months before his death, and asked him about this issue, he answered, "It's hard for me to just talk about what Jim Garland did."

I cannot believe that Jim omitted the details of his adult life because they were difficult for him to remember or embarrassing for him to record; his memory poured over with open recollections. Nor can I conclude that Garland's decision was entirely humble; he was a generous, but not self-effacing, man. I do think that, while admitting his scanty formal education, Garland wanted to assert a critical understanding of his region. He had not written down the jokes, remedies, recipes, and games of one man's emblematic life just so that others could extrapolate the large ideas. He felt entitled and equipped to draw conclusions.

In this respect, Garland's book differs from the personal recollections of Verna Mae Slone's *What My Heart Wants to Tell* (New Republic Books, 1979), and from Nell Painter's sociopolitical oral history *The Narrative of Hosea Hudson: His Life as a Negro Communist in the South* (Harvard University Press, 1979). In her introduction, Painter describes how only as the interviews proceeded did Hudson, "a unique informant," "come to see — or to admit — that his experiences beyond the Party held an interest for readers that equalled his importance as a symbol of the Communist party. Still, Hudson was recording a political autobiography. I wanted to write southern social history using Hudson's life as an illustration" (p. 36). Jim Garland, on the other hand, was well aware that mountain life outside of political organizations was politically important. As author of his own book, he set out to describe the circumstances of this life and interpret them in the light of his own political experience. He wanted to write social and political history himself; I wanted to get his manuscript into print.

Only after the fact of the original typescript was Garland convinced that political autobiography could enliven his history and improve his manuscript's chance for publication. For truthfully, most publishers were not ready to pay for political analysis by a man with such unorthodox credentials. Garland may, out of the seriousness of his politics, have been driven to write a book about his people rather than about himself. But I suspect that Garland also made his choice understanding that the writers, not the informants, command our sense of the political past. By avoiding autobiography, he hoped to achieve the distance he felt credible analysis required and to win for himself a larger kind of authority.

In the spring of 1968, Margaret Garland Harrington, Jim's and Hazel's eldest child, retyped the first three chapters of his original typescript, correcting spelling, but for the next eight years, the manuscript lay undisturbed and relatively unnoticed. In 1976 Mark Wilson, a professor at the University of California, San Diego, published excerpts in the brochure accompanying Sarah Gunning's LP, *Silver Dagger* (Rounder 0051). Jim showed portions of the manuscript to Irwin Silber of *Sing Out* in New York and to Bess Lomax Hawes during a folk festival in Portland, Oregon; however, not until 1977 was the entire manuscript laid open for serious consideration.

Bess Hawes, director of the Folkarts division of the National Endowment for the Arts, had long known the Garland family as musicians. She contacted Jim and asked to see the full manuscript. Garland told Bess that he needed to return to Kentucky to conduct interviews with old friends and relatives to corroborate his remembrances and to add information. Jim also wanted to speak with young mountain people in order to further his story. Finding the contents of the original book worthy and believing "the world of the arts owed Jim a trip home," Bess Hawes and the Folkarts program provided funds for Garland to return to Kentucky and conduct interviews; the grant also set aside money to hire a driver, a typist, and a writer to aid in editing the manuscript. The grant was to be administered by Appalshop, an arts cooperative in Whitesburg, Kentucky. Jack Wright of Appalshop, when asked to suggest an editor for the manuscript, contacted Bill Bishop, a former reporter for Whitesburg's *Mountain Eagle*, who had also conducted an extensive oral history study of the W.B. Jones organization in Harlan and Bell counties.

Bishop retyped the first ten chapters of the original, standardizing spelling, punctuation, and sentence structure, and, finding that Jim had also made some tapes as part of his book, had these transcribed. The taped material, according to Bishop, consisted of Jim's reading his manuscript into a recorder, material identical to the written version save an occasional sentence. Where songs appeared in the manuscript, Jim had sung them onto the tape.

After reviewing the manuscript, Bishop contacted Jim, then in Eastern Kentucky conducting his interviews, and encouraged him to write down the autobiographical material concerning the National Miners Union (NMU). Bishop also recommended that Jim write an introduction to explain the impetus and plan of the manuscript. These additions Garland completed in the fall and winter of 1977-78.

In April 1978, Bill Bishop contacted me and asked if I, who had assisted in his oral history of the Jones organization and who, as a teacher of English composition at that time, was more practiced in the kind of editing which Garland's book required, would be interested in assuming the work. I agreed to take it on.

Ordering all the material I had according to Jim Garland's written specifications — the tape transcriptions, the interviews, the recently written account of the NMU, the original chapters — I began to record page by page the contents of the book. I found that, on the whole, Garland had structured his manuscript chronologically, beginning with the settlement of the mountains, moving into stories of his maternal grandfather Wilson Lucas, then to the biographies of his parents and stories of his half-sister and half-brother, Aunt Molly Jackson and Bad John Garland. Jim had used these "characters" to vivify the routines, the rituals, the play, and the occupations of mountain people.

For example, Garland discussed the tenets of the Missionary Baptist faith within the written account of his father's life, since Oliver Perry Garland had been a Baptist pastor. He brought up children's games while chronicling his own youth in the coal camps. This logic being so prevalent in the original, I chose to impose the pattern throughout the entire manuscript, even when it meant shuffling paragraphs out of their original sequence. As an instance, Garland described all mining methods, from simple coal digging to the implementation of sophisticated machinery, in two chapters near the end of the original manuscript. I relocated the explanations of the more primitive mining procedures in the chapter that concerns Jim's father's experience as a miner. Since Jim and his brother worked as entrymen, shooting coal from the solid, the description of that procedure enters the narrative when Jim himself goes to work in the mines.

I have applied the same principle when situating jokes and songs in the manuscript. Jim was inclined to tell one joke about a Baptist minister when it indicated something about behavior in the mountains, but then to become caught up in joke-telling itself. Because Garland made so many attempts to explain what such stories revealed about mountain society, I have moved those tales for which he offers no such analysis into positions where I feel, by their very juxtaposition with more serious matters, they may prove illuminating as well as entertaining. The only exception to this method is the string of stories in "Here We Come A Roving"; I have kept these running contiguously as in the original manuscript, hoping thereby to reflect his mother's rich store of narratives.

Oddly, Jim neglected to include the lyrics of his own songs in the manuscript, even though several songs are explicitly mentioned. Because, for example, after telling the story of Harry Simms's death, Jim writes, "I include this song here," yet fails actually to write down "The Ballad of Harry Simms," I believe he felt these lyrics could handily be added later. Hazel Garland supplied me with the lyrics of many songs after Jim's death with the assurance that these were the originals (several have been misquoted in other sources). Where Jim mentions the writing of a certain song, I have inserted the lyrics. Those songs about which he offers no such background, I have inserted in the book as they parallel themes.

Wilson Lucas, Oliver and Elizabeth Garland, Molly, John, and Jim himself comprise the limbs around which the details of the story grow; however, in reading the hand-written notes he made on the transcribed interviews, I feel certain that the identities of these sources were to be subordinated to the themes of the book. Tom Inman's interview, since it deals primarily with mining machinery, was to "go with" Jim's chapter on mining methods. Myrtle Garland, though a contemporary of Jim's, was to be introduced as he dealt with the Straight Creek strike. In one case, Harvey Valentine, Garland did note where the interview was to be placed, but I countered his decision. Valentine was an old friend whom Jim obviously identified with NMU advocacy; for this reason, Jim had located the interview alongside the National Miners Union material. The bulk of the interview, however, concerns the Holiness Church, Valentine being a pastor of that denomination. For this reason, I moved most of Valentine's comments into the chapter "Holiness People," including only a few pertinent quotations from his discussion later in the chapters dealing with unionism and the '32 strike.

I have omitted three interviews. One, with Pauline Inman, a dear relative of Jim's, mainly describes her work in the Bell County school system. While this kind of catching up was imminently important to Jim, indeed prompted his trip back to Kentucky, I felt her comments were too detailed and isolated to fit clearly into the rest of the manuscript. Jim also interviewed Elwood Carr about mountain plants and herbal remedies; since this material primarily asserted Carr's expertise, I decided it veered too far afield to be included. The other, an interview with Popeye Garland, amounted to an explanation of the portal-to-portal pay system, information which I think the Tom Inman interview covers sufficiently.

Throughout the manuscript I have used italics to offset pertinent but secondary material (jokes, songs, interviews) from the trunk of the narrative. At worst, this method will seem patchwork, a melange of vaguely related details; I hope that apt placement has avoided that effect. At best, this device can convey Jim's eclectic intelligence and his digressive style. Ideally, readers will find these details embellishments rather than deviations. Since Jim's original chapters contained a multitude of such digressions, I feel this method follows a precedent in the original, and because Jim wrote so little introductory or transitional material, I felt this the only accurate way to retain his anecdotes without intruding editorial fiber.

My aim was to retain everything. Aside from the three aforementioned interviews, I have omitted very little. I left out the few stories and jokes I felt carried nothing more than a flavor of mountain humor; to this purpose, the book now offers many fine examples. I left out several of the songs Hazel sent me and six or seven square dance calls. At the publisher's recommendation, I also removed a number of process explanations (how to make gritted corn bread, how to construct a thump keg still, etc.), recognizing that this information exists elsewhere in finer detail. I regret excising them because they show the fullness of Garland's experience and concern, though I think the edited book retains a good measure of thematic breadth.

I have added to the manuscript material garnered from two interviews with Jim himself. During one, conducted by Bill Bishop, October 12, 1977, in Arjay, Kentucky, Garland commented in broad terms on his political past and expounded his theory of economics; I spliced most of these passages into the book's final chapter. Bishop and I conducted another intensive interview in

June 1978 at Bishop's house in Louisville. At this time we tried to elicit a detailed calendar of events during the years 1930 through 1940. Chapters 13 through 19 in particular contain this material.

I have corrected the manuscript's spelling and punctuation, the only exceptions being a few words in the jokes. I also standardized the grammar, save some passages of directly quoted material. When I met Jim in the summer of 1978 and recommended this standardization, he agreed immediately. Because Garland's errors in grammar, spelling, and punctuation were inconsistent, I see no violation of his style in revising toward standard English rather than away from it. I have also combined sentences to achieve a greater density and variety than exists in the original work. Some may suggest that incongruent subjects and verbs, choppy sentences, or the absence of parallel constructions adds precious color to writing. Without examining the motives or the effects of such a view, I can insist that it was far more important to Jim Garland that his ideas be taken seriously than that his uneven writing style be cherished.

I have changed very little of the diction. To have done so would have been to invent details. I have used synonyms to break the monotony of some paragraphs, but I have taken great care that my substitutions were words within Jim's lexicon, words that appeared elsewhere in the original text. The only nonstandard form I have retained is "kindly," used by Jim to mean "rather" or "kind of." It appeared consistently throughout the manuscript. In addition, I have heard Jim's wife, Hazel, and sister Sarah use this form and so believe it to be a viable one.

Though Garland had kept in close contact with his Kentucky friends and relatives, he had not resided in the mountains for forty years. Jim realized that while he had, since moving away, been a champion of his mountain people at folk festivals and political conferences all over the country, he needed to go back to legitimize his writing. In a two-page note written upon his return to Kentucky, Jim Garland, in a confessional tone that rarely entered his writing, contemplated the difficulty of his dual role: a mountain man who had made history and a traveler come back to evaluate it.

"As I drove by the place where I was born, I looked at the little flat place where the mining camp had set, and to the filthy water where my mother was baptized, and I said, 'Dad, I will do the best I can.'"

Jim Garland died September 6, 1978, his manuscript a sprawl of tapes and papers in the possession of a near-stranger. Since the confusing, discouraging night I heard of his death, many people have helped turn his work into this book. Bess Hawes, director of the Folkarts Program at the National Endowment for the Arts, had the foresight to fund Garland's return to

Kentucky and to pay for an editor. I thank her, and the people of Appalshop in Whitesburg, Ky., for administering her decision. Bill Bishop, David Walls, Anne Campbell, and Jim and Sharen Branscome contributed their invaluable expertise and *moved* in the crucial early stages of this work. Archie Green, David Dunnaway, Mark Wilson, Richard Reuss, Joseph Hickerson, and the people at Roundup Records helped faithfully with the discography which this novice could not have compiled without them. I thank Mark Wilson, Anne McKinnon, Chip Martin of Alice Lloyd, and, at the University of Louisville, Andy Anderson and his staff for help locating photographs; I also appreciate Gary Sampson's fine work reproducing many of them. For their generous contributions to the typesetting of this book, I thank the John Edwards Memorial Foundation, Al Smith, the Woody Guthrie Foundation, Pete Seeger, Rounder Records, and other friends who wished their donations to remain anonymous. To William Ray Evans and, especially, to Pam DeVoe who surrendered so many hours to this project, I am enormously grateful. Hazel Garland and her family, particularly Betty Garland Roy, Margaret Harrington, Pauline Inman and her late husband Tom, have all contributed unceasingly and patiently as this project inched along; their trust finally made my work possible. Thanks to Tom Bethell whose feisty wisdom has added so much. What part of this book is mine I dedicate to Archie Green and Bill Bishop.

*JIM GARLAND'S STORY
OF THE KENTUCKY MOUNTAINS*

Introduction

I have read many books about the mountains of Eastern Kentucky, most of them written by college-educated people. Some may ask why I, who did not even receive a high school education, should write another.

First and foremost, I am a true mountain person; in fact, if you looked all over those mountains, you could not find an entire family as typical as mine. Though my earliest Kentucky ancestors were landowners like most of the first white settlers, we had to turn to sharecropping as land became more and more concentrated in the hands of fewer and fewer Kentuckians. Later, as the family grew and farming on a small scale became an impossible way to make a living, we worked in the coal mines.

We were religious people, some of us, and some of us were atheists. Some were teachers of singing schools and others could not read or write. Most of us went into the mines, some as early as nine years of age, but others scorned the very thought of mining as an occupation and became tramps and hobos instead. But there is one outstanding characteristic which all of the Garlands have been noted for throughout their history in Kentucky, and that is the ability to sing and talk. Many folks, especially the coal operators, called us the Big Mouth Garlands.

Yes, we were an average Kentucky family until it became time to organize the miners into a union. Then, I am glad to say, we were no longer typical. We have been at the forefront of this action from the beginning to the present day — from the old Knights of Labor to the AFL-CIO and the United Mine Workers of America. My father did some of the first organizing for the United Mine Workers union in Kentucky and was a member as long as he lived, serving in all levels of local office and helping to set up a new local as late as 1922, not long before he died. It was in this tradition that I grew.

Down through the years, I have seen Daniel Boone lionized as a national hero while the average mountain people were slandered. On radio and television, they were pictured as filthy drunks or ignorant louts. The movies dramatized stories of the mountain feuds — damned lies more than anything else. And all of the books I have read about mountain people, all of them written by well-educated, middle- or upper-class authors, have only kept alive the same false picture of mountain life. I have not seen one book written from the workingman's or uneducated mountaineer's viewpoint. That viewpoint should be brought to people.

Since I have spent many years writing, singing, and collecting songs, I have included the lyrics of many of them in this book. They should serve to show what people thought was important at different periods during the settlement and industrialization of the mountains. The tales that have been handed down by our ancestors, their chores and pastimes also tell the story of mountain life.

I have tried to give a more factual account of the history of mining and to show its effects on the daily lives of mountain people: how the small mine operators, in an attempt to rebuild southern slave society, considered themselves the benefactors of the men who worked for them, and how many of the early miners felt the same way. I show how later, when the big companies came in with absentee operations, this neighborly relationship between miner and owner swiftly vanished. In order to give as full a picture as possible, since my experience as that of any man is limited, I have included information given to me by friends and family members who were more involved in certain movements and occurences than I was.

I have not referred to specific dates too often. Rather I have organized time according to the happenings within my own family: when my father and mother were married, when my brother was killed in the mines. This is the way most of us tell time anyway.

After much thinking and urging from my friends, I began writing down what I had been told and what I could remember of the mountains' history because I believed much of it was important. Later, I found that the National Endowment for the Arts would grant me some funds; I realized that I could be paid to write about those things that forty years ago almost landed me in jail. Most of the things I was advocating back then — old-age pensions, home relief for those unable to work, aid to dependent children — have been won. They have been won not by big hearts but by organizations. To keep what we have gained, we must be ever ready to stand together and fight again.

Long Live the Good Mountain People,

JIM GARLAND

Washougal, Washington
1977

1. The Wilderness

The time in history had come to settle the Appalachian Mountains. Most of the land east of them had been homesteaded or acquired otherwise, but in the mountains and west of them, there was virgin land for the taking. "Taking" is just what I mean, though, for the Indians who still lived and hunted on this land were not about to give it up without a struggle.

Contrary to his reputation as an independent pioneer, Daniel Boone, like many others, was hired by large land companies to guide groups into this new territory. Bringing with them wagons, cows, chickens, hogs, and all the implements necessary to form a settlement and begin farming, they came through the Cumberland Gap and traveled the rivers wide enough to move their equipment. Boone led a number of people to the banks of the Kentucky, there establishing a fort and naming the settlement Boonesboro.

When Indian hunters came around, curious to see what was up along the Kentucky, in the usual manner of the English colonists, Boone and his company gathered up rifles and began killing the Indians off. This reaction naturally led to open warfare between the Indians and the white settlers, with white renegades (white men who had joined the Indians, whether by adoption into the tribes or for their own gain) betraying the whites and renegade Indians deserting their tribes, mostly for the white man's whiskey.

The vast mountainous region lying along the border between Virginia and what is now West Virginia, and extending from Pennsylvania in the north to the Big Smokies in the south was known as the Wilderness. Since such rough and unknown terrain held little interest for the eastern financiers, Boone's company and other hired settlers continued west to more level land. Still, this immense watershed contained some of the prettiest rivers and valleys to be found on the North American continent. The Wilderness beckoned to a different type of settler than did the treeless land farther north along the Kentucky. Into this Wilderness came hunters and poor men who had not been chosen to travel with the well-financed groups. And of course, it attracted those people who had always loved the mountains.

Some historians claim that the only routes into Kentucky were the Ohio River and those larger passages taken by Boone and his party; those were the best routes for large companies transporting tools and animals. But the trappers and hunters who sought the Wilderness lands came with very little: a pack mule perhaps, a hound dog, parched corn, salt, string and fishhooks. They found other entries by crossing the Blue Ridge Mountains and walking the tops of the ridges. All through the Appalachian range, you will find hilltop paths made by the passing of wild game. Even today you can walk these paths quite comfortably all along the major ridges like Pine and Black mountains, the same trails that gave the early mountaineers entry to the Wilderness. So while Boone was struggling with canebrakes and rivers in flood, the mountain men were traveling high and dry.

My ancestors had landed in Boston, Massachusetts, in 1637. From there, the Garlands split north and south, the southern branch of the family settling in Virginia. These hunting Garlands walked from Virginia across to Kentucky. They liked what they saw. Game was plentiful; they found the turkey and the mourning dove, the raccoon, the possum, and the fox, fish in the rivers and creeks. Chestnut trees covered whole sides of mountains with their burrs bursting and hurling down the tasty chestnuts. Beechnuts and acorns lay on every hand. The sugar maple was there to be tapped. Wild honey bees buzzed around the poplars, blossoms so sweet that the pioneer could almost taste honey on his tongue. Softwood stood fifty feet high and straight, ready for the axe to build the mountain man a home. There were wide, fertile creek bottoms on which to raise grain or any other crop. Hogs would grow fat on the mast in the mountains. With 160 acres of valley or river bottom staked out, a pair of chickens, and a good mountain girl or Indian bride to share his home and start a family, what more could a mountain man want?

Unlike the settlers along the Kentucky River, these mountain hunters for the most part lived peaceably among the Cherokee Indians, exchanging ways of hunting and medicine. Many a settler preferred to marry an Indian girl who had come with a hunting party from the Cherokee nation over in North Carolina or Eastern Tennessee, rather than to return to Virginia for a wife. One of my own great-grandmothers, in fact, was a full-blooded Cherokee. Very few Indian braves married white women, though, for the very good reason that there were so few white women there to marry.

Not long after a settlement of any size had been formed, the circuit rider would appear and spend the night in a new cabin. He was always welcome. Because many Indians had to some extent adopted Christian religion by this time, he might spend the night in their hunting camps or hold religious meetings jointly with the Cherokee people and the whites. In this way, the circuit rider also served as a peacemaker.

Most of these traveling preachers were doctors, too. Generally they could heal a cut or a gunshot wound or set a broken leg. In a pinch, they even delivered babies or doctored sick horses and mules. Circuit riders were also prime sources of information, often being the settlers' only contact with Virginia for a year or two at a time. As devoted religious men, they never expected any pay for their services, and they received none, other than food and lodging.

The first sects to enter the mountains, the Baptists and the Methodists, were both represented by traveling ministers in the early days. Though the Methodists use the sprinkling of water in baptism and the Baptists advocate total immersion, the two denominations were similar in most other ways. Mountain folk have always interpreted the Bible literally, no matter which church they ascribed to, believing hell to be an actual fiery place where a grinning devil with horns and a tail prods wicked souls with a pitchfork to keep his flames burning.

Jethro Smith, a very ugly man, and Bill Jones were talking with their preacher one afternoon about life after death. Bill asked his pastor if people kept their same features in the next life. "Yes they do," answered the preacher, "but why do you ask?" Jones said, "Oh, I was just thinking, won't the devil leave home when Jethro Smith goes to hell?"

The Primitive Baptist or Hardshell Baptist Church was among the first branches of that denomination to enter the mountains. I believe that to this day its members have retained the original methods of worship more fully than has any other mountain sect. Unlike the Missionary Baptists, who believe that man can save himself by faith, the Primitive Baptists claim that man cannot save himself. Some say that the Primitive Baptists also believe in predestination.

With reference to visits I have made to Primitive Baptist churches and through recollection of stories told to me by my family about this early church, I believe that I can reconstruct a typical church service of the settlement days.

More than likely, the service was held in the school building, a log construction near the center of the community. Although the service might have been held on any night of the week and in any season, we will set this particular service on a Sunday in the summer at six o'clock p.m. so the folks will have time to get home before black dark.

People began to arrive by four o'clock in order to exchange news and visit with one another. The women visited together and the men gathered in the yard or under a shade tree to discuss everything — crops, hunting, horses — or to tell a smutty joke or two. Very young children stayed with their mothers, older ones played around the school building, and those of courting age made eyes at one another, trying to set up dates to walk home together after church.

The preacher, or elder as the Primitive Baptists call their minister, arrived a half-hour before the service began. To each and all he gave the "handshake of fellowship" so that no one would feel slighted, and since he was traveling far from home, he worked to finagle an invitation to spend the night.

After the handshake, all came inside and attended while the preacher made quite a show of searching through his Bible to find an appropriate text. When the time arrived for the service to begin, the preacher called on a man or woman in the congregation who had "the gift of leading songs" to start the singing of one or two hymns. Most of these songs were drawn from the old Thomas Hymn Book.

The first settlers had brought this particular song book with them to the mountains from the eastern states, and today, over 150 years later, it remains the hymnal most often used in the Primitive Baptist churches. The book contains songs made in six-line, all of which are sung virtually the same way, and songs in four-line, which also use nearly identical tunes. Dr. Watts wrote the best known four-liners, but the Thomas Hymn Book also includes songs by Belldone, Cooper, and Ludley. The hymns concern a range of themes, the Gospel, salvation, the Fall of Man, prayer, and Christian love, just to name a few. All of these songs are quite long, and since most of them tell stories or, as it were, preach their own self-contained sermons, no verse was ever omitted by the church congregation. When no minister was present, folks might gather just to sing their own sermons and prayers using the Thomas Hymn Book.

In the early church services, as in the Primitive Baptist Church today, there was no choir. Once the leader began singing, people sitting all over the church house sang along in unison, just as slowly as possible. On one of my visits to the Primitive Baptist Church on Williams Branch in Bell County, Kentucky, I encountered a man with the most powerful voice I had ever heard. When I asked him how he was able to sing so loudly, he told me that his power to sing came from "The Great I Am."

After one or two songs, the preacher asked someone in the congregation with "the gift of praying" to lead a prayer. All church members knelt at their seats and prayed aloud with the leader, after which all were seated and the preacher rose to deliver his sermon. If another minister were present, the two would usually share the time for sermonizing.

The typical preacher used many scriptures to prove his message, working the texts together to heighten the emotions of the congregation. A sermon had to be sentimental or the people would be disappointed and would return home calling the service a dry one. These early Baptists were much more hysterical than the latter-day Baptists. The old women, in particular, shouted, jumped up and down, and hollered "Glory! Glory!" Today a congregation in the mountains is still likely to encourage the preacher with "Amen!" or "Preach the word! Go on, Brother!" but in the early churches, the shouts tended to get more excited. One I liked was, "You are plowing mighty close to the corn, Brother; go right on plowing!"

At the end of his sermon, the preacher usually asked if anyone wished to be prayed for. Those who did would rise and give the preacher their hands. Next, the elder asked if anyone wished to join the church. If there was none, the song leader would be then called on to conduct the singing of another hymn.

The last day of a preacher's stay in any one locality, he usually drew the service to a close with a hymn called "The Parting Hand," another song from the Thomas Hymn Book. For the sake of those who either could not read or did not own a hymnal, this song might be lined out by some particularly good singer in the group.

The liner read or quoted from memory one line at a time, giving a bit of the rise and fall of each phrase; then he or she waited for the congregation to respond. Some liners would go ahead and sing the congregation's part also.

> Liner: My dearest friends in bonds of love
> Our hearts in sweetest union prove.
> Congregation: *(very slowly)* My dearest friends in bonds of love
> Our hearts in sweetest union prove.
> Liner: Your friendship's like a drawing band
> Yet we must take this parting hand.
> Congregation: Your friendship's like a drawing band
> Yet we must take this parting hand.

I'll give you the rest of the song so you can line it out yourself. Just remember to read one line and then sing it as slowly as possible.

> Your presence sweet, your union dear,
> Your words delightful to my ear,
> And when I see that we must part,
> You draw cords around my heart.
> How sweet the hours have passed away
> When we have met to sing and pray.
> How loathe I have been to leave the place
> Where Jesus shows his smiling face.
> O could I stay with friends so kind,
> Would it cheer my struggling mind.

But duty makes me understand
That we must take the parting hand.
And since it is God's holy will,
We must be parted for awhile,
In sweet submission all in one.
We'll say "Our Father's will be done."
Dear fellow youth in Christian ties
We seek for mansions in the skies.
Fight on, you'll win the happy shore
Where parting hands are known no more.
How oft I've seen the flowing tears
And heard you tell your hopes and fears.
Your hearts with love have seemed to flame
Which makes me hope we'll meet again.

I have reproduced this song, an early favorite, directly from the old Thomas Hymn Book. Coming to Kentucky with the first white settlers and circuit riders, this song can still be heard in the Primitive Baptist churches of the mountains, the church at Williams Branch, for example. That particular parish was set up in 1817, just two years after the Battle of New Orleans. But despite its age, it carries on exactly the same as of old. No wonder those folks are called Hardshell Baptists. I say more power to them!

2. The Logger's Away, The Miller's at Home

By 1800, community life was well established in the mountains of Kentucky. People had taken up along the mountain sides or on farms along the creek bottoms. Unlike the trappers who had lived almost entirely on the animals, nuts, and berries found free in the mountains, this next generation survived by the cultivation of crops, corn being by far the most important. Corn, in fact, was the base on which mountain life at that time was built. Corn fed the cows and hogs; the family ate corn in the late summer and fall; men set up moonshine stills; women made the tasty gritted bread from corn and buttermilk.

A farmer was one day gathering his eggs when he noticed some markings on them; on several of the eggs he saw what he made out to read "GPC." He ran inside to show his wife, telling her that God had called upon him to take up preaching. "This 'GPC' means 'Go Preach Christ.'" He left the farm to pursue his new-found calling, but in just a few days, his wife saw him returning to their house. "What's the matter that you're not preaching?" she asked him. He answered, "After I started, I found out I'd misinterpreted that message. Instead of 'Go Preach Christ' the eggs were really saying 'Go Plow Corn.'"

One of the first industries in the mountains was the gristmill, located on a stream, its stone burrs turned by a water wheel. Arranged on the mill were sifters that separated the bran or, as it was called, "bolted the meal." The miller became the mountains' first businessman. As his toll for grinding a bushel, the miller would take between a gallon and a peck of ground corn and, in some cases, would keep the bran, the best livestock feed, as well. As usually happens when some people get the chance to dictate how much of another fellow's labor they will take for themselves in return for their own labor, time, advice, or perhaps just their own friendship, many of the millers became greedy. Quite a few stories and songs attest to their stinginess and dishonesty.

    1. *There was an old man who owned a little mill*
    And when he died he made up his will.
    He called up his oldest son.
    "Son, oh Son, I am almost gone.
    I will will you my mill and money you will make
    If you tell me the toll you intend for to take."
    Sing a Rack Fa Diddle I Day.
    "Father, you know that my name is Jack,
    Father, you know that my name is Jack,
    Father, you know that my name is Jack,
    Out of a bushel I would take a peck."
    Sing a Rack Fa Diddle I Day.

(Chorus) *"Son, oh Son, my foolish son,*
    I am sorry that you ain't learned my way,
    And to you my mill, I won't give,
    For by such a toll no miller can live."
    Sing a Rack Fa Diddle I Day.

    2. *He called up his second son.*
    "Son, oh Son, I am almost gone.
    I will will you my mill and money you will make
    If you tell me the toll you intend for to take."
    Sing a Rack Fa Diddle I Day.
    "Father, you know that my name is Jase,
    Father, you know that my name is Jase,
    Father, you know that my name is Jase,
    Out of a bushel I would take it half."
    Sing a Rack Fa Diddle I Day.
    (Chorus)

    3. *He called up his youngest son.*
    "Son, oh Son, I am almost gone.
    I will will you my mill and money you will make
    If you tell me the toll you intend for to take."
    Sing a Rack Fa Diddle I Day.
    "Father, you know I am your darling boy.
    Taking tolls is all my joy.
    If a fortune I should like,
    I would take the whole turn, swear I never saw the sack."
    Sing a Rack Fa Diddle I Day.

> "Son, oh Son, my good wise son,
> I am glad that you have learned my way."
> "Hallelujah!" the old woman cried,
> And the old man lay back on his ears and died.
> Sing a Rack Fa Diddle I Day.

Here is another song, a smutty one, that tells of the miller's tightfistedness:

> There was an old woman, lived under the hill.
> She shit in her stocking and sent it to the mill.
> The miller swore and proved by his wife,
> He never took toll from a turd in his life.
>
> There was an old woman, God bless her, God bless her.
> She threw her leg over the dresser, the dresser.
> A ten penny nail hung under her tail
> And tore off half of her pisser, her pisser.
>
> Old Granny Hare, what are you doing there?
> "Setting on a dog turd, picking out a nail.
> I picked out one, I picked out two,
> I picked out three, I picked out four,
> If I had my specs I could pick out more."

Millers began to expand their businesses. They freighted corn and livestock out of the mountains to Pittsburg and London, Kentucky, where the produce was exchanged for cloth, trinkets, needles, thread, thimbles, and combs. With these new articles, many gristmill owners started their own grocery stores, the first of their kind in the mountains.

At this time, the only other merchant in the mountains was the pack peddler who would come out from the larger towns, carrying the enormous pack. In great demand among the young boys were the Jew's harp and the French harp, or mouth organ. The pack peddler also brought the Barlow knife, a one-bladed, bone-handled knife which sold for fifteen cents. A man was just not a man until he got one of these knives.

As mountain society became more firmly rooted, individual families grew enormously. Schools would have to be built. The local school was built in just the same way that a house was built for a couple of newlyweds — everyone pitched in. They raised a big log building which would serve not only as a school but as a church, a voting place, and a dance hall. The schoolhouse was the social center of the community.

There always seemed to be someone available to teach, though usually the schoolteachers were men. Using whatever book might be obtainable and using slate to write on, the teacher taught his students everything he knew. When he had nothing more to offer a pupil, that student was released and considered capable of teaching school himself. School lasted six months out of the year, starting in the fall after the corn was laid by and running through the winter. This schedule allowed children to work in the fields during spring and summer.

Despite the hillbilly image put forth in the comic strips and movies, mountain people did not then and do not now dress in a raggle-taggle way. True, if you had passed along a cornfield back then, you might have seen a man plowing his corn, dressed only in a long-tailed shirt made of linsey or wool which had been spun and woven by his wife and dyed with the berries of native plants. If he were wearing pants, they probably would have been out of the same material. In the winter, he would probably wear a buckskin jacket and pants, or a coat of sheepskin. A farmer might be plowing barefooted, though I doubt it because of all the rocks, sharp sticks, and briars in that country.

Early mountain families depended on the traveling shoemaker to provide for them. With his pack mule, mule cart, or wagon, the shoemaker would arrive at the settler's cabin and live there until he had made shoes for the entire family. Most of the time, he furnished the sole leather, which had to be brought in from along the Ohio or from across the mountains in Virginia. The rest of the shoe he made from hides tanned by the settler himself: cow, horse, calf, even wild animal hides. Rabbit skins made nice baby moccasins. Groundhog hide made awfully good shoestrings.

Here is a song about the end of the one-man shoemaking trade. The awl was a tool that punched holes in the leather, holes that the shoemaker fitted with wooden pegs.

It was in 1801, peg and awl,
It was in 1801, peg and awl,
It was in 1801, pegging shoes was all I done.
Hand me down my peg and awl, my peg and awl.

It was in 1802, peg and awl,
It was in 1802, peg and awl,
It was in 1802, pegging shoes was all I do.
Hand me down my peg, my awl, my peg and awl.

They have invented a new machine, peg and awl,
They have invented a new machine, peg and awl,
They have invented a new machine.
Prettiest little thing you ever have seen.
Hand me down my peg and awl, my peg and awl.

It was in 1803, peg and awl,
It was in 1803, peg and awl,
It was in 1803, that little machine it set me free.
Hand me down my peg, my awl, my peg and awl.

It was in 1804, peg and awl,
It was in 1804, peg and awl,
It was in 1804, I will peg them shoes no more.
Threw away my peg, my awl, my peg and awl.

Now it is 1805, peg and awl,
Now it is 1805, peg and awl,
Now it is 1805, do anything to stay alive.
No more peg and no more awl, no more peg and awl.

This song recounts very clearly the ending of the small craftsman's job, although the one-man shoemaking trade did not end quite this early or this suddenly. A friend of mine says his grandfather was a shoemaker in the Middle West until 1860, though surely in the larger cities, the machine had replaced the peg and awl method long before the middle of the nineteenth century.

Grandfather Wilson Lucas, my mother's father, grew up on Goose Creek, the headwaters of the Kentucky River, in Clay County, near Manchester, Kentucky. He and his sons worked logging. All winter, they, along with several neighbors, would cut trees and tie them together into rafts. When the high tides of spring came, they rode these rafts down the Kentucky River, onto the Ohio, and as far away as St. Louis, returning on foot to the mountains with their pay in their pockets. After all the work of winter and the danger and toil of rafting the logs to market, many a man would be robbed by gangs hiding out along the river banks. (I have been told that Jesse and Frank James started their careers by robbing loggers along these rivers.)

Rather than walk inland many men chose to risk returning home along the rivers in order to enjoy the bawdy houses, established along this route for the pleasure of just such traveling men. These houses were lively places with much singing and drinking, along with the other usual things. Leaving some of their pay in these houses, the loggers carried back to the mountains many bawdy songs.

The log rafters also brought back the banjo from down on the Ohio and Mississippi settlements. This musical instrument took the mountains by storm until soon, everyone was trying to play some kind of banjo. Very few finished banjos were brought into the hills; if a logger could bring back the hoop, brackets, and ring, a mountaineer could fashion a banjo head from groundhog hide and carve out a suitable neck. Some even tried to make banjos out of gourds, though these didn't sound very good.

Of course, along with the banjo came the banjo tunes as sung and played along the river. "Old Zeb Coon" and virtually all of the white and Negro songs of the rivers found their way into the hill country. Likewise, the mountain tunes, songs like "Darling Cory," "Loving Nancy," and many of the Old English ballads which had first come to the hills from Virginia were taken down to the river settlements. There they met with versions of the same songs which had drifted south and west by way of the New England states, Pennsylvania, and Ohio. For this reason one finds so many variations of the same song.

After making one of these logging trips down to St. Louis, my Uncle Dan Lucas brought back a song book with notes, the old shaped notes, the likes of which no one in the mountains had ever seen before. Uncle Dan had taken a few singing lessons while in St. Louis and, as he was a good singer in the old method of lining out songs, people prevailed upon him to teach a singing school using these new shaped notes. As far as I know, this was the first of such singing schools in Clay County.

In the 1830s, medicine shows started to travel through the mountains, bringing sea shanties from the East Coast and the songs of the Negroes in the Deep South. These groups stopped their wagons and set up shop in any settlement large enough to make it pay, attracting people from miles around. As part of almost all of these shows, a Negro boy danced and performed as a comic, and a small group of players with banjos and fiddles provided music. Always, there would be Dr. So-and-So spieling about the wonders of his own elixir or tonic that could cure anything from amaze and grace to a floating opportunity, baldness, or housemaid's knee. To keep the medicine from souring, the Doctor always spiked the stuff with some of his own whiskey. The medicine shows, as well as entertaining folks, introduced them to new songs and kept them in touch with all parts of the nation.

Many people, authorities, as they claim, in American folklore, would ask us to accept the theory that the mountain people were isolated back in the hills, that they developed a strange culture that kept the old English and Irish ballads more pure than could the English and Irish themselves. This is hogwash, pure and simple. There was no period between migrations or wars that was long enough to establish such an isolated culture there. Many mountain boys fought with Jackson at the Battle of New Orleans and, in fact, gave such a good account of themselves that the broadside song "We Are the Heroes of Kentucky" circulated widely. Before the Civil War, the mountains witnessed the settling of homes by a variety of white races, the beginning of commerce by the millers, the bartering of mountain goods for supplies outside the region, and the travels of log rafters, circuit riders, pack peddlers, and carnival entertainers — all of which should prove that the isolation theory of mountain culture is almost as false as comic strip hillbillies.

Just when the first sawmills appeared in the mountains is hard to determine, but they were probably the second industry of the hills and the first industrial employer: the gristmill had been run by the owner alone. The sawmill gave a big boost not only to logging but to the job of ox driving as well. And lest I forget to give credit where credit is due, I must mention the role played by the mister of the cattle family. This slow but powerful beast of burden cleared most of the mountain farmland and forest. So well suited to the job, oxen were used to log with even after World War I.

The oxen hold a warm spot in the heart of every true mountain person. Some of my fondest memories are of a pair of bull calves given to me when I was only about six years old. Jim Stewart, then married to my sister Molly, made a yoke and helped me break them in to work; soon I was hauling in small logs for stove wood. These calves got so used to being yoked together that, even when I let them loose, they walked and grazed side by side. When they were a year old, my father sold them because he thought they were getting too big for me to handle. (For quite a while, my father did not rate much above whale manure with me.)

Bates's bull was said to have outpulled a team of six horses, just one of many tall tales about the ox that are told over and over again the mountains. Of course, many songs praised the animal or spoke of the hard work of ox driving.

Woa back Buck and yea back Sam.
Who made your back band, who God damn?
Buck's no good and Sam won't pull,
Gonna have to cut that other little bull.
Sixteen oxen in my team,
Worked old Buck, before,
Worked old Buck, till his tail pulled off,
I'll work old Buck no more.
I was going down the road,
A tired team and a heavy load;
I cracked my whip and old Buck sprung,
And he did da-da on my wagon tongue.

It seems that the owner who had worked old Buck on the tram road finally decided to kill him for beef. A lot of high mucky-muckies were at the ox driver's house for supper, and as a joke, because this ox driver was such a loud, cussing man, they asked him to say the grace. He looked around at them and then bowed his head:

*Well done, old Buck,
What brought you here,
You hauled pig metal for twenty years.
You have been abused,
And took abuse,
And now set up for table use.*

With the sawmills in operation, bigger and bigger homes could be built; small towns and villages sprang up around the mills. Carpentering became the chief work of many men and others got good at working stone, building chimneys of stone and clay mortar. The mountain people began to make their livings, as did people sooner or later in all frontier communities, by branching out into many special trades. When this time arrives in any community, the basis of exchange changes; instead of just helping their neighbors and trading off goods, people begin to hire out for wages. In the mountains, as in all other frontier settlements, once the bartering system began to disappear, huge changes took place in mountain society.

3. Bad Blood

My Grandfather Lucas was half-Irish and half-Cherokee. His mother probably would have been sent on the March of Tears to Oklahoma if she had not been married to an Irishman; even as it was, she did not live very long, grieving for her people who were forced to leave their homes and move to reservations. Let all white men hang their heads in shame for the dishonest and cowardly way they treated the good Indian people, a race, in my opinion, far more civilized than the whites. The Indians adopted prisoners, sometimes they killed their captives, but they made no man a slave.

Wilson Lucas was one of the most well-liked men in the community, even though he was always playing jokes on his friends. They would try to get even with him, but usually he would turn the attempt to his own favor and get his neighbor's goat once again.

Grandfather Lucas seemed to get away with tricking about anyone, even Ardill White, the miller of Raider's Creek. One day Ardill White, who also thought himself quite a jokester, saw Lucas coming to the mill and told all the men who were waiting to have their corn ground that he was about to have some fun with my grandfather. As Grandfather Lucas rode up, White called out, "Wilson, Miss Kate" (that is what White called his own wife), "she wants to see you down at the big house" (that is what everyone called the miller's home). My grandfather knew that this was all part of the joke, but he decided to play along.

When he got to the big house, he told Miss Kate that Ardill needed a dollar in change sent up to him at the mill. White's wife gave Grandfather the money he had asked for. As he rode back toward the mill, he could see that White and the other men were laughing.

Ardill asked, "What did she want with you, Lucas?"

My grandfather answered, "Oh, she just wanted to give me this dollar in small change," and rode away leaving everyone laughing, except Ardill White.

During another trip that Grandfather made into Manchester, he ran into a neighbor who had been married just a short time. When this particular friend kept bragging about how his wife never got jealous, Grandfather Lucas had to play a joke on him.

The next time Lucas was in Manchester, he rode by this friend's house and found he was not at home. He said to the wife quite calmly, "I just came by to get a little scrap of that cloth your man bought for you in Manchester last week. I thought it was the prettiest cloth I ever saw." Of course, she was astonished because her husband had not brought home any cloth at all and she told my grandfather so. "Oh yes he did," Lucas insisted. "He bought it the same day he bought you the shoes." She began to swear, "That no good so-and-so didn't bring me no shoes," at which Grandfather looked perturbed and said quietly, "Maybe I have talked too far." Then he rode away. When her husband came home, that woman met him at the door with the broom and gave him a good beating before he could explain that this had just been one of Wilson Lucas's jokes.

In spite of all his joking, my grandfather never brought harm to anyone; in fact, these stories of pranks are typical of a simpler time in the mountains. They reveal what community life was like before the problem of the feuds raised its ugly head. The potential for wide-scale feuds had always been there, I suppose, because almost all of these mountain people prided themselves on their self-sufficiency, many of them having come to the hills initially to get away from subservience to others. Still, no mountaineer of these early days considered himself to be any better than his neighbor who lived over the hill or ten miles away down the river.

They were independent in spirit, but they were generous with one another, with a strong tradition of ready lending and borrowing. Before the Civil War, people would even borrow fire, carrying a live coal from a neighbor's oven for a mile or two to their own stoves if they were out of matches. Since stores were few, if a mountain family ran out of food, often one member would go to a neighbor's and borrow a mess or two to hold his people until one of them had time to get to the store. Even mules were loaned among neighbors. Everything was paid back or, in the case of utensils or tools, returned — all, that is, except salt. It was bad luck to repay salt.

This system of neighborliness lasted until there remained no more unclaimed farmland for people to take up. Until just before the Civil War, the average family had held 160 or more acres, but with all the land accounted for, parents had to divide the family acreage among the children. The typical farm became smaller and smaller until the average farmer had little more than forty acres and a mule. When the land along the hillsides washed away carrying off the topsoil, an even greater scarcity resulted.

With this scarcity, the desire for land became much greater. People combined treaties and ran surveys to see if they couldn't prove that their neighbors' lands had been incorrectly marked. There were disputes over which trees, which rocks marked a property line, especially after "land trees" were cut down and stone markers moved. Of course, this made for bad blood among many mountain families. Rather than someone to share with and depend on, a neighbor became someone to be mistrusted.

As in any situation of this kind, there were those who benefitted. Through hook or crook, some, like the Harrods, acquired more than one house, more than one farm, while others, because of bad management, bad luck, illness, or some other reason, found themselves with nothing. In order to make a living, those who had lost their land turned to sharecropping on the property of others. Traditions of helpful friendship started to disappear, and in their place grew a sense of superiority in those who had more and a resentment on the part of those who had less. Within mountain society, which before had functioned under the ideals of independence and equality, two classes of people emerged.

This division usually cut along family lines, but in some cases individual families were broken apart. One family branch that had gained more property under this new system might try to sever relations with poorer cousins. I have heard some people swear that their family origins were completely different from the lineage of others with the same name.

The richer folks began to educate their children better, even sending them away to school. These children in later life came back to the mountains to become doctors, politicans, teachers, or merchants, and to enjoy a sense of themselves as a class apart from the common folk. Rich men did not want their daughters to marry below their station, a class snobbery that, of course, led to fights, even killings.

These were the people who inevitably owned much of the land rich with coal seams. When investors from outside the mountains came to open up the mines, this upper class, hungry for the gains to be made in royalties off the tonnage, became willing tools of the operators in exploiting the resources of the region. The upper-class people would be elected sheriffs, jailers and judges, assuming all those positions from which they could better force the poor mountain people into the mines to work as wage slaves. The folks with no land left had very little to say about the fate of the beautiful hills where their families had settled years before. Thus, even before the coal operators came into the region, mountain society had begun to disintegrate.

But instead of sticking together against the richer folks and perhaps staving off some of the poverty that was, even then, coming to the shills, the poor people fought against each other. Feuds broke out for all kinds of reasons, one major cause being that people drank too much. Part Irish, they liked a good fight, part Indian, many couldn't handle their whiskey, and all of them were armed.

Many a feud began as just a brawl. In the early days men were more likely to pull off their coats and have at each other bare-fisted until the better man won. Being religious people, most mountaineers did not want to kill anybody, but there were others, well-known mean men, who didn't want to fight; they wanted to kill, just like the bad men of the Old West. A few of these mean men, especially after they had drunk some moonshine whiskey, could bully a whole community. Some would disrupt church services and try to run the preacher out. If anyone were shot or killed in a disturbance like this, a feud was certain to start immediately, since the mean men usually had brothers just as bad at home.

Both sides would call out their families, the hiding and scheming would begin, and soon a bloody feud was raging. Distant cousins would be drawn into the fighting; all family members were involved, often until one side had completely killed the other off. Even if there were just children left, fourteen or fifteen years old, the family that had won would expect these children to pick up the battle again once they had grown large enough to handle guns.

As a fight continued, both sides eventually tried to get to the law for protection. If a man could get arrested and sentenced to jail, he could be safe from the guns of the enemy family. In the last feud that I witnessed, three feudists and five bystanders were shot, but none of them killed. Both families, the Lees and the Georges, limped into the courthouse, surrendered in the high sheriff's office, and were put under arrest.

The feuds began before 1860 but became much more intense after the Civil War. Kentucky gave many soldiers to the Union side (more than did Ohio) and just as many to the side of the south. Not only did this deepen the divisions between many feuding families but it split individual families as well; I for one had a grandfather on each side of the battle. The two were friends before the war and, thank goodness, friends once again after the war was over.

Most mountaineers agreed on the slavery issue, for it was against all the beliefs of the mountain settlers and the Indians with whom they had intermarried to enslave any man. Of course, neither was slavery very profitable in the hills; farms were so small and families so large that often even relatives had no work to do. My grandfather Lucas bought two Negro women in Tennessee, but after learning that one of them had been separated from her baby, he sold them back for less than he had paid. He just could not own a slave.

Only the better-off people owned slaves, and I might add their neighbors thought very little of them for doing so. Though they treated their slaves fairly well, many of these wealthier men were morally weak. They expected complete fidelity from their wives, but many of them had children by their women slaves. For this reason, many black and white families in the mountains share the same name. One will also find people in the hills with a yellowish skin color, descendants of white men and black women.

One old man who owned quite a number of slaves was preparing to die. He called his attorney in to his bedside in order to make a will and asked for all his slaves to be freed. His lawyer asked, "Do you realize how much these slaves will be worth to your children?" To this the dying man replied, "It is bad enough that they are not getting a share of my property. Many of them are my children."

Due to the slavery issue, the majority of the hill people took the Union side, though the Bluegrass region of Kentucky went for the Confederacy. Ardill White, the miller of Raider's Creek, recruited a squadron of men for the Union army, the company in which my Grandfather Lucas served throughout the war. He fought in the "Battle Above the Clouds" near Chattanooga and was among replacements rushed to Gettysburg. For the most part, Grandfather Lucas worked as what we would now call a medic, setting broken legs, digging out bullets, and laying out and dressing the Union dead. When possible, he would slip home on furlough, a dangerous trip since the mountains were so heavily traveled by both Rebel and Union soldiers that, at any one time, no one could tell exactly who had control of the hills.

The mountain people feared the Rebel army because Confederate soldiers, living almost entirely off the land, would ransack a community, taking pigs, chickens, cows and mules and searching family cabins for money. These soldiers were constantly on the lookout for snipers, armed mountain men who fought them from hidden places in the brush along the hillsides. Anyone of these bushwackers, if captured by the Rebels, would be hanged without trial or court-martial.

The Union forces also got supplies and animals from the mountain women but paid for what they took, meaning that whenever the Rebel forces were coming through, folks would hide everything they could, but when the Union army approached, women would bake pies and cakes and set up shop along the roads.

Deserters, both Union and Rebel, slipped back home through the mountains, and since the code of the hills was to mind one's own business and expect others to do the same, the mountain folks would not turn in a man who had had enough of the war. He could travel through the region safely.

Other migrants through the mountains during the war years were slaves escaping north to freedom by way of the underground railroad. Most mountain Negroes had already been set free by their owners before Lincoln's proclamation, and most all of them who were able went to war for the Union.

At the Battle of Cumberland Gap, as I was told by an old Confederate soldier, the bodies of Negro soldiers were stacked ten feet high for half a mile. All of them were buried in a common ditch. These men were good citizens, no better and no worse than their white mountain neighbors. Very little discrimination had been shown to them in the hills because there the Negro man and the white man had for many years worked side by side. As a result, the mountain people fed, hid and helped north most run-away slaves who slipped into the region.

After a war is over, you may ask why it was fought. You can best find an answer by noting what prize the victor takes. The Civil War was not fought to free the slaves — far from it — for if it had been, the victor would have freed them. Instead, the Negro was released from chattel slavery only to be made a wage slave. What the victor did claim was southern cotton for the mills in the more industrialized north. Instead of exporting fiber and other raw materials to England, the South was pried open for the benefit of northern business.

Grandfather Lucas returned to his wife and seven children in Clay County after the peace was made, only to find that the feuds were even more violently tearing the mountains apart. Wilson Lucas managed to remain neutral during all this fighting, mainly because all sides needed to call on him for the medical skills he had acquired during the war. When feuding families shot each other up, they sent for Uncle Wilson, as they called him, to heal their wounded. After he had doctored the injuries of one family, he would visit the other and tie up their wounds. Both sides would probe him to see how badly the other family had been hurt, but he never would tell. He would just say, "Boys, this is not my fight; I'm not in it. I'm here to help your wounded people and that's all I'm here for." Lucas walked a tightrope between the feudists and got by with it because they needed him; he had no enemies in Clay County.

Feuds were to continue for many years after the Civil War; neither the law, nor the church, nor any other movement of goodwill had any effect on them. To this day in the mountains, there exist families at odds with each other, but they seldom resort to shooting anymore. The only force strong enough to stop the feudists in their violence was industrialization. When you go to work in a coal mine, the boss doesn't ask, "Are you a Jones, a Griffin, or a Fisher?" He puts you to work, very possibly pushing a coal car alongside a man from a family that you fought against only weeks before. When the slate falls on you, the man who helps to drag it off may be of the feuding family next door. In an industrial situation, where a man must depend on others for his income, his health, his life, feuding cannot continue. This was one of the only positive effects of coal mining in the Kentucky mountains.

4. Meat Skins

Since the war to open up the South was over, the railroads rapidly began to build lines for the transportation of southern cotton to the industrial North. Soon these routes were built around and through the mountains; Pittsburg, Kentucky and London, Corbin, even Pineville and Middlesboro had railroads by 1880, only sixteen years after the Civil War.

Oh buddy, won't you line 'em,
Oh buddy, won't you line 'em,
Line 'em boy,
Oh buddy, won't you line that track.

The lining out method of singing, which mountain churches and loggers had used, was also heard during the building of the railroads. A good liner was in great demand on the railroad section gangs because by either lining out an old song or inventing a new one about the scene at hand, he could coordinate the individual workers and speed them up on the job. The gang would answer him:

Push 'em over and line 'em back.
Oh buddy, won't you line 'em,
Oh buddy, won't you line 'em,
Oh, buddy, won't you line that track.

A liner would be paid more than the ordinary railroad worker for his skills, and because his role was well accepted, in fact, appreciated, the other men didn't dispute his higher wage.

In his best talking voice the leader would line out:

Come tell me of your ship and what is her name,
Do tell me happy sailor.

The group would chant the same line just as slowly as they could possibly sing, holding the last note while the liner spoke the next phrase:

*Come tell me of your captain and what is his fame,
Oh tell me, happy sailor.*

After the gang sang this line, the leader would line out the chorus:

*It is the old ship of Zion, hallelu, hallelu,
It is the old ship of Zion, hallelujah.*

The group and the leader sang out these lines in unison to end the first verse. After each of the rest of the verses, all sang the chorus without the liner's prompting.

The railroads were the first companies to enter the mountains with the purpose of mining coal. Since by this time, most engines were coal fired, railroad outfits opened their own mines and consumed the fuel themselves. One such mine, at Walsend, Kentucky, remained in business until the 1930's when I left the state.

The railroads had not been mining long, though, before many other small companies learned of this land's richness. Many beaus came a'courting the virgin mountains, seeking favor with her guardians, the new wealthy class of mountain people who had acquired most of the land. Even before the large coal companies sent in their agents, small operators leased land in areas where the railroad, at that time, was not even expected to pass, at prices as low as twenty-five cents an acre. The landed mountain people assumed that underground mining, paying them an additional royalty per ton, would make worthwhile their leasing lands for so little money. The grandchildren of these sell-outs, though, learned the full consequences of the railroad's entry and of these early coal leases.

In this song I tried to show what some of those consequences have been:

SAD THE DAY

Sad the day I saw the steam shovel a'coming,
The sound of its wheels as it rattled along.
Deep in my heart a voice seemed to be saying,
"Good-bye my sweet home, you soon will be gone."

In 18 and 80 my folks were rejoicing,
They had sold the mineral rights on the farm.
Twenty-five cents an acre they paid them.
My folks did not know it would cause any harm.

This farm it was the home of my father;
His father too was born and raised here.

Now they are at rest beneath the green willows
Along with their wives and children so dear.

Let them alone. Please do not disturb them.
Don't dump the yellow clay dirt over their graves.
The law may say that you have a right to
Because of that twenty-five cents that you paid.

I looked and I saw them up on the mountain
As they dumped the yellow clay and rock down the hill.
Soon every living plant will be covered.
My beautiful valley soon will be filled.

Don't force me to leave the house I was born in.
Please don't destroy my home dear to me.
Please take back the twenty-five cents an acre
You paid for the mineral rights and just let us be.

Where did most of the small operators come from? Many of them were sons or grandsons of former plantation owners. After the war, northern carpetbaggers had descended on southern lands, buying up plantations as delinquent taxes, taxes which the owners could not pay because they had sunk all their money in Confederate bonds. The children of these fallen southern aristocrats longed for the former system of landowner and slave and saw in mine operation an opportunity to regain it. With its company store, its mine shacks, and its company scrip, a small mining camp certainly resembled a plantation in the Deep South.

Of course, other small businessmen were eager to take up mine operation as well. Some were latecomers from the Old Country. Even some Welsh coal miners drifted in who, because of their experience, were in great demand as managers and foremen; many of them later became operators themselves.

Most of the small operators considered themselves good friends of the miners, although a step above them socially. When a miner went on a drunk, disturbed the peace, or broke the Sabbath, the coal operator would just get in touch with the county judge (who more than likely held his job due to the operator's support) and would tell the judge to turn his "boy" loose. The operator often stood a miner's fine, usually withholding that amount from the worker's pay.

One old coal miner I knew, Granny Reed, was quite a strong early union man, though he was kindly lazy too and so was always in Dutch with the coal operator. One particular fall, Granny was out of a job. With his old shoes tied around his feet, being pretty thin on clothing, Granny was out on the porch of the company store one day, stamping his feet to try to keep warm. Mosey Coleman, the coal operator, must have had a tinge of conscience: he walked over to Granny, told him to go in the store and have George Jones fit him up with a pair of shoes on credit. Granny did this at once. As the old miner came out of the company store wearing his new shoes, Mosey Coleman looked at him and said, "Granny, a year from now you can look down at those shoes and sing 'How Firm a Foundation.'"

And Granny answered, "Mosey, five years from now you can look down at your books and sing, 'A Charge to Keep I Have'!"

The early operator lived in the mining camp, but in a much larger and sturdier house than any miner. Usually he had one or two black servants, a cook and a housekeeper at least. For his workers, the small operator had shacks built and often a community church house too, but he and his family would never attend services there. Neither did the operator's children go to the public school. The sons and daughters of mine foremen and superintendents, however, attended the local school in the elementary grades; many of the children born to this middle class of managers traveled away for more education, later to return to the mountains as lawyers with an interest in politics.

Who worked in these early mines? The vast majority were sharecroppers, landless men who after giving up half their crops were still in debt to a landowner. At the offer of steady work, many sharecroppers grabbed up jobs in the mines.

Other men hated mining. They hated the dirt and they hated the loss of independence. Farming had allowed them a certain amount of leisure time for hunting and in the winter, lots of socializing with neighbors. But there are many ways to force a man with a big family to do what he does not want to do. Starvation is a dreadful whip that has been used to exploit working people down through the years, and starvation was exactly what faced most sharecroppers as the alternative to working in the mines. Some people went farther west, many, like my Uncle Bob Lucas, moving into the piney woods of Arkansas. Those men who had run into trouble with the law were especially inclined to travel west.

Unable to make a living farming and unwilling to enter the coal mines, my father, Oliver Perry "Peoria" Garland, still chose to remain in Kentucky. With his uncle, he went to work operating a general store at East Bernstadt, Kentucky. As was the way at that time, the store carried everything from horseshoe nails and harnesses to men's shirts, house furnishings, and a full line of food. He and his first wife, Deborah Robinson Garland, had two children: Molly, later known as Aunt Molly Jackson, born in 1880, and John born two years later at East Bernstadt. Two other children died in infancy.

My father sustained his family very well until the miners at East Bernstadt came out on strike and attempted to organize a union. Since my father was pastor of the Missionary Baptist Church there, the miners counted on him for support. My great uncle, who owned the majority of the stock in the store, also sympathized with the miners' cause. "Peoria," he said to my father, "these are good men. Let them have what they want on credit and they can pay when they go back to work." As happened so many times, the men lost their strike and couldn't pay; many of them, barred from returning to work at the East Bernstadt mine, were forced to move away. As a result, my father and uncle went broke, losing the general merchandise store.

In order to avoid mining, my father, like so many others of his generation, resigned himself to sharecropping. The forty acres allotted to the typical sharecropper could produce only about thirty or forty bushels an acre, and of this, half reverted to the landowner. With a wife and five, six, maybe even seven children at home, the small farmer could barely sustain himself.

My father's first wife died, leaving him to care for Molly and John, two rambunctious children to say the least. Soon, however, he had remarried, to my mother, Elizabeth Lucas, daughter of Wilson Lucas. Within less than six years, there were three more children in the family: Bob, Dick and Lonie. Dad was sharecropping during these years for Ardill White, the same Raider's Creek miller who had organized the Clay County squadron of Union soldiers. In addition to working his portion of White's acreage, my father worked both days and nights at other jobs for White until he became entirely dependent on the landowner for survival. I have been told by my mother that at the end of each day, White paid my father off with fifty cents and a bunch of meat skins. My father accepted this payment because he had no choice.

Tobacco was and still is the money crop for the farmers in Clay County. Most families raised ten acres, often dividing the plot into smaller patches so that the teenage boys could work some land on their own and pocket some money after the fall market.

Tobacco is a difficult crop to raise. If the plants survive the attacks of weeds, worms, and hailstorms until they are full grown, the tobacco is cut and the stock is split through with a stake. Then the plants are hung in the barn to dry. The leaves will get so dry that if you holler loud enough, you can hear the tobacco shelling off the stocks. After this drying period, the leaves will dampen again because of the humidity in the late summer air. This process is called "coming into case." At this time, the tobacco is "put down," meaning piled in one corner of the barn and heaped over with green corn, which keeps it moist.

Now the tobacco is ready to hand; a hand of tobacco refers to a bunch of leaves of the same grade. Since the price you will get depends a lot on how carefully your crop is handed, the work is most often done by skilled crews of thirteen, one worker for each grade of tobacco.

The bigger farms were always able to hire the handing crews first and so were the first to put their crops on the market. Big companies would buy this leaf at a good price. But by the time the small man got his tobacco to sale, the price would have sunk to about half. Still, the sharecropper could do nothing but sell since every day that his tobacco spent on the market floor would cost him.

Tobacco is sold in an auction house, the one we used being in Richmond, Kentucky. After paying a fee, the farmer puts his tobacco on the auction floor. The auctioneer uses a chant to call the prices as buyers walk through, flipping the leaves, examining the hands, and deciding how much they will pay for each batch. If the farmer refuses to sell his crop for the price offered, he must withdraw it from the floor and put it on again later. In the meantime, his leaves are becoming more and more shopworn, putting him further at the mercy of the buyers and the auction house.

One small farmer hauled his wagon load of tobacco into the auction house for sale, bringing with him a few chickens. Once his tobacco was sold, the auctioneer proceeded to figure up the fee charges. "Well, the way I figure it," the auctioneer said, "you owe me one dollar."

"But I hain't got a dollar," answered the farmer. "Could you take these chickens instead?"

This the auction man did. The very next week, back came the small farmer to the auction house, his wagon loaded with more leaves and two more chickens to hand over for the fee.

Though this story exaggerates a bit, it is true that the small farmer could not compete with the rich producer. This situation brought on direct action in Kentucky during the Tobacco Wars. Once the small farmers realized that they had been frozen out of the market, they organized the Night Riders and resorted to burning down the tobacco barns of large farmers. The Night Riders could be considered the first farmers union in Kentucky. (They are not to be confused with those other night riders who, like the Ku Klux Klan, did violence against Negroes, immigrants, and members of the Catholic Church.)

Another job that my father worked for Ardill White's fifty cents and meat skin was digging coal. It had been that folks just dug coal for their own use, but as mountain society divided into the wealthy and the poor, some people found that they didn't like to wallow in the mud and wade in the creeks. My father dug about five tons of coal by each fall to set White up for the winter.

The first men to get coal from the ground were called "coal diggers" because they simply dug the coal out with a straight pick, about as heavy as a dirt pick. In the small branches and larger creeks, water washed the dirt off the tops of coal seams, leaving them exposed in the streambeds. With only a simple tool, men dug up this soft coal, what we now call "outcroppings," and carted it away. Before the railroads came, most of the coal went to homes or to blacksmiths' forges as it made much hotter fire than wood.

The places where coal was exposed or very near the surface were limited and soon were dug out, so the coal diggers, many of whom had become quite handy at this kind of work, began to pick away at seams beneath rock. A small man found this much easier than did a larger man because many of the coal seams were only 28" or 32" from top to bottom. As they ventured deeper into the earth, the early miners found that the coal became progressively harder and that their hand-sharpened picks could not pry it loose. It became necessary for a blacksmith to sharpen the digger's tools every day. The blacksmith heated the pick's end in his forge and beat it out into a very small, sharp point. Then, with one lick of his hammer, he would make a little burr on the tip and dip the point, while it was still hot, in water to temper it. Even with these sharper picks though, the coal diggers' tools could not get at coal very far underground.

Sharecropping to support a growing family was hard enough, but my father's money problems were doubled because of his preaching. Though he was not ordained until years later, my father had been a preacher in the Missionary Baptist Church since he was sixteen years old. Many mountain boys felt called upon to preach at an early age, and those who could speak well drew big crowds. To understand the child preachers and their popularity, one must realize that the mountain people believe a man is called to preach the gospel. If he can, he is supposed to read the scripture, but if God wants him to preach, even if he cannot read or write, his mouth will be filled with the gospel.

Those of my father's generation who could not read or write often knew entire passages from the Bible by heart because they had heard passages read and discussed so often around the fireside at home. Any mountain boy who attended church had heard the same passages used over and over again in local services and had probably listened to scriptural arguments among people in the community. The Bible, the only book in many mountain homes, became part of a young boy's store of knowledge.

Preachers of different denominations, and many who were not preachers at all, made quite a hobby of "arguing the scriptures." Every man felt that he had a God-given right to search out the scriptures for himself; if he discovered something that others had not found, it was his Christian duty to inform the whole world. This duty led usually to a heated discussion.

I recall one such argument between my father and a Holiness preacher named Crank. As was the custom, there was preaching going on over on the courthouse lawn. A certain blind man had been holding forth preaching, claiming that if he made any mistake in his references to scripture, one of his listeners should correct him. Once the blind man had finished, Preacher Crank asked how a man who could not even see could search the scripture. My father stood up and answered that the blind man already knew the scripture and so had no need to search. At this, Crank said to my father, "You have preached a lie."

My dad drew back his fist saying, "Take care, take care." Crank dared my father to hit him, and that's exactly what my father did. The Holiness preacher turned the other cheek, and Dad hit that side too. After that incident, my father never did like preacher Crank, he would say, "Crank, Crank — a handle to grind a stone. Garland — a wreath of flowers."

The child preachers were something like the whiz-kids of later years and the movie stars of today, with one exception: they were never paid great sums of money. A preacher was given only food, shelter, and clothing for his services; in fact, to pay him for doing what God had called him to do would have been a sin. For this reason, the child preachers, in spite of their popularity, escaped many of the evils that plague the young movie stars of today. Most of them grew up and married quite normally. Early preaching had little effect on their lives, except that most of them, like my father, continued to preach until they died.

Many mountain preachers had led very sinful, immoral lives. Some had been married several times, others had killed someone. It seems that many of these men were determined later in life to become the most upright members of the community. Such reformed bad men became immensely popular as preachers since folks believed that any man who could change so drastically just had to be saved, called directly by God to preach. And who is an ordinary person to question the wisdom of God?

Most of the early Baptist preachers were not ordained. A man could just read the Bible and listen to other preachers as his instruction; then, if the regular pastor were unable to come to church one Sunday, this man could fill in. If he could speak well and pray loudly, often he would later be ordained by the deacons of his local parish.

One mountain preacher of the amateur variety could not pronounce his words very well because of a speech impediment. During one service he was conducting, he had all the church members down a'praying when he got his secrets caught between two of the benches.

"Oh my cod! Oh my cod!" he yelled. The church members, thinking he was ecstatically praying, all joined in: "Oh my God!"

"Not my heavenly Cod," he yelled, "but my cod below."

Even though the board of deacons hired the pastor, a rejection by them did not stop any man who wanted to preach on his own initiative. In this respect only, the Missionary Baptist Church has changed since its early days. Now many young men attend ministerial college, at Clear Creek Spring, for example, rather than simply beginning to preach and being ordained later by the local board of deacons. I suppose another minor change might be that in the present-day Missionary Baptist churches, solo singers more often come to the front of the church to perform hymns.

In Kentucky, the church found most of its new members at revival meetings, highly emotional gatherings held on successive nights for a week, sometimes for an entire month. One traveling revivalist came to a vicinity where some wild young men had made a practice of chasing preachers away. As he began to preach, this salty old man pulled out his Bible and laid it on the rough table serving as a pulpit, saying to the congregation, "I will lay my sword right there." Then he pulled back the tail of his coat, took out a big .45 pistol, and laid it down next to the Bible saying, "I'll use whichever one of these you wish for me to use. But when I turn the other cheek, it is to listen to see if the man I shot is still breathing." Needless to say, this man was not molested. It came back to me that this salty old preacher was my father, and while I couldn't certify that it was, I wouldn't have put that past him.

My father was sometimes away for weeks on end preaching revivals, often during the harvest season. The field work then fell to my mother and her older children. My father would return home without pay, bringing with him only the little bit of food he could carry on his horse. My mother said that during the years my father sharecropped, the family literally became naked. When someone had to go to the store, all the family's garments were pooled so that this one person would have enough to wear. They couldn't have a shoemaker move in, for that would have meant another mouth to feed. Instead, the women would share one pair of shoes and the boys would tie just anything around their feet for protection. Sometimes they tried to make moccasins out of old scraps of animal skin. My mother told me that when the family saw visitors coming, they would hide until the people had left because they were not decently dressed enough to be seen.

The wives of preachers often resented the attention their husbands received from their congregations, and when left alone with the children, would resort to feeling sorry for themselves. I believe these wives' feelings were well justified. The Bible does not give much voice to a wife, but neither does hunger wait for the revival meeting to end. Many mountain preachers' wives even left their families, their children growing up to be some of the toughest kids in the community. Having witnessed the hardships of a religious family, very few followed in their fathers' footsteps. My brother Bill, who later became a Missionary Baptist pastor, was an exception.

I believe the only people who ranked higher in the confidence and respect of the mountain community were the early mountain doctors, perhaps because there were fewer of them. Before the advent of the railroad, there were very few doctors who had been educated as such. Medicine was generally practiced by two methods: faith healing and herb doctoring. Those who practiced the former claimed that one could be healed of sickness by praying and by the laying on of hands. Many mountain people still ascribe to this method of healing, though usually they undertake it in conjunction with modern medical practices.

Another type of faith healing was practiced early in the mountains by those believed to be witches. "Boxknocker" Monhollen, one of these self-proclaimed doctors, received his nickname because of his supposed feats as a medium, having, according to some, made tables walk and boxes rattle. Witch doctoring became a dangerous practice when these mediums were entirely convinced of their powers.

I remember when one of our neighbors cut a large artery in his foot with an axe. Boxknocker Monhollen arrived to cure the young man, claiming he could stop the blood by sticking the axe in the ground. Finally, someone who knew a little about first aid wound a tourniquet around the boy's leg before he bled to death; my Aunt Martha Fisher took the boy to her house and arranged for a different sort of doctor to come stich the wound.

Unlike the witch doctors, herb doctors claimed to have gotten their knowledge from their Indian ancestors, and indeed many of their herbal remedies were borrowed from the Cherokee. Certainly, they practiced medicine far differently from doctors today. The herb doctor would not just ask about aches and pains and write out a prescription; he would diagnose the trouble and mix doses of medicine from the powders in his little black bag, as well as being a friend and confidant.

My father was one such herb doctor, and a veterinarian also. In later years he acquired and worked from a true textbook of medicine but he never claimed to be anything but an herb doctor, devising most of his remedies from mountain herbs, berries, and vegetables. The Indian remedies and herb medicines have a lot to speak for them; in fact, even with the advent of modern medicine, herbal remedies continue to be used to some extent in the mountains. In my father's time, though, most everyone knew the medicinal properties of the native plants, probably because doctors were so few and since paying for a doctor was often impossible. Very few people ever went to the hospital. Most ill people stayed at home, died at home, and were dressed and buried by their neighbors. My father, for example, though he lived to be sixty-five and spent the last twelve years of his life a very sick man, never went to a hospital.

My cousin John Herd was boarding with us when the whole family came down with smallpox — everyone except me. With only a half-dozen bumps, I claimed smallpox wouldn't hurt good flesh. John Herd, though, was sick in bed. He owned the prettiest watch that I had ever seen, and I wanted very much for him to give it to me. One day he said, "Well, Jim, if I die, you can have the watch, but you had better keep an eye on the other people around here or they might beat you to it." I was tickled to death, thinking that my cousin was about to die.

Outside playing, I'd begin to wonder if John Herd had passed away. Every so often I'd run inside and call out, "John Herd, are you dead yet?"

Each time he'd answer me, "No, not yet, Jim, but keep checking. I'm liable to go any time."

One afternoon when I came in to check on my cousin, I found my brother Bob standing above his bed holding the watch. I can still remember how mad I was at them both. "Well, the devil to John Herd," I yelled. "There was no use in him dying if I wasn't going to get that watch." Of course, just then my cousin opened his eyes and he and my brother had quite a laugh on me. This story shows how mountain people typically will continue to joke, even when they are lying on their deathbeds.

Herb doctors like my father, though highly respected and trusted, rarely delivered babies in the mountains. Only the women herb doctors and midwives, "granny women" as they were often called, could do this, unless, of course, a medical doctor could be found (and afforded). Even in such cases, midwives were often called in to help.

My Aunt Martha Fisher was a midwife; so was my sister Molly from about 1910 until 1932. She delivered far more babies during those years than did all the doctors on both Horse Creek in Clay County and Straight Creek in Bell County. According to Molly's own estimate, she attended over 5,000 births.

Midwives, usually middle-aged or older women, were mostly tough old girls. Aunt Martha, for example, wasn't afraid of anything. She shot one woman who was running around with her husband and threatened to shoot him too if he took one step toward that woman again. He never took that step.

Even if mountain women took care of the birth themselves, they generally wanted a midwife to check them over, to be on the safe side. Lots of times, granny women would stay over after the women had delivered their babies, doing the housework until the mothers could do for themselves. Aunt Molly was highly thought of as a midwife; in fact, many women preferred her help to that of a doctor. Serving at the births of two of my children, she did quite nicely.

Folks of my parents' generation suffered from an ill effect of the Civil War few people realize — the lapse in education. The war had taken all the schoolteachers and doctors, except for the few who couldn't possibly serve, leaving the mountain children without teaching for four years. Some will point out that after the war, young men ended up in classrooms with very young children in order to catch up in their learning, but for the most part, those who had missed school during the war years never returned for any education. My mother, for example, could barely read for the very reason that she'd never had a teacher; her older sisters could not read at all. My father became an excellent reader, though, having taught himself by reading the Bible.

These uneducated people were also those met by outsiders coming into the hills to look for a supposedly isolated culture. When scholars entered the mountains and found poorly educated men and women and children, like my sister Molly, they immediately assumed here was a culture that had preserved the songs and traditions of the Old World, a lost generation. As I have said before, there never was a worse lie. Uneducated or poorly educated as they were, my older brothers and sisters were quite aware of the world outside the mountains; my brother John joined the circus and traveled all over the South, and my brother Dick, in the long tradition of mountain support for third parties, voted for Eugene V. Debs on the Socialist party ticket.

Another hindrance to the education of mountain children after the Civil War, especially for children of poor men devoted to farming like my father, was the constant uprooting of families. My father could survive sharecropping for at the most, two years at a stretch before he would have to return to coal mining at any place that would hire him. His children left school to follow him to each new mining camp, but it seemed as soon as they became a part of one caol camp's classrooms, they again were moving, either to another coal camp or back to the farm.

These children of the Civil War and their children, who grew up in the period of transition from the sharecropped farm to the exploratory mine, perhaps needed education more than any other mountain children had before or have since. They would be called upon to develop a whole new way of life; they were the parents of the first generation of coal miners. They had to decide whether to send their own illiterate children into the mines. They needed to stand against the unscrupulous outsiders who, with all their wealth and education, were determined to exploit the rich seams of bituminous coal and the mountain people as well.

5. The Feast

Before the 1890s, no one truly knew whether coal, aside from its use to fuel the railroads, would be a paying proposition. The mountain people who had been forced from the land knew that the mines meant wages and that the railroad meant an increase of goods and money flowing into the area. Because of these encouragements, in spite of what some may say, the early miners would bend over backward rather than do anything to hurt the first small operators.

Individual investors were willing to take a risk on coal since the outlay for an early mine was so small. If a man had good credit, he could open up an operation for $2,000, just enough to build a tipple, buy a couple of mules, pay a half-dozen miners, and lease the land. With only twenty-five to fifty cents per ton reverting to the landowner in royalties, the small operators soon began to make considerable profits. And as the small operations grew, so did production — to three or four, sometimes as many as ten fifteen-ton gondolas (railroad cars) per day.

At the first exploratory mining sites, miners initially used picks and shovels much like the coal diggers' tools. But soon, as they encountered the harder coal farther underground, new mining methods had to be established.

Digging coal haphazardly is quite different from a mining operation, all of which works according to a blueprint. The mining area is charted off. At the center is the main entry and branching off of it, the cross entries which are driven to the end of the leased property. The cross entries are numbered 1st right, 1st left, 2nd right, 2nd left, and so on, although some coal companies would not have cross entries numbered 13. The last right and left entries were made within two hundred feet of the property line, as nearly as that could be ascertained. Because the rugged terrain of the mountains made such calculations difficult, mining engineers surveyed from both the outside and the inside of the mines for accuracy. Even so, someone was always claiming that his coal was being unlawfully mined.

My father used unslaked lime to blast the coal loose, a method which most people today have never heard of, but which my friend Tom Inman says was used in Laurel County until 1890. Using a breast auger, the miner bored a hole two inches in diameter and six feet deep into the coal, filling the back two feet with unslaked lime. The hole was bored starting at least one foot from the bottom and angling down for six feet, ending, if possible, at the seam bottom. A steel needle, six and one half feet long, was then placed in the hole, one end touching the lime. With a tamping bar (an iron rod, six or seven feet long, which is wide at one end and tapers into a handle at the other), the miners tamped two feet of damp clay dirt into the hole and filled the remaining two feet with water.

The steel needle was then removed from the hole, leaving a pencil-sized opening through which the water could run down into the lime. After a period of time, sometimes as long as a day, the lime would eventually have pushed the coal loose enough to dig. This method was abandoned fairly soon, probably because it was so slow.

The next to come along was black powder. This procedure worked in much the same way as had the lime, except that it loosened the coal much more quickly. The needle was still used, but the hole reduced in diameter to an inch and a quarter, and coal dust rather than clay was tamped into the hole. The miner made a squib by twisting black powder into the end of four or five inches of paper. The last two inches of the twisted paper contained the black powder and were covered with sulfur. The needle was removed and the squib placed in the hole. The sulfur end, when lit, would burn very slowly down to the powder charge, finally blasting out the coal. With the advent of the use of black powder, mines could be driven to practically limitless depths under the mountain.

The first track laid in the mines consisted of two by fours or two by threes sawed at the local lumber mills. The miners had to push cars into their working places and push the loaded cars, which in the early days held from 1,500 to 3,000 pounds, back out to where the mules could be hooked up. This pushing was one of the hardest things a miner had to do; whether on an upgrade or a downgrade, he, with the help of a "buddy," would have to get down with his shoulder against the coal car, hold onto the rail with his hands, and push with his feet.

In the early days, three or four miners would share a mule. Later, this gave way to mule-driving as a special trade within the mine. During the days of the mule-driver, the average coal output per man was about three and one half tons per ten hour day.

Many of the early miners thought of the small coal operators as benefactors and fell for the old line: "You should appreciate the man who gives you a job." The hill people's traditional satisfaction with, "Well, I am making a living" worked all right as long as they stayed on the farm. But this was not good enough for the industrial worker, moving from good working conditions to bad ones, working an average of only 155 days per year. Yet it was hard for the early miners to realize that the small operator, no matter how concerned he seemed to be, was still making a good deal of money off their labors. For this reason alone it was hard at first to organize into a trade union.

Too, unions were a new idea. Logging had never been organized because of the nature of the work, most of it contracted by men who owned the oxen necessary to haul the logs to the mill. The sharecropper's firm obligation to his landowner had not fostered organization.

Generally there are two kinds of labor unions. The craft union theory espouses that all union members should share the same line of work. The railroad industry unions are examples of this kind, with railroad engineers in one union, brakemen in another. Industrial unions work from a different theory; they claim that all who work in or around the industrial situation should be organized as one.

The acceptance of industrial unionism provided the only hope in organizing mine workers. Craft unionism could not work because, especially in the early days, one day a worker would be loading coal, the next day running a machine, and the next working as a timber man. Since the first coal mines were not specialized operations, according to the craft union theory, a man would have had to belong to fifty different unions.

The old Knights of Labor was the first attempt to organize workers in the same setting into one union. My father became a member in the last days of his sharecropping for Ardill White. Later, when he was working at Pittsburg, Kentucky, in the low-vein sulfurous coal, about twenty-four to thirty-six inches high, he joined the Knights of Labor miners' affiliate there. My friend Tilman Cadle, who helped to lead the 1932 strike in Eastern Kentucky and whose father was also a member of the Knights of Labor, recalls that its president or "master" was Terence V. Powderly.

The Knights of Labor was more like a lodge than a union. In the tradition of the old English and German carpenters unions, the Knights of Labor held to apprenticeship. In my father's case, this meant that after he had become a miner, he took young boys down in the mine and trained them. If the present-day miners union has any sense, it will go back to this principle, creating a brotherhood, as the Knights of Labor called itself, rather than just a strict trade union.

My father's membership in the rather loosely organized Knights of Labor was short-lived. He was working in the mines when the miners at Coal Creek, Tennessee, went on strike. The operators there forced local prison inmates to resume the work at the mine, a ploy which indeed worked until the union members, early United Mine Workers of America advocates, set all the prisoners free. Two of the prisoners stayed hidden in my father's house for three weeks, until the search for them was abandoned. From this time, 1896 on, my father, whether he was working in the mines or just living in the mining camps, was always in the union, the UMW of A. He went on to become the local president in his mining camp at East Bernstadt.

The thirty years that followed were busy with expansion. The railroad pushed into all the hollows, busting right through at Corbin and moving into Bell County whose East Jellico seam was about the best grade of bituminous coal in the country. The railroad headed into Knox and great Harlan County.

The union was organizing, but mostly underground and with uneven success. For this reason, there were many small-scale wildcat strikes, more or less local affairs over specific grievances. In a strike situation, the operator always brought forth the same strong argument: "Boys, you are only hurting yourselves and your operator as well, for while we are on strike, my orders are being filled by the competition down the road." Often the miners would agree to go back to work, but with each strike they learned something.

The mountain people had always thought that if their employer didn't treat them well, they should quit, or in some cases, give the boss a good whipping. But more and more, as the number of competing coal mines grew, mountain people began to see they had to stick together or they would never win anything. They had fallen into the trap of believing that making a living was a goal in itself, but in the years that ended the nineteenth century, they were to realize that this slogan was an enslaving lie.

In the change from a farming society to an economy based on mining, many people were left out completely. Those hardest hit were old people, too feeble to be of value as sharecroppers, who had no children to move in with. Sometimes, if the landowner were a good Joe, he wouldn't go to court to put such old-timers off his land. They would be allowed to live on in a shack of some kind.

But many folks were not so fortunate. Put out with no place to live, they would wander around the hills, staying a night or two with anyone who would keep them until eventually, they would end up on the poor farm.

Old people could not just take up a spot on one of these poor farms; they needed first to be admitted, assigned by the county judge. People who were starving or sick with no resources to care for themselves could notify their local magistrate; he in turn could bring their cases up before the county board if he chose to. If this board decided to grant help to a needy person, the county judge would write out a voucher, usually for a very small amount, to be used for food. The beneficiary would then try to find local merchants, or perhaps a doctor, who would accept the county's voucher as payment.

This same board had the power to issue admittances to the poor farm.

Even when an assignment had been made, old people usually had to wait to be admitted since the poor farms' two-room shacks were scarce. An old person might have to wait until some other old man or woman died to make room. This was the very deepest of poverty.

Some may think of the poor farms as rest homes where old people could go to stay out the rest of their lives in comfort — far from it. The people assigned to the poor farms worked in the fields and were expected to raise most of their own food on the plots assigned to them. Those who were able cooked on their own stoves. Those who couldn't care for themselves ate in a communal kitchen run by the stronger inmates. Some of the women made quilts at the poor farm, while the men made chairs and axe and pick handles. All of their crafts were sold to help with the general expense of the place.

Though some poor farms were not as bad as others, all of them were uncomfortable. Those who ran the places were supposed to make the farms unattractive so as not to encourage more old people to petition their magistrates. Many terrible stories were told about life there, some even claiming that when old people became incapable of caring for themselves, they were given the black bottle (poison). I have also heard that if an inmate became ill between the doctor's visits, he or she would simply be left to wait until the physician's visiting day. Undoubtedly, many of these stories were untrue; probably they were spread deliberately to scare away other eligible old people.

The poor farms were the direct effect of the small farmers' and sharecroppers' leaving the land for work in the mines. The old people could not generally handle the work of mining, and besides, the coal companies wanted to train young men, boys who lived with their families, rather than old men whose relatives were dead and gone. The coal companies liked large families of males because more work could be squeezed out of one household. An old man and his wife were hardly worth the company's furnishing a house.

You may say that mountain people would not have put up with this kind of treatment even if they were old, that a mountaineer would more likely shoot anyone who tried to treat him like this. And of course, a few men indeed wouldn't submit to these conditions. Instead of ending up on the poor farm, they would just take enough from another man's field to subsist on. As I have said before, though, hunger is a dreadful master. When you take the means of making a living from a man, you take his manhood away. This is true whether he be a mountain man or a man living in the city's ghetto.

A few poor farms were still in operation as late as 1926 (I remember one in Bell County at that time), but I think they have been discontinued now. The poor farms were not created because people had a right to them, because of age or need. They were used as a charitable political tool with which the men in office could show they cared. Maybe some politicians even did care. But nothing, no one was to stand in the way of the coal industry.

There were no mines in Harlan County until about 1890 or '95, I believe. But once the area had been opened up by the railroads, all the big names — U.S. Steel, Henry Ford Company, General Motors, Black Diamond, and a little later, Peabody — were swarming in for the feast. Some big mines were brought into Mingo Hollow by the English very early. On the basis of the knowledge the small, exploratory operators had acquired, these large conglomerates sent in agents to lease land and to begin to exploit the people and the mountains.

Unlike the operators of the exploratory mines, these people did not care for the country; they didn't live there. The large operators made little pretense of friendship with their workers, running their mines through hired men who, once given their orders, had little or no power to deal with the miners' complaints. The owners did not care how much coal was lost through sloppy mining practices, nor did they care how many miners lost their lives because of unsafe working conditions. With the consent and help of mountain landowners, these outsiders destroyed the beautiful hills and reduced a once proud and self-sufficient people to the poverty-ridden folk of today.

The corporations opened up mines quickly, threw up flimsy plank shacks, and began recruiting people for work. They built company commissaries and issued company scrip. The miners were to work in their mines, live in their houses, be served by the company doctor, and vote right on election day. Although the war to free the slaves had been over for thirty years, here was a system, set up legally, that was as vicious as chattel slavery.

Though the United Mine Workers of America was young, the coal operators knew what was coming to labor in the mountains and soon began to organize into coal operators associations, not only to fight against the miners' union, but to compete more successfully against other coal operators for the huge orders to the Great Lakes. This region is where most of the coal was sent during the summer.

The operators of Harlan County created the Harlan County Coal Operators Association and the operators in Bell and Knox counties, the Appalachian Coal Operators Association. In the struggles between the two, those who suffered most were the coal miners. One group would cut wages in order to underbid the rival association, and as a result, the competing group would cut wages even lower. Small-scale strikes accomplished little. The big companies held so many mine fields and had brought in so much new equipment that when miners of one district went on strike, the orders could simply be filled in another.

Only in the small, once exploratory mines had the union built up any degree of real strength. These operators had become accustomed to dealing with union groups. But in their attempts to give miners at least a bare sustenance wage, such small mine operators were being edged out of the market; some could no longer afford to stock their company stores with food. The miners would then go out on strike again, and eventually the small mine would be eaten up, taken over by one of the large outside corporations.

According to this pattern, large companies quickly gained dominance in the mountains. Good men were killed, ballot boxes were stuffed, votes were bought. The companies corrupted the political organizations of several counties and even those of the state by giving money to the officeholders they could control and browbeating those they could not buy. The state militia was used to break strikes and to aid company guards. Many of these company gunmen were murderers the company officials had taken from penitentiaries and held in bondage, threatening to send them back to prison. Those miners who did not buckle under were blacklisted, hounded, or killed. The union fought back as it could, winning a few strikes but losing many more. Churches were corrupted, many of the ministers being persuaded to side with the operators against their local parishioners.

My father, after his many attempts to return to farming, was forced to recognize that he, and in all likelihood his children, would work in the mines. Yet he had also resolved to stick by the union. As U.S. Steel, Peabody, and the others were tightening their grip on the hills, he preached a sermon, one which today would probably cast him as a Communist: "Come now, you rich men, weep and howl for your torment that has come upon you. You have heaped up together treasures and the rust of them shall eat your flesh as if it were fire. You have held back by fraud the wages of those that labor in your fields and the cries of them have reached up to heaven against you."

6. The Legendary Bad John Garland

Mountain people were superstitious, believing in good luck and bad luck, in ghosts and in witches. Many planted their crops by the moon and no one planted during the first three days in May as these were considered barren days. Being crossed by a black cat meant bad luck, but throwing salt over one's right shoulder could sometimes lift the curse. One neighbor of ours who drank quite a lot would just swear and be damned that some witch was turning him into a horse when he slept and riding him all through the night. When put in water, a hair from a horse's tail would, according to some, turn into a snake. Killing a toad supposedly made one's cow give bloody milk. The seventh son of a seventh son, some still believe, has the power to cure a baby's rash by blowing into the infant's mouth.

My mother claimed that she cured a rash I had as a child by using a magical remedy. She found a peddler woman in the vicinity who led with her a mare and a young colt. My mother helped this old woman milk the mare and fed me a pint, following the ritual of the superstition. She promised me that the remedy took effect immediately.

I certainly would be in error to say that all mountain people were quite this superstitious; in fact, there were other mountain people just as determined to explain away all the ghosts and cures the superstitious folks believed in. As for myself, I am not too quick to agree with either of these ideas. One man claimed, "Why buddy, there is no such thing as ghosts. People just can't come back after they die." To this, a fellow of another persuasion replied, "I know that, and you know that, but what worries me is — do the ghosts know it?"

A certain preacher was holding a church trial of an unmarried young woman who was going to have a baby. In her own defense, the young lady stood up in front of the church and claimed that she was pregnant by the Holy Ghost. At this, the preacher very indignantly asked the church gathering, "Is there anyone here that has had sexual intercourse with a ghost? If so, raise your hand please." One old fellow sitting in the back shot up his hand. The preacher looked at him in disbelief: *"Brother, do you mean to say to all of us that you have indeed had sexual intercourse with a ghost?"*

"Ghost!" the old man shouted, *"I thought you said goat!"*

My Grandfather Lucas was one of those people who was always exposing a perfectly good ghost as something plain and ordinary. People in his community swore that every time they passed a certain empty house, an old woman would stick her head around the door and then jerk it back once she'd been seen. Even though half of his neighbors claimed to have seen this woman, my grandfather was not one to be easily convinced.

He passed by the house one evening and, sure enough, witnessed what appeared to be a real ghost, just as his friends had described. He walked back behind the house to investigate and, in doing so, trampled down the weeds and brush that had grown up around the house undisturbed. It seemed that these white-topped weeds, when blown by the wind, wavered against a back window, which was visible through the front door of the house. All my grandfather's stomping around brought an end to the ghostly, white-haired lady.

Once when he was coming home on furlough during the Civil War, Grandfather Lucas told of seeing a woman with no head, dancing in the moonlight. He told me that he looked and looked, wanting to run, but that his mind urged him, "Don't be foolish. There can be no such thing." Several times he began walking toward the dancing girl, only to run off again in fright, until finally he ventured up close, his musket cocked. He found a white-faced cow with long horns, rubbing her neck against a tree.

Shortly after my parents were married, they, along with John and Molly, moved into what was known as the Press Hindrickson House at Fourmile, Kentucky. Rare in its time, the place was a two-story log and plank house, complete with a separate guest room.

Press Hindrickson had built the house and raised a large family of mighty mean children in it. His son John Hindrickson, in fact, was probably the toughest Kentuckian of his day. John, along with his brothers Press, Jr., and Willy, caused lots of trouble, but they were so notoriously mean that the county sheriff was afraid to arrest any of them by himself. He finally decided to call on the state militia for help.

As soon as the militia men approached the house, the Hindrickson boys opened fire from hiding places along the hillsides; John, who always wore a big western-style hat, was firing an old .45 and waving the smoke away with his Stetson. The Hindrickson boys made it so hot for the law that day that the militia started running and kept running, all the way out of Fourmile hollow.

Many breathed a sigh of relief when later John was put away for life, only after he had killed several men and scared many more half to death.

As tough as they claimed to be, none of the Hindrickson children, once they were grown, would live in their father's house — nor would anyone else. The place was supposed to be haunted. The story goes that old Press Hindrickson had killed a group of pack peddlers who had stopped by the house to collect some money he owned them, and though none of this was ever proved, folks in the vicinity were all inclined to stay away from the place, all except — you guessed it — my little old dad. At only five foot six, he still was not afraid of anything. If a ghost had come around, my father would have just preached it such a long sermon that the spirit would have fallen asleep.

It never occurred to my father that the rest of his family was not as brave as he. Once when Dad had been away for about two weeks at a revival meeting, he returned home unexpectedly, as he often did, but found the house empty. My mother, who had been visiting at a neighbor's house that evening, was just then returning home as it was getting dusky dark. She had to pass a graveyard on the way back to the house, and scared at the idea of ghosts, especially since my father was not with her, she closed her eyes and began running past. Meanwhile, my father, figuring that Mother was out visiting, had decided to walk up the road to meet her. As he saw her running toward him, he spread out his arms. Of course, she ran right into him, scared to death.

"Elizabeth, didn't you see me?" Dad asked her, once he realized how frightened she was.

Mother said, shaking, "How could I see you with my eyes closed?"

My older brothers and sisters must have had a miserable time living in the Press Hindrickson house because, as in any old house, there were bound to have been strange noises. Maybe it was the creaking of the house itself as it contracted and expanded; maybe it was the board shingles on the roof being blown by the wind; maybe it was the screech owls in the trees; or maybe it was the souls of the departed peddlers, gleefully scaring the daylight out of my poor little mother, who never harmed a flea. But when tales of ghosts have been told and retold, especially to children, all kinds of odd sights and sounds begin to take on mysterious meanings.

When John Mills was courting my half-sister Molly, he spent a night in the Press Hindrickson house. In the middle of the night, he got scared out of his wits and began hollering, "Mr. Garland, Mr. Garland!"

My father thought John Mills was a dimwit but got out of bed anyway to ask what was the matter. "Mr. Garland, make a light," John Mills whispered, "A tall, stoop-shouldered man was bending right over your poor wife."

"John Mills, go to sleep," my dad said. "You didn't see anything."

Once the house had quieted down again, John Mills a second time began to yell, "Mr. Garland, Mr. Garland! Please get up. That man is back again."

My father called out to Mills in the dark, "John, there is nothing there. You're just seeing rats. Go to sleep."

"But Mr. Garland, my eyes don't let me see rats. Can I build a fire?"

"There's no wood for a fire."

"Then Mr. Garland, can I burn the bed slats? I'll get you some more wood in the morning."

John Mills sat up all through the night. My father would wake up and find him each time praying or talking to himself. Mills came back to visit Molly, married her, in fact, but never again did he spend a night in the Press Hindrickson house.

My half-brother John spent only one night in the place himself; he was so convinced that he had seen ghosts there that he insisted on moving in with the Bracket and Hindrickson families until my father and mother moved. Both of these other families had some very tough older boys as I have shown already, and I'm quite sure these early friends contributed to John Garland's later pattern of life.

John was not more than fourteen or fifteen when he and Tom Bracket went away with the carnival show that came through Bell County. When they were down in Georgia, the boss over the roustabouts ordered my brother to feed the snakes, not knowing John's terrible fear of the creatures. When John refused the order, the boss struck him with a whip. John responded by hitting his boss on the head with a brick (a brick or a rock was his favorite weapon) and then, along with Tom Bracket, left the carnival grounds running. Together they bummed and hoboed back home. This was the first of John's many escapes.

Not long after the carnival caper, my brother began running around with Happy John Hindrickson, the same man who had whipped the state militia at Fourmile. The two once went to a dance together at a neighbor's home. The man of the house, once the guests entered, insisted on taking everyone's pistol and laying it on the bed in order to avoid any chance of a shooting. John Garland wasn't carrying a pistol, but John Hindrickson handed his over to the host, at which the rest of the guests were much relieved.

The party was carrying on just fine until all at once, John Hindrickson let out a yowl. He jumped into the middle of the bed piled with guns and started to empty all the pistols through the roof. When all the guns were empty, and after most of the guests had fled, he picked up his own pistol, threw the rest of them in the yard, and the two Johns left.

As they wandered home, Hindrickson turned to my brother: "John Garland, a boy like you ain't got no business running around with me. I'm no damn good. I'm mean as hell and can't help it." Still, my brother continued to be Hindrickson's good friend. For some reason, they were never together when John Hindrickson killed someone. My father always said that Hindrickson didn't let John Garland really become involved in his troubles, mainly because Hindrickson had so much respect for my father, whom he called "Uncle Preach." You may think that John Hindrickson or General Mays or even Jesse and Frank James were supermen. Not on your life. They were just mean, ornery people who didn't think twice about killing.

In later years, my brothers John and Bob worked together on the night shift in the Chenoa Hollow mines as part of what was called the "mucking crew," removing slate that had fallen on the haulways. There was one big loudmouthed fellow on the crew who liked to ride everybody, calling them dirty names and saying dirty dozens about them. Now one thing that my brother John would not do was call a man names, insult someone by calling him a "son of a bitch" or a "bastard"; and neither would John Garland take this kind of treatment from anyone else. Bob saw that John didn't like this loudmouthed man and when he got a chance, warned the guy to lay off John. "Listen, you can joke on me as much as you like — I don't care. But you had better leave John out of it."

The fellow just hooted at Bob and said, "Oh, let him get his rear end up if he wants to."

One night at work, this guy asked by brother John a question. But when John answered him, the fellow replied, "That ain't what your sister said when I had her out behind the barn."

John had been breaking the slate with a sledge hammer while the loudmouth shoveled rock. John hit two or three licks quickly on the slate and then stepped back for this man to shovel it up. Bob saw what was coming and hollered out to John, but it was too late. John smacked the guy right in the back side and knocked him onto the slate pile. Both my brothers thought the guy was dead. Before anyone else knew what had happened, they made for the boarding house where they'd been staying, got their clothes, and left immediately for West Virginia.

Bob came back to our family in Fourmile shortly after and found that the man had not died, though two years after the incident, the fellow was still walking on crutches. John got the news but decided to stay in West Virginia and work for awhile.

After an illness, pneumonia I believe it was, John returned to his Kentucky home and soon regained his reputation as a drinker and tough man. Shortly after he had come back, John accompanied my father on the way to a revival meeting. My father held his Bible under his arm while John, who had been doing some drinking, followed one or two steps behind, his big .45 in hand. When folks along the road saw the two of them, they were immediately curious.

"Where are you going, Mr. Garland?" they asked.

"Oh, I'm going over to Flat Lick to hold a revival meeting."

"And where are you going, John?" they asked.

"I am going along with Dad. When he gets one saved, I'm going to kill it before it has time to backslide."

John never really intended to shoot anyone. Rocks and fists had always served him just fine. Once at Ealy Hollow, after fighting two men, John sat back, having whipped them both. An onlooker asked, "John, why didn't you shoot them fellers? You had a pistol."

"Well, doggone, I did have one," John answered, surprised. "I forgot all about it."

Another time John walked in among a group of friends, wearing six hats on his head. Of course, the folks wanted to know how John had managed this one. "Well," he said, "I was walking alongside the railroad track and all these highfalutin fellers stuck their heads out of the train window as they passed to have a laugh at me. I just raised a brush up and swept these hats off their heads. The train went right on and I picked up all six. That way I was sure to get my size."

John served for three years as a deputy sheriff. I guess that the local people thought the toughest man among them would make the best enforcer of the law. Often this rule holds true, but in the case of my brother, the deputy held a Judge Roy Bean notion of his own authority.

Lots of warrants that John received would become mysteriously lost, or the man whose name appeared on a particular warrant would somehow find out about it in plenty of time to make a getaway. John would let a drunk get by with just about anything, I suppose because he was such a drinker himself. But once he would serve a warrant, John enjoyed making an enormous show out of it.

In one instance, a group of mothers came to my brother and demanded that he arrest a certain woman of ill reputation who was living over in High Lonesome, an old abandoned house up on a hill. It seemed that a number of the local lads were supplying her with food and taking turns visiting her, John's own stepson among them. John promised to take care of the situation.

He watched until he spotted some of the boys making for High Lonesome and decided in the course of fulfilling his promise to have some fun. Though he didn't have a warrant for anyone's arrest, John had taken a few drinks to put him in the proper mood; he followed the young men anyway. He found a group of them with this woman in a wooded hollow below High Lonesome and, pulling out his pistol, John scared all of them stiff. Instead of putting the woman under arrest, John began to act like a wild man.

He yelled that he wanted the woman for himself and dared any of the boys to move. Then John forced the woman at pistol point to lie down on the ground. Of all things, he began to bellow like a crazed bull. He backed down the hillside, got on all fours, and then began rushing toward the terrified woman. Running about twenty-five feet toward her, all the while bellowing loudly, he then stopped and began to paw the dirt, throwing it up over his back.

The poor woman could stand no more of this; she took off up the mountain and was never seen around the coal camp again. Completely shocked, the boys, sneaked off home. John told their mothers that he had gotten rid of the prostitute, though he never explained how. I'm quite sure, too, that this craziness accomplished much more than any arrest could have.

John was once called on to arrest a man who had gotten drunk and was beating his wife. Once John arrived at their house, the drunk came after him with a razor, with a swipe cutting off one of the galluses of John's overalls and slicing my brother's hat brim. John hit the drunk's hand, knocking the razor away, and then roughed the guy up enough to make sure that he would leave his wife alone. After he left the house, John could laugh about coming so close to being cut; he would have forgotten about the whole thing if this man had kept his mouth shut. Instead, though, the fellow had to go bragging about what he had done to Bad John Garland. A certain motorman who brought coal cars to the spot where John worked told my brother about the man's boasting. This was just the kind of thing that burned John up.

My brother immediately sought the braggart out at work, pulled him off the coal-cutting machine, and beat him unmercifully. To make sure this fellow wouldn't be waiting for him with a gun outside the mine at the end of the work day, John forced the man to walk ahead of him all the way out of the mine. None of the miners thought that John had acted wrongly.

John got to running around with one girl who turned up pregnant. When my father insisted that John marry her, he did, though John later left the woman, after their baby was born. Eventually she brought the child over to my dad's house and left her. Soon after this, John's wife took up with another man outside of marriage, came back to my father's house, and took the baby back with her. When John heard about this, he got drunk and went down where she and this man were staying. He shot up the house completely, picked up the baby girl, and dared either one of them to as much as look at the child again, threatening that if they did, he would kill them both. John called this his custody case. I suppose John's favorite saying was, "Doggone, buddy, this world is a goose, and if you don't pick it, you'll get picked."

John's attitude toward labor unions was a mixture of beliefs, in both organization and direct action. He had the deepest contempt for any man who would scab and if the opportunity presented itself, would give any such man a beating. For this very reason, John was no help on committees formed to hold talks with the operators. I remember when John served on one such committee, he only wanted to whip the operator into agreement. An Irishman who was then serving with John to represent the miners announced to the rest of the committee members: "And be glorra, Mr. Chairman, I don't think we should send Mr. Garland anymore to talk with the boss. And be faith, I thought John was going to strike him in spite of us all."

John's narrowest scrape was once when he feared he would be picked up for a murder at Cary, Kentucky. About a week before a certain man was killed, John had been followed coming out of Pineville. About one mile out of town, this man stopped John and threatened to cut him with a knife. John pulled out a .32 special squeezer pistol and forced the man to throw down the knife. He tried to make the man run, but the guy just sat down on the railroad track and dared John to harm him. John shoved his pistol against the man's head and held it there until one of his own friends rushed up to stop him. As the friend grabbed John, by brother's pistol fired a hole through the top of the man's cap. I don't know whether John intended to kill this man or not.

A week later, John and Wild Bill Jones were walking home and found this same man beaten to death beside the railroad track. Of course, no one would have believed in John's innocence, especially since he could have been traced to the scene of the killing; so the two of them left the man as they'd found him. Later, Boxknocker Monhollen, the self-proclaimed medium, discovered the body, but the murderer was never found.

My brother John was the subject of many more wild tales, all of them typical of the mountain bad man. As far as I know, though, my brother never killed a man, and even though he was always in trouble with the law, he was never sent to the penitentiary. My father used to say, with good reason, that it was more good luck than good conduct that kept his oldest son out of prison.

John died after forty years, a young man, but one who had done more living than most men twice his age. A man named Silus Collet killed John, shot him with a .30-30 rifle through by brother's own front door. Collet owed John for a milk cow that my brother had let him have on credit.

7. Here We Come A'Roving

Many people hold the view that life in the coal mining camp was the next thing to life in the penitentiary. Not true. The coal camps were just like any other small towns except much friendlier. All the men, and the women too to some extent, worked together every day and came to know each other almost as well as they knew their own families; the people of one coal camp often were of the same family if they traced the generations back far enough. After growing up in such a community, you not only knew your neighbors but their grandparents, aunts, and uncles as well. You knew the good ones and the bad ones, those who were sulky and hard to get along with and those who were jovial and good to joke with. If a mine worked a hundred men, average for the early exploratory mines, about fifty or sixty families would be living in the same camp; in most households, a father as well as one or two of his sons would be working at the mine.

All families lived in houses built on the board and batten style. Planks, one by eight or one by ten, were set up to frame these houses; no two by fours were used. Over the cracks were nailed smaller planks (the batten), three or four inches wide. This alone was the wall, was support, was everything. The miners covered the insides of the houses with a rough blue paper, fastening it to the planks with little tin buttons and nailing it down. The board and batten style is still used (I've built horse barns this way), but I don't think that houses this flimsy are built anymore.

After the small operators worked out the mines and abandoned the mining camps, there was still coal left in some seams. Large companies like Peabody and Whitfield took over the coal leases and, in some places, bought the land. The old mining camp houses were no longer used for miners in that no local mine was running, but even so, the county began to assess the houses as dwellings, meaning the companies had to pay taxes on them. To avoid this expense, the companies sold off houses for whatever anyone would pay, usually about $100. Some people bought them only for the lumber. The houses that were not bought were simply bulldozed down. Now these aren't good houses, but they are a lot better than the shacks that some mountain people live in.

In the last fifteen years, as the old houses were being destroyed, the government has been putting in apartments for older folks. But if half, maybe even a tenth of that money could be spent repairing these old houses, retired miners with their black lung and Workman's Compensation benefits could afford to buy houses in which to live out their lives. Even though sanitary conditions were bad and insulation was poor, some folks lived twenty years in these places and had their own garden spots. The government, at very little expense, could drill a half-dozen or so wells, put in water and toilets and septic tanks, and let these old miners have houses of their own.

Here's a song I wrote a few years back, after seeing many of the old houses torn down.

Chorus: Where can I go? Where can I stay?
They have knocked down my mine shack and hauled it away.
No more can I work in that dark dreary hole.
I am just an old coal miner left out in the cold.

When I was a young man and things looked so fine,
I started to work in the dark dreary mines.
I worked forty years in that dark dreary hole.
Now I am just an old miner left out in the cold.

I go to the city and try to get by.
I look for a job. Oh Lordy, I try.
But I can't read the street signs, don't know where to go.
Just an old coal miner left out in the cold.

I will go back to my hills so green and so fair.
I know they are not much, but they will always be there.
Oh no, the steam shovels are tearing them down,
And all the old miners hang out around town.
(Chorus)

Now I'm getting old and my hair's turning grey.
I soon will fall down and be hauled away.
No more to work in that dark dreary hole,
I am just an old coal miner left out in the cold.
(Chorus)

When I get up to heaven to the pearly gate,
Old St. Peter will say, "Old timer, why are you so late?
You had all your hell in that dark dreary hole.
Just come right on in, friend, out of the cold."

Mountain children seem to grow up quicker than city children. The miner's sons and daughters usually didn't even finish the eight grades of common school before the boys followed their fathers into the mines and the girls married and began to raise families of their own.

I was born April 8, 1905, at Fourmile, Kentucky, the twelfth child in a family of fifteen. My parents discovered my bad eyesight by the time I was about six months old; this weakness prevented me from going to school until I reached age nine. My folks thought that my poor vision would completely prohibit me from learning in school, but since I wanted to be like the other children, I went on my own initiative.

In my first school year, I had a chart reading class. I could barely see the chart, much less read it at first, but my hearing and my memory were so good that soon I had it memorized and could fake the reading when I was called on. Boyd Wilson, my first teacher, soon sent word to my parents to buy me a primer, but they said it was no use. Instead, I borrowed a copy from one of my classmates, who coached me on the first two or three lessons. After this, Mr. Wilson helped me. In four years, I completed all eight grades of the common school.

I had made arrangements to attend the Red Bird Settlement School the next year; the school supertintendent, John Hays, had promised to give me some lower grades of school to teach so that I could afford to finish at Red Bird and then go on to Berea College to finish my education.

I went to work with my oldest brother Bob for one dollar a day and board in the mines at Fox Ridge, Kentucky, planning to work there for six months only and then go ahead with my education at the Red Bird School, but fate intervened: my father, who had been ill for the past seven years, took another bad spell and had to go to bed again. I needed to keep on working to support my father, mother, and younger sister. I don't grieve too much about this. I have used what learning I have to the best of my ability and have read widely. I cannot say that I have a bad remembrance of my childhood.

One thing about mountain people, miners especially, and the one thing that I most go looking for each time that I return to the mountains, is that they are never too busy to talk. A lot of people don't read the newspaper, some can't read too well in any case, so the news is passed by word of mouth. While with the advent of the automobile, this custom may be less prevalent now than when I was growing up, people still meet along the road or by the railroad track to talk for quite a spell. I knew my father to stop between Cary and Coleman's, a matter of about three miles, to talk with people all along the way as we walked to my brother's house. As a small boy, I was kindly bothered by this, but now I do much the same thing when I'm visiting in the mountains.

When I was growing up, people made their own entertainment. Older boys, and some of the parents and grandparents too, would bring together fiddles and guitars, banjos and Jew's harps, and while they might not have been the best of musicians, people from all around would come hear them play. Sometimes one among the group would have an old-time organ to play, another might bring an old squeeze box, or early accordian. I remember gatherings like this, many of them, that grew to thirty or forty people on and around our own back porch.

Whenever I hear people talking about the good old days, I think first of the stir-offs in the fall. Everyone was welcome to come take away for free the foam on top of the molasses, and I was always there with a little bucket for my share of the skimmings. A little bit of baking powder stirred into the molasses with a fork would turn it a nice brown color. With butter and hot biscuits, we would have a feast.

Mountain children got together to play games during all the affairs that brought their parents together. The larger children joined in on whatever work was being done, but the smaller ones did mostly as they pleased. If there were an empty house nearby, the children would use it to play Kitty Wants a Corner. Gatherings of more than five often played Crack the Whip. Mountain chidren enjoyed many singing games, some of which were outlawed at school because they contained verses that referred to kissing: Drop the Handkerchief, Go in and out the Window, and Post Office, for example. Because many Christians in the community frowned on these games, the schoolteachers usually made the children cut out the kissing verses. (I might add that it was much more difficult to get the boys to play these games than to get the girls interested.)

One game, Here We Come A'Roving, divided the girls and boys into separate lines about one hundred steps or more apart. The boys' line walked forward, singing:

> "Here we come a'roving,
> A'roving, a'roving,
> Here we come a'roving,
> My fair ladies."

The girls then sang:

> "What are you roving here for,
> Here for, here for?
> What are you roving here for,
> My fair sirs?"

The boys' group answered:

> "We are roving here to get married,
> Married, married,

We are roving here to get married,
My fair ladies."

After this, the girls asked:

"Why don't you take one of us, sirs,
Us, sirs, us, sirs?
Why don't you take one of us, sirs,
For to be your bride?"

The boys responded:

"You are all too black and dirty,
Dirty, dirty.
You are all too black and dirty,
For to be our brides."

Here the singing stopped and the race began. The girls chased the boys with switches and, if they got within reach, gave those boys a few whacks.

The mountain boys alone played other games, one of them being Go Sheepy Go, played at night. They divided into two teams, each group choosing a captain. One captain would take his side away to hide, after inventing a bunch of calls or yells to mean either "lay low" or "creep around." The hidden group's intent was to beat the group out searching for them back to home place. When their captain thought that the other group had strayed far enough away from home in search of his gang, he would yell, "Go Sheepy Go!" and all boys on both teams would race for home. If those who had been hiding all reached home before the other boys arrived, they would have the chance to hide again. If the other side, the hunters, came home first, they would get to hide.

Because livestock ran freely in the mountains in my young days, people who were trying to raise vegetables had to build fences to protect their gardens. We boys were always growling and griping about how this cut down on our places to play. I guess we hated fences just about as much as the coyboys of the Old West did.

Mountain boys played many marble games, some for keeps and others, like Roly Hole, just for fun. In this game, four round holes were dug, two or three inches wide and about that deep. The first three holes were spaced apart at equal distances, but the fourth hole was dug twice as far away. A head taws mark was drawn from which all players would shoot their marbles. To decide who would shoot first, players would "lag up" by shooting the taw or marble toward the head taw line; the boy who got closest began the game. The purpose of the game was to see who could first get his taws in each of the holes, up and back. If one player missed a hole, the next would shoot. Each player could "kill" any other by shooting at that fellow's taw with his own. If this happened, the one "killed" would have to start all over again at head taws, and the boy who "killed" him would get another shot. The first one to complete the trip up and down the four holes won.

Keeps was played in a ring, just a circle drawn as round as possible on the ground with a stick. Each player put the same number of marbles into the ring at the beginning of the game, and all players lagged up along the circle to determine the starting positions. The taws were flipped with the thumb from a still position along the ring of the circle and aimed at the marbles bunched or lined up in the ring's center. The purpose was to knock as many marbles out of the circle as possible, for those would be yours to keep. "Fugging" was not allowed. This meant shoving your fist forward as you let your taw go, giving more power to your shot. All players had to "knuckle down," meaning keep their fists on the line of the circle. If someone tried to creep his hand up a little bit to get a closer shot, he would be called.

Later, marbles came to be made of glass and steel balls, but when I first played, we used chalk eyes and clay eyes. Some marbles were even made from stone, usually slate rock, with a wooden marble-grinder. Since it took a boy days to grind a round rock to a smooth finish, one of these stone marbles was as valued as ten of the others.

When a new boy came to the neighborhood, often the local boys would play a dirty game on him called Playing Fox. One of the local boys would act as the fox while all the others were hounds, the purpose of the game being to catch the fox by the tail. While the new kid wasn't watching, the fox would take the bunch of stick weeds or branches he was using as a tail and dip it into the manure of an outside toilet. Then the race would begin. Of course, the ones in the know would put on a big show of trying to catch the fox, but they'd make sure that the new boy caught him by the tail — with unpleasant results. This game sometimes initiated a new boy into the coal camp.

What time we had as children was never dull. Of course, we had the usual games of strength and speed (Indian wrestling, weight lifting, running and jumping contests) as well as Ring around the Rosey and baseball during recess at school. But in addition, we had some games that were particularly mountain in nature. When the mines weren't running, we would sneak back into them, especially in the summer because it stayed cool underground. Finding an empty coal car, we would push it back into the mine and ride it along the downhill grades. I am sorry to say that some children were hurt this way.

We would construct minute imitations of the mine company's inclines that transported the coal down off the mountains. Since many mines were several hundred yards up the hillsides, track had to be laid up and down these inclines. To the loaded cars up on the mountain would be fastened a long rope which then passed several times around a big drum. At the other end of this rope would be fastened a like number of empty cars that sat at the tipple at the bottom of the hill. The loaded cars, being much heavier, would, as they descended, pull the empty cars up the incline to the mine opening, the speed of descent being controlled by a long break lever on the drum.

Using sardine cans for cars, stickweed stalks for rails, and large spools for drums, we boys would run loads of rocks up and down the plank inclines. It became quite a contest to see who could make the best incline, tipple, and head house where the drum was mounted.

Though hunting is thought of as entertainment for grown men, I remember improvising my own hunting games as a child. My friends and I especially went in for catching rabbits and ground squirrels. One thing there is about ground squirrels: when you first catch one, it will try to bite you, but if you keep it around and pet it awhile, it will get used to you. It won't bite then unless you squeeze it. In fact, you can even put a string around a ground squirrel's neck and carry one around in your pocket; many mountain boys did. This trick made me realize that snakes, too, might be handled, though I never did so myself. Birds, on the other hand, will try to bite as long as they live. And don't trust a wild hog or a range bull.

I remember from my childhood that the lightning bug would come in May and would still be around when the June bug put in his appearance. Mountain children catch the June bug and tie a string to one of its legs. As the child holds the string, the June bug flies around, making a noise called "zumming." Some children will catch a tumble bug by mistake, but of course, a tumble bug will not zum.

Mountain girls were more likely to play Ring Around the Rosey, hopscotch, or the game which has been played by most every little girl growing up in the world — housekeeping. In one game mountain girls played, called Cooking a Dumb Egg, the little girl did everything as she faced backward. She put an egg on to boil, her back to the stove, took the egg up and opened it behind her back. The yolk was removed and the white filled with salt and eaten. Then the girl was to go to bed and see the boy she was to marry appear in her dreams. If instead she saw her casket brought into her dream, the girl was to believe she'd die soon.

The children didn't usually stay out late at night, but if they did, it was because someone was playing a harmonica or up telling tales. Without a radio or television, people crowded in to hear a good tale-teller like my mother. My father would not often tell stories, though when he did, they were always good ones. One he used to tell was a bit dirty, but since he told it, being a preacher, I suppose so can I.

An old man and woman had a son named John who was awful mean, so mean, in fact, that his own folks were afraid of him. Since John was making life miserable for his poor parents, the old man decided that something had to be done. After the couple had gone to bed one night, the old man waited until he heard their son John go up the ladder to the loft where he slept before he turned to his wife to discuss what they should do with such a mean boy. But the old woman had gotten into bed already and gone to sleep with her feet up toward the head of the bed, something the old man had not noticed. Now, they had eaten a mess of beans for dinner which was beginning to gas the old lady.

The old man said to her, "Old woman, old woman, what are we going to do with our son John?"

When he got no answer, he asked her once again, "Old woman, old woman, what can we do with our mean son John?"

About this time, the old woman let out a little gas. "Old woman, will you quit blowing your breath in my face and answer my question!" her husband yelled. But the old woman let out a little more gas.

The old man, who was getting mad by this point, said, "Old woman, if you blow your breath in my face like that again, I will slap your face." And again, she let go with some.

The old man slapped her in what he thought was her face, causing her to let out a little bean. At this the old feller became terrified and began to holler, "John, John, get a light quick. I have just slapped out your poor mother's eyeball!"

My father did not sing love ballads since he was a Baptist preacher and the Church looked down on such singing. My mother, too, was a member of the church, but she was far more liberal about such things than Dad. She would often sing the old love songs and ballads, and I'm forever glad that she did; among her favorites were "Lord Bateman," "The House Carpenter," "Never Make True Lovers Part," "I Have a True Love in the Army," and "Loving Nancy." Mountain men and women alike were careful not to sing anything smutty in mixed company, and for this reason, many of the good mountain songs which people considered dirty were lost. Still, though, I remember several of these songs which we used to sing together as a family. "Jim Bolin" is one which I include here, an old fiddle and banjo tune. I have left the dirty verses out and made some new ones to take their places.

Jim Bolin and his father and his mother
All went out to shop together
Some bought this and some bought that,
But Jim came home with the tail of a cat.
The tail was long and the tail was thin.

"It will do for a whip," said Jim Bolin.
"It will do for a whip," said Jim Bolin.

Jim Bolin had no britches to wear.
He took him a sheep skin and made him a pair.
He put the hairy side out and the skinny side in.
"They are pretty good britches," said Jim Bolin.
"They are pretty good britches," said Jim Bolin.

Jim Bolin had no watch to wear.
He took him a turnip and made him one,
And he put a cricket within.
"It will do for a ticker," said Jim Bolin.
"It will do for a ticker," said Jim Bolin.

Jim Bolin had no wife to cook,
So he ordered him one from an ordering book.
Her nose was long and her ears was thin.
"She is a pretty good wife," said Jim Bolin.
"She is a pretty good wife," said Jim Bolin.

Jim Bolin and his wife and his mother
All went out to eat together.
Some like it thick and some like it thin.
"In with your paddles," said Jim Bolin.
"In with your paddles," said Jim Bolin.

Many evenings my mother would sit up for hours, telling us stories, tales of many things: there were the ghost stories, the bad men stories, stories of the good fairy, of Tom Thumb, of giants, of Indians, and of fights where the good people won out over the bad. Some of our favorites were tales of Foolish Jack and his older brother Wise Peter.

Wise Peter sent Foolish Jack to the store to buy some hearts, liver, and lights (lungs). When Foolish Jack asked his brother, "How will I remember all that stuff?" Wise Peter whipped him and told him to get going, that to remember the order, Jack needed only to repeat, "Hearts, liver and lights . . . hearts, liver, and lights" all the way to the store.

Jack set out, repeating the list as he had been told, when after awhile he came upon a sick man who was heaving up his last meal by the side of the road. "Hearts, liver, and lights," Foolish Jack called out. At this, the sick man became furious: "You want me to heave up my heart, liver, and lights?" And he set to whipping Foolish Jack. Confused, Jack asked him, "Well, what shall I say then?"

"You say," answered the man, "'I hope they will never come up.'"

Foolish Jack continued toward the store, doing as he had been instructed, when he came upon a man planting turnips. "I hope they will never come up," Jack called out. The farmer immediately turned on Jack and whipped him saying, "So you hope my turnips never come up, do you?" Poor Foolish Jack asked him, "Well, what should I say then?"

"You must say, 'Lord, send thousands,'" the farmer insisted. So Foolish Jack proceeded along his way saying aloud, "Lord, send thousands . . . Lord, send thousands."

Soon he passed a man who was trying to scare crows from his cornfield. "Lord, send thousands," Foolish Jack repeated. "You want thousands of crows eating up my corn?" the second farmer exclaimed. He, too, whipped Foolish Jack, yelling, "I will beat you till you heave up your heart, liver, and lights." At this Foolish Jack was much relieved. He thanked the farmer for reminding him what he was to purchase at the store and resumed his walk, calling out, "Hearts, liver, and lights . . . hearts, liver, and lights."

My mother used to tell a story of a couple who found at their door a raggedy, dirty man who needed a place to stay the night. They didn't like the looks of the stranger and turned him away. The next morning, they woke up and looked across the road to see that, lo and behold, their neighbor's little log shack was gone. In its place was an enormous, fine house. When they ran over to find out what had happened, the neighbor told them that he had put the raggedy man up for the night and that the same traveler had turned out to be a good fairy. In return for the hospitality he had been shown, the fairy had given away three wishes. The neighbor's first wish had been for a fine new house, and sure enough, there it stood.

The man and woman jumped on their horse immediately and hurried to catch up with the stranger to ask for three wishes of their own. It was kindly getting late when they found him. After apologizing for having turned him away, the couple begged the traveler to come back and stay with them for a week. "No," the man said, "I must be getting on, but since you are so sorry about turning me away, I will grant you three wishes. But you must remember that the first three things you wish for will be exactly what you will receive."

The couple thanked him, started home, and began to talk excitedly about what they might wish for, when their horse took a big stumble. The man yelled out angrily at the animal, "The next time you stumble like that, you old nag, I wish you would fall dead." So soon enough, the horse did stumble again and just as the man had foolishly wished, it fell dead in the road.

Furious at having wasted one of their wishes, the man and his wife continued home, the man carrying the saddle. He began to tire after they had walked quite a distance, and because his wife was still scolding him for having been so stupid, he murmured, "I wish this gosh darned old saddle was off my back and on yours, old woman!" Immediately, his wife was carrying the saddle, just as he had wished.

"Look what you've gone and done, wasted another of our wishes!" she yelled at him. "And anyway, this old saddle is much too heavy for me to carry all the way home. I wish you would take it back." Only then did she realize that between them they'd foolishly used up all the good fairy's wishes.

Another story my mother told was about a hill man, about twenty-five years old, who had never owned a pair of store-bought shoes in his life. Finally, he traded a hog for a pair of nice button-up shoes. He was so proud and wanted so much to admire his new shoes all the time that he walked backward everywhere he went. Eventually he walked backward all the way across the state of Kentucky into Ohio. Well, when the natives of Ohio saw him walking backward, they thought he was some kind of nut and put him under arrest. That was until they saw that he could count to one hundred without taking his shoes off. They were amazed at such learning. At once they put him to teaching school in one of their universities.

In another story a certain sermonizing preacher called out to his congregation the question, "Who here wants to go to heaven? All in the house that wants to go to heaven, hold up your hands." Everyone held up their hands except one man. The preacher, not knowing quite what to think of this, asked, "All that would want to go to hell, hold up your hand." Still this man didn't move a muscle. Finally the preacher had to ask, "Brother, you did not hold up your hand for either. You must give us some answer one way or the other."

"But preacher," the man said, "I don't want to go either place. I am doing fine right here in Kentucky. If it's all right with you, I'll just stay here."

While my mother told these stories, we children would use our imaginations, making even the tallest tales real. The hours would pass away until every head began to nod, to dream of the farmer's wife and the gingerbread boy.

8. Woman's Work

As I have mentioned before, young folks in the coal mining camps grew up quickly. In a family of six or seven children, a thirteen- or fourteen-year-old girl would not have too much work to do around the house, and so as not to be another mouth for the old man to feed, she would look for a husband. Most mountain boys considered themselves men by age sixteen, though many entered the mines even younger. But as long as they lived with their parents, mountain children obeyed their fathers and mothers (or got ready to lick the old man). Soon the childish games were put aside for grown-up work and other more important pastimes, like making moonshine whiskey or squirrel hunting for the family table.

Many a happily married couple first met at a quilting bee. While the married men usually took this chance to go possum hunting, single fellows hung around the women and girls as they worked, hoping to see their favorite girls home.

Mountain girls did not have much to look forward to except marriage since the rule of parents was ordinarily quite strict. Once married, most of them began to raise their own large families of coal miners. Since there were no Beatles to swoon over and no movie heroes to worship, mountain girls took up the folk songs and stories that had been passed down to them by their mothers.

Partly as a consequence of this tradition, my half-sister Molly grew to become one of the mountains' best known singers and storytellers. As anyone who ever met her can tell you, Molly was always causing an uproar. When she was just a girl of twelve, she blacked her face and went down to Bill Lewis's house, scaring his wife half to death. The Lewises got a warrant out for her, and though Molly ran off for awhile, she was arrested as soon as she came home again. My father could have gotten her released any time, but he decided to let her stay in jail for a few days to teach her a lesson. While she was locked up, Molly made what was, I guess, her first song, a plea to Condiff, the local jailer.

Last Monday morning, thought I would have some fun.
I blacked my face, put britches on.
Went down to Bill Lewis's and made them run.
Mr. Condiff, won't you please turn me loose.

The very next day, they got out a writ.
Out to Clay County then I did split.
Mr. Condiff, won't you please turn me loose.

In about three days I came back to old Clay.
The sheriff arrested me the very next day.
Mr. Condiff, won't you please turn me loose.

They threw me in that old county jail.
Had no one to go my bail.
Mr. Condiff, won't you please turn me loose.

The nits and the lice were hanging from the jiste.
One turned over and said, "Jesus Christ!"
Mr. Condiff, won't you please turn me loose.

My mother, only eleven years older than Molly, found handling this stepdaughter was hard work, especially when my father left the house. Brother John, even though younger than Molly, took it upon himself as her full brother to whip the stuffing out of her when she gave my mother too much of a hard time. He liked my mother. But Molly didn't and would tell all kinds of lies about her, trying to make my father angry with his wife.

Once when Molly went to a neighbor's house to spend the night, she told these folks that my mother wouldn't let any of the children eat meat. Molly said Mother would take a meat skin and rub it all around our mouths to make my father think that all of us had eaten. Molly also claimed Mother would tie a meat skin to a piece of string, force us to swallow the meat, and then pull it back out of our throats. Of course, the shocked neighbors told Dad what his daughter had said; he assured them that all the tales were Molly's making up. After he came home and mentioned the pitiful stories, and once John agreed that all of them were lies, Dad gave Molly quite a whipping.

The next time my father left home, Molly raised up a quarrel with my mother about having gotten whipped. When John told his sister to lay off, she turned on him and threatened to leave home. She went outside, mounted Old Kick Belly, a mare we had at the time, and began to ride off. That was until John knocked her off with an ear of corn. He hit her so hard that Molly was out for awhile; my mother thought she was dead. By the time Father returned, Molly was fully conscious and ready to describe every bit of how she had been mistreated. As was my father's habit, he spoke with John for another side of the story. Once again Dad decided that Molly had gotten exactly what she deserved.

When my sister was about thirteen, she decided that she wanted to marry a neighbor boy not much older. Mother tried to talk Molly out of this, explaining that both of them were too young, that they wouldn't have any way to support themselves. Molly wouldn't hear of this. She insisted that no matter how they would have to live, she was determined to get a marriage certificate; Molly, though, pronounced it "stiffidick."

When my dad came home, Mother explained Molly's plans. Immediately Dad went outside and cut a nice, long hickory switch, came inside and laid it on the mantel saying, "Now right there lays Molly's 'stiffidick,' and if I hear again of her wanting to get married, I intend to give it to her just as long as that lasts." I suppose all these experiences were good training for Molly's later life as a midwife and a working-class songwriter.

As a matter of fact, Molly did marry quite young, to a man named John Mills. During their courtship, Mills worked on the railroad section gang and boarded in one of the section houses. One evening when my father was beginning to think Mills had overstayed his welcome, Dad asked, "John, don't you think you had better get back? The men will go off and leave you in the morning."

"Oh no they won't, Mr. Garland," John Mills said. "Right now I have on at least thirty of their shirts." Sure enough, Mills had put on a shirt of about every man in the section gang to make sure they wouldn't take off without him.

Once Molly married John Mills, she found he was so foolish and stingy that he lived only on corn bread and jallop, a gravy made from cornmeal. Molly told him one time, "John Mills, if you don't get something to eat around here, I'm going to leave you."

"Lord have mercy, honey," her husband said, "I hain't got nothing less than a five, and if a man breaks a five-dollar bill, it's gone in no time." As it happened, Molly did not eat jallop much longer. Soon she quit Mills and married Jim Stewart.

Aunt Molly Jackson wrote many union songs and many other types of songs as well. She was at the height of her glory when she was giving someone she thought was no good a hard time. If she believed someone was taking advantage of his or her position in life, whether that was a coal operator, a husband who beat his wife, a man who would not work to support his family, or a bookkeeper who denied some needy family scrip to buy food with, she made her feelings known. These troublemaking instincts led her to write many a fine song.

One such song, "Fare Thee Well, Old Ely Branch," Molly wrote while married to Jim Stewart. The two of them then lived at Ely Branch because Jim was working at the Houghes mine. After writing out several copies of the song, Molly decided to drop them all down at the spring where the local miners' wives came to get water each day. But all this was too good to keep secret. Molly let the word out and, of course, Jim Stewart was fired.

Later, after they had moved to Bell County, Molly found out that a family with several children had been denied scrip. When my sister saw the mother of this family crying in front of the company store, she marched the woman back inside, ordered a basket full of groceries, and walked out with them. The store clerk followed Molly out and demanded the food back, but she cursed him with every "Belly-robbing son of a bitch" she could lay her tongue to. This time, no one waited for Jim Stewart to leave the mines in the afternoon. The bosses sent for him and had his pay ready when Stewart arrived at the company store.

Molly had quite a sense of humor. Once when she was in the company store, she noticed that the clerk had his pants unbuttoned. She commented, "The office door is open, young man." The clerk was a smart one: "Look and see if you can find the bookkeeper." Molly answered him, "No, all I see is a little dried up clerk sitting in there on a bag of nuts."

Molly didn't have any children of her own who lived past infancy, but she was always taking someone else's child in for awhile and claiming he was her own. Her third husband, Bill Jackson, had four children whom she raised. Jackson was quite a character, a large, cross-eyed man with a big red nose, and the only man Molly married whom she couldn't control. When my sister got to raising Cain with him, he would get out his old .45 pistol and shoot under her feet. No wonder people called him "Forty-Five Bill Jackson." They separated in 1932, though they didn't intend to do so permanently. Molly went to New York to speak for miners' relief and found that she liked the city too much to come back to Kentucky. Bill Jackson decided to get himself a new woman.

In most cases, the woman's life in the coal camp was harder than her husband's, since with many children to take care of, she was too busy with house chores for much recreation. The wife's duties were many and varied. She was expected to be the first one up in the morning in order to cook her man's breakfast (and a miner eats as much for breakfast as he does for any meal of the day). She had to pack him a big lunch, called "dinner" in the mountains. If she didn't have anything that morning to put in his dinner bucket, she would have to pack it later and send it to him by the mine's motorman. The miner's dinner bucket was a five-quart tin container with a center cup which held the main part of his meal, a pie pan on top for his bread or dessert, and a bottom section which could hold about three quarts of water, the mine water being too sulfurous for drinking. Some of the smaller mines were shallow enough so that the men could come home for dinner between 11:00 and 12:00. In that case, a wife would have her husband's dinner cooked and ready.

After the man had gone to the mines, his wife went about all of her many chores: washing dishes, making beds, cleaning house, and scrubbing floors. The miners' houses had no carpets, just 1'x10' wood planks, usually of oak. Mountain women scrubbed these floors nice and clean with lye.

She usually washed the family's clothes down by the creek, pumps being so far away from the house that it was simply easier to carry clothes to the water than to haul all that water to the house. Too, the creek water was softer than the more sulfurous pump water. Set up by the creek side would be a water boiler where all the clothes were boiled and washtubs in which the women scrubbed the clothes up and down on washboards. Since several women would be washing clothes at the same time, on the same day, this was also an opportunity for the women to visit and talk with one another.

The clothes were then hung out to dry on clotheslines, which were stretched either between two trees or between two miners' houses. The clothes had to be watched closely because free-running cows could easily pass under the line, forcing a woman to do all her work over again. Other times a wind would come up, blowing so hard that the line broke, sending all the clean clothes down into the dirt. I have heard a few women out-curse a red eye, as the saying goes, when this happened.

After all the house chores were done, a miner's wife went to the company store to trade scrip for food, a daily task because miners rarely earned enough credit to pay for more than one day's food at a time. In most cases, she would serve supper at about five o'clock, right after her husband had finished his bath. Of all working people, I don't think any surpasses the coal miner in being able to put away food, unless it would be the logger, who can also put down a man-sized meal three times a day.

A mountain woman also had to carry in water every day from the pump, typically a quarter of a mile from her house. Usually she would have to wait her turn to fill up her two ten-quart buckets since there were so few pumps in each coal camp. There was kindling to split and coal to haul in for the stove. Think, too, that this woman whom I have described had no small children. More often than not, though, the mountain wife would have two or three children hanging to her dress tail.

One may ask why this woman's husband did not help with some of the chores once he came home from the mines. The truth is that a man who has worked on his knees all day in thirty to thirty-six inch coal is about pooped out. Most wives would work themselves almost to death before asking their husbands for help with the housework. The result was, in fact, that many a mountain man outlived both his first wife and a second.

If her family were fortunate enough to have a milk cow, it was the wife's responsibility to milk the cow, churn the milk, and make the butter. It usually fell to one of her older sons to drive the cow in off the mountainside every evening. I had this job at our house. Sometimes I would find a daddy longlegs spider to help me. Holding him by one leg, I would ask, "Daddy, Daddy Longlegs, show me where my cow's at." Then I would check to see which one of the spider's legs pointed out farthest and would walk in that direction.

The most sought-after houses in the mining camps were those with small gardens. Again, if her family were lucky enough to have been located in such a house, the mountain woman raised the garden after her husband had helped spade the ground. If there were larger children in the family, they helped too. Mountain women enjoyed gossiping over the garden fences, passing all the latest news faster than most any newspaper could manage.

I went down to Corbin to interview a woman whom I will call Hanah. She is eighty-seven years old, can neither read nor write, and has lived on Stinking Creek or in Corbin, Kentucky, all her life. She has two children; each one had a different father. Having worked all of her life, Hanah has never asked anybody for help of any kind, in spite of her handicap in not being able to read. She became a first-class cook at a leading Kentucky hotel and was known as their special cake and pastry baker. She worked at that hotel for fifty years, was even offered a job cooking for a congressman, but turned it down because she didn't want to leave Kentucky.

These days social security pays Hanah $138 per month. Over the years she has been able, she proudly told me, to put aside $40,000 in the bank as well as paying for her own house. She still tends her vegetable garden, refuses to have electricity put in her house, and heats her home with the wood she can scrounge out of trimmings off her neighbor's trees. If you saw this woman on the street, you would want to walk right over and give her a handout, but Hanah does not give a hoot what her neighbors or anyone else thinks of her. The clothes she wears around her house are virtually in rags, but in the closets she has nice dresses neatly hung up.

Some time ago her neighbors, thinking she was destitute, began to bring things to her house. Hanah told me, "Jim, I didn't know what to do. If I told them I had money, some of those damn neighbors would probably have tried to come in and rob me. So I just let them go along, bringing the food and stuff, until one day a boy saw the banker helping me sign up for a $20,000 bond. He spread it all over town that I had lots of money, and was those neighbors mad! Hell, I never asked them for a damn thing."

This lady is a paradox, a combination of generosity and stinginess. She saves almost all of the interest on her money and a large part of her social security check until I or someone else comes around to count it for her and see to banking it. Once she was burglarized, the thieves getting away with about

$200. But the next time they tried to rob the old lady, they met a hail of .38 bullets fired through the door. Luckily, Hanah did not hit any of them. When the police came, all they did was take away her pistol, but she managed to buy another one soon enough. The robbers don't come around as often as they used to.

The first of May, 1977, I went to see about Hanah, having heard that she was suffering from trouble with her feet. When I got to her house, I saw that she was in a bad way. Her feet and legs, almost up to her knees, were all red and covered with blisters; it looked as if the outer skin had just fallen off. I thought that she had sugar diabetes for sure since her brothers had both died from it. Both her brothers had had their legs cut off because of this malady. Hanah told me that she had just had corns on her toes at first but had contracted all this trouble after using a mountain remedy suggested by one of her neighbors. The neighbor had evidently recommended that Hanah use Epsom salts on her feet, but instead she had packed her feet in table salt, which had poisoned her. The salve she was using only made her feet sorer and created more blisters.

I was so sure that her feet would have to be amputated that I persuaded Hanah to go home with me to Washington state to see my doctor there. She had never been anywhere on a bus, train, or airplane, so I expected for her to be scared on the trip. Not on your life — she just drank her little bottle of whiskey and mine also.

Once I took her to visit my doctor, he found that she had no sugar diabetes, no high blood pressure; in fact, he found that the old lady was in fine shape except for her feet. After she took a prescription for a month, her feet were healing and she began to sing, "I want to see my old Kentucky home." I had to bring her back to Corbin.

I tell something of Hanah to point out that many mountain people, without the aid of an education, have been very able and determined to survive the torment of their lives. Women especially lacked education in that so many of the old mountain men, their fathers, did not see any need in sending girls to school. Here is what Hanah has to say about it: "Jim, my daddy never let us girls go to school. We lived on a three-hundred-acre farm; my father worked on this farm and so did we girls. There were four boys and seven girls in my family. Most of the boys were sent off to the little one-roomed schoolhouse, but we girls were just not allowed.

"My father didn't provide well for us. If I got one dress a year, I would have to get it by digging ginseng or mayapple root. I never had a pair of girl-type shoes. For the money I could make digging ginseng, I could buy some coarse, boy-type shoes, one pair each year.

"When I was sixteen, my father kicked me out, and I went to Pineville where I worked for my room and board. It was here in Pineville that I had my first child, a girl. Soon after this, I went to Corbin and was able to buy a house for $1,500, paying so much per month. I let my mother have my first baby; she raised her because I was working ten to fourteen hours a day in the hotel and was not able to take care of her. Later, when my second child was born, I kept her with me."

I asked Hanah how many times she had been married. "Jim," she told me, "I have never been married to any damn man. I have the same name I was born with, but I have had the best of it all."

I left Hanah, thinking that if it were as cold in the winter to come as it had been the previous winter, she would surely freeze to death. But maybe not — she has stood many a cold, hard month in that little house, heated with the neighbors' tree trimmings. Oh, yes, she is a paradox; she virtually starves herself to death to save money, but she offered to give me a couple hundred dollars if I would take it. I said, "Hanah, if I ever really need it, I will ask you for a loan, but otherwise, no way would I take your money." This old lady is a true mountain woman, independent as hell, and she cusses like a red eye when she gets riled up. Long may she live; we have too few like her left.

9. Cocks, Hounds, Foxes, Kick-outs

While their women were occupied with house chores, the mountain men enjoyed a good many sports and games in their spare time. Few people know it, but chicken fights were immensely popular; as a matter of fact, these contests are still held in the mountains, though it's now unlawful to fight chickens with steel spurs. When I was growing up, most every man I knew had a fighting cock, but the one I remember best was my half-brother John Garland's big Dominick. Bad John called him a clubfooted Dominick because that breed has such large feet. This rooster weighed at least eight pounds, quite large for a fighting cock, but having such small spurs, he fought best by using his beak and feet.

Most of the fellows had good game cocks: Roundheads, Black Devils, Arkansas Travelers, Irish Greys, Grey Tormentors, Bacon War Horses, and all the crossbreeds of these. One afternoon as they were all bragging about their game cocks, John mentioned that he had a good rooster; of course, at once the men wanted a fight. John agreed to bring his rooster in if these men would put up the worth of his animal. The fellows agreed, setting his value at one dollar. Had they known that John's rooster was indeed a big Dominicker, not a game cock, they would have only put up 50 cents. In fact, it would have been below their dignity to fight their fine game cocks against a farmyard fowl.

A little four or five pound Roundhead was brought to fight John's chicken. When the men saw what John had brought to fight with, they began to cuss and swear, "Why that scrub won't last two flys against a fighting game cock!" But since the wager had already been arranged, they all decided to hold the fight anyway.

The contest was held in an empty house, giving the Dominicker an advantage since he was not going to be doing any flying anyway. When the fight began, the little Roundhead was anxious to go and went right into John's big rooster, hitting him along the wing. He didn't do the Dominicker any damage. The big rooster looked him over and the next time the Roundhead came on him, John's Clubfoot took hold of the little bird's head so that it couldn't get loose. The Dom then began to walk on the little Roundhead with those big feet and to eat away at his head. Well, Roundhead was dead game and would, no doubt, have died game had he been fighting another game cock with steel spurs. He just couldn't handle this big rooster that did nothing but bite and walk all over him. He was down under the Dominicker's feet when he hacked and began to sing like a hen. John's old Clubfoot was not even breathing hard.

This got the boys mad. Determined, they came every week with another game cock which John's rooster would go about beating into submission or unconsciousness. Ten weeks later and ten dollars richer, John had become the most talked-about man in the chicken fraternity. Then, John made his first mistake, and the last one for old Clubfoot.

Bad John took his rooster to Fourmile for the next fight and found when he got there that the boys had come up with a little Arkansas Traveler. The fight was to be held in an open field. Now, these Arkansas Travelers are chickens that run and fight, taking off at a distance, then turning and hitting, then running again. The old Dom was not accustomed to this style of fighting. Once the contest began, he waited for the game rooster to get close enough to catch hold of, as he had done with the Roundhead, but the little Traveler was too smart. He flew over the Dom a couple of times without making contact. Then he hit the Dom and bounced back to his original position. He had decided to wear the big chicken down.

Clubfoot kept trying to catch hold of the Traveler's head, but couldn't manage to. Off they took, the little game cock in the lead and John's Dominicker running after him. As the Dom stopped and turned his head, the Traveler let him have one; the blood began to flow from a good cut in the Domer's comb. He went for the Traveler again, chasing him up on a rock pile. The little game cock, taking advantage of the height, caught the Dom by the comb and sent a spur along his head, almost to the nose. John's Domer was hurt and hurt bad. He was still game, but the blood was beginning to bother him.

The little rooster, seeing this, moved in and on the next fly caught the Dominicker in the eye. The spur came all the way through the head; the Traveler was hung to a dead rooster. John turned away and came as near to crying as he ever had — over just an old, scrub, clubfooted Dominicker of a rooster.

Another favorite pastime of the mountain men, during the summer months particularly, is Set Back, a card game that resembles bridge in an abbreviated form. Many evenings, miners would gather to relax, play cards, and meet the train on its second trip of the day through Straight Creek. The world championship Set Back game is still held each year at Straight Creek, in the home of Al "High Pockets" Wilson.

During the years when I was joining in on the Set Back games, the radio was just being talked about. Of course, the coal operator owned the first one in our mining camp, but not too long after, a few miners bought them too. I remember hearing my first radio broadcast — the Dempsey/Tunney prize fight in 1927.

Aside from trying to catch ground squirrels, rabbit hunting was the first type of hunting that I, and most other mountain boys, ever did. I remember when I was six years old and my brother Bill was ten, we made rabbit boxes out of wide split boards. These boxes were about two feet long and eight inches square. We tacked a piece of tin with holes poked through it over one end of the box and on the other end attached a door, hinged with leather at the top. We would raise this end, propping it open with a stick, and then set the box in a rabbit hole. A likely spot was under a rock or in a hollow log. By stopping up all of the spaces around the box, we knew that when the rabbit wanted to leave his hole — since he could see the daylight through the holes we had punched — he would hop right into our box. Once he went in, he would knock out the stick, and the door would fall shut behind him; next morning, we'd have a rabbit.

We also had a rabbit-hunting dog, a hound bitch too old to run foxes and so slow that she actually couldn't even hole many of the rabbits that played around our briar patch. Once when she was running a rabbit, we all took after it, chasing the rabbit ourselves into a hole in a tree. We twisted it out, cleaned it, and were eating the fried rabbit while Old Muse was still on its trail.

My brother John was a possum- and coon-hunting man who, like many other men in the mountains, was willing to pay quite a price for a fine possum and coon dog. I remember once when I was staying with him, he and two more fellows spent $45 for such a dog; half hound/half cur, white with red spots, Old Bounce was what John named him. After making this investment, John warned my brother Bill and me that we were not to take Old Bounce rabbit hunting.

One day, Old Bounce got loose and followed us; the first thing we knew, he had taken off after a rabbit. John had told us proudly that Bounce would not even look at a rabbit, being so expertly trained, but the dog sure was looking at this particular animal. Old Bounce, in fact, ran it down a hole before Old Muse had even gotten started. In all, Bounce holed three rabbits that we managed to trap in our boxes by the next morning. Of course, we were afraid to tell John what had happened.

A couple of days later, when John saw Old Bounce running a rabbit, he was fit to be tied, swearing that we had ruined his expensive coon-and-possum dog. But when John took the dog hunting that night, and on every other night, Old Bounce would not look at a rabbit, even if one jumped right in front of him. There are many hunting dogs that will act this way: rabbits in the daytime, coon and possum at night. Especially good hunting dogs also learn that when a man takes down his shotgun, he is going squirrel hunting, and they show they know it by acting frisky, almost talking.

Many of the mountain methods of hunting differ from those in other parts of the world. Take fox hunting, for example. In the mountains, fox hunting does not mean riding to the hounds as it does in England. The same breed of hound dog is used both in the hills and in Britain, but that is about where the likeness ends.

The purpose of the fox hunt is not to catch the fox — far from it; the hunters just about know the foxes by name, calling them Old Bushy Tail and Old Smart Eye. The enjoyment of fox hunting is in the music of the dogs' voices sounding off in chorus, some low, some high, and many in-between. Each man listens for his dog, proud if his animal is leading the pack, sad if his dog is not talking.

Men will go to the highest mountain to turn their dogs loose. Once the animals open up on a fox, the hunters usually build a fire and prepare to spend the night, since if the fox is a red fox, he won't take cover for six or eight hours. Old Bushy Tail, in fact, will seem to enjoy the hide and seek as much as the dogs do.

The fox moves in circles, going out of earshot along one ridge and coming back into hearing along another. Sometimes these circles will be six or eight miles around. Other times, the fox may keep within hearing distance for hours, tricking the dogs by dodging in and out of thickets or wading the creek branches to hide his trail. But eventually some wise old hound will find him. I have known foxes to keep the hounds running for forty-eight hours, so that a dog in good flesh at the start of the hunt will be skinny when at last the fox goes to a hole.

Some dogs will get smart and, figuring out the fox's usual route, will leave the pack and cut down from one ridge, up another to be waiting for Mr. Fox. Even then, the dog will rarely catch the animal. If a hunting dog cuts on a fox like this a few times, he is retired from the pack, since cutting is unfair both to the fox and to the other dogs.

Setting open traps in the mountains is a good way to make enemies. Some very fine hunting dogs have been caught in steel traps like this and starved or thirsted to death. After this happened to Uncle Jack's dog, my uncle got so mad that I'm sure he would have killed whoever was responsible.

As the bottle of shine goes around, there is a lot of bragging around the campfire about present dogs, dogs once owned, once known. As the stories are swapped back and forth, it becomes obvious that the members of the fraternity of fox hunters are not the least bit sorry for themselves; they consider their sport the greatest in the world, and everyone becomes very sad when one among them, because of sickness or age, can no longer join in the hunt. That man will sit on his porch, whittling on a stick, and strain his ears for the sound of the dogs on the mountains. He must be thinking of fox races past and of dogs many years gone to the good hunting ground. I'm sure that if there is a heaven for the fox hunter, he will want Old Mat, Old Tige, Old Sam, or Queen to be there with him. And if he doesn't find at least a few red foxes to hunt, he'll be very disappointed.

There were and are many different breeds of hound dogs, and each man champions his favorite: little black-and-tans, big black-and-tans, the blue tick, or the white spotted hound known as the Walker. In addition, there are any number of crossbreeds, though only a cross between a hound and a fox hound would be allowed to run in a fox hunt.

One old fox hunter used to claim that his dogs barked in a special dog language. As the hounds were running, Old Heck would hit a cold trail and open up saying, "He's been along here . . . He's been along here." Old Spike would answer, "He's been a long time traveling . . . He's been a long time traveling." Old Queen, in a different voice, would ask, "How old is he? . . . How old is he?" to which the little tan would answer, "About two or three . . . About two or three." According to the old hunter, his dogs would repeat this sequence over and over again. You can try this some time as a round.

I heard the story of a dog so smart that when his owner would get down his gun, the hound would go get a sack. When the man mentioned in the hound's presence that he was going fishing, the dog would run around behind the barn and dig a can of fishing worms.

A certain mountain girl claimed to own an educated dog. One day when she and a young neighbor boy were playing, the dog came through the gate, obviously having hurt itself, as it was holding up one of its paws and hopping on its other legs. The boy asked her what her supposedly educated dog was doing.

"Oh," said the little girl, "he's just adding, putting down three and carrying one." After this the dog sat down and, as dogs will do, began to drag its rump along the ground.

"What is he doing now?" asked the boy, rather confused.

The little girl looked and answered: "Oh, he just made a mistake and is erasing it."

Once I remember going possum hunting with a man named Gunther Smith on Buzzard Creek in Clay County, close to a settlement that was called

Hell-For-Certain. Gunther had just traded a peck of soup beans for what he had been told was a good possum dog, and we had immediately taken the animal out in the woods and let him loose. As was the possum-hunting method, we sat down to wait for the hound to strike a trail, but we waited and waited and nothing happened. Finally, when we decided to search for the dog, we came up to a big log about fifty feet from where Gunther had let his new hound loose. There behind that log lay Smith's dog, sound asleep. Gunther was so furious that he raised up his gun and shot the hound right there, saying, "Damn you, I would kill you if you cost me a bushel of beans!"

Many mountain women complain that their men like their hounds more than they do their wives, and in a lot of cases, this may be the truth. I once asked a friend of mine, an ardent fox hunter, what he got out of hunting. He told me, "Ah buddy, if you had a quarreling wife and a house full of kids like I have, you would know the peace and enjoyment I get just listening to my old hounds run." The chorus of hunting dogs is the mountain man's grand opera.

To pick the best hunter for the year, mountain communities held dry hunts. Each entrant was allowed to take only some salt, his gun, and his dog with him into the woods and so had to live just on what he could catch and on those nuts and berries growing wild in the mountains. The contestants weren't allowed to accept food from anyone they might meet along their various routes through the hills. The man who could sustain himself the longest was considered for that year the hills' best hunter.

Thus far I have divided the sports and games children enjoyed from those enjoyed by adults, but in the case of the annual county or tri-county fair, this division can't be made. The first such fairs date back to the years just after the Civil War, but they have continued for many years to be popular with mountain people of all ages.

There were carnival rides for the children, games of chance, the traveling sideshow with curiosities like the dog-faced boy, a carnival wrestler who took on all comers, and, of course, there was the hoochy-coochy show. For the most part, though, the county fairs brought family entertainment: a brass band, clowns, and a singing group, usually called the Old Plantation Show. These musicians brought many songs into the mountains; "Old Kentucky Cradle Me" and "My Old Kentucky Home" probably came to the hills by way of such traveling musicians. Again, this disclaims the idea that the mountains were ever long isolated from the rest of the nation.

Shooting matches were popularly held during the county fairs, though they might be held at any other time of the year as well. Most of the men in my day used the pig rifle, better known as the Kentucky rifle, which used a cap and ball. These guns were first bored to a .32 and then rebored, as the rifles became leaded or pitted, to the next larger size until they were .45 or more.

The contestants' prizes were the meat cuts from some animal, usually a cow or hog that had been butchered, dressed, and divided into five choices: the best shots received the first choice, the second best got second choice, and so on. The hind quarters went to the first and second best shots, the front quarters were third and fourth choices, and the fifth best shot received the heart, liver, and lungs of the animal. Sometimes, too, a sixth choice would be offered, some little bit of money called a "pony purse."

Those men knew their guns. I have seen the first four shooters in a contest all hit their cross marks so that the judge would have to cut a ball, insert it in the bullet hole, then draw across the bullet with a sharp knife, and use a caliper to determine the winner. I have seen Old Stuttering John Mills win the first four choices in the match with only eight shots.

These shooting matches were a real joy to mountain men. Some, like my father after he had been injured in the mines, would pay a fee to have someone else shoot for them. I am very sorry to find that shooting matches of this kind are things of the past; even the pig rifle, once used by all the men, is now a collector's item since so few remain in the mountains. The modern .22s and larger rifles would outshoot the old Kentucky rifle, but you could never convince the old timers of this. When they were still alive, they continued to shoot the pig rifle against the more modern guns.

Horse races were also held at these fairs, though the horses entered were all farm animals and the wagering never rose to very high stakes. Since the mountain horses and mules were not raised to buck and since the cattle were of domesticated breeds, in the old days there was never a rodeo.

Many of the older men attended these annual fairs but not for the carnival; they came to the Jockey Ground for horse trading. Anyone with an animal to trade would ride his horse or mule around until someone flagged him down. Then the two would begin the procedure of offer and counteroffer.

In horse trading, it was considered all right to try to fool the fellow you traded with, just as long as the horse's ailment was something a good horse trader should be able to recognize. Take boot and give boot, but watch your step! My father was a leading plug horse trader, primarily because, being a horse doctor of sorts, he always was keeping crippled or sick animals around and trying to cure them. He was one of the few mountain men I knew who could cure a horse of fistula. This condition, caused by a poorly fitted collar which bruises the horse, will stiffen an animal's shoulders and if not cured quickly, may completely destroy the horse's usefulness. My father had a remedy for everything: he would stitch horses for string halters in the hind legs, cut them for ring bone in the front feet, burn them in the mouth with a hot iron for lampers, drench them for bots by pouring a homemade mixture down their noses, and burn feathers under their noses for distemper. Many times these remedies succeeded; in other cases the cures themselves killed the horses.

My father could tell a horse's age by looking into its mouth. Until it reaches four years, a horse will still have its baby teeth, while the teeth of a horse between four and seven years old will have coops in them. A mare's wisdom teeth will come up out of each side of the jaw at seven years and sink back in as she approaches eleven. One saying, "Smooth at seven, hock at eleven," provided a good general rule for judging a horse's age. By examining the corner teeth, one can estimate that a horse is close to seven years old if one edge of the teeth is longer than the others. As the horse nears eleven years, these corner teeth become increasingly square.

My father double-checked his estimate of a horse's age by examining its ribs. Starting at the rear and moving up toward the horse's head, he would check to see how far the animal's ribs had separated. He believed that for each three years of a horse's age, an additional rib would have spread a little in the animal's back.

Beyond these types of examinations, a wise horse trader will also check the feet for ring bone and stifle, look for stiffness, saddle sores, lampers, and fistula. Open spaces around the hooves could mean that the horse or mule has been water foundered. The horse's eyes must be examined, too, and its nose tested for distemper. All of these considerations should be thought of before anyone gets down to serious bargaining.

Since people came to trade for all different kinds of reasons, naturally some trades came off quickly and easily while others didn't come off at all. Some men were there simply for the money that could be made, while others were looking for an animal to match another they had at home, needing a pair or team for the two-horse turning plow or a two-horse carriage. Some would bring a milk cow, if they had more cows than they needed, and hope to trade for a riding horse, maybe a gaited horse like a run-and-walker (now called a Tennessee Walking Horse), a pacer (a good racking horse which many people liked to show off by riding), or a three- or four-gaited horse. Some tried to trade off a no-good nag for something better, while other preferred to trade a good horse for a worse one and the boot (cash). A family man might want to trade a mean horse for a gentler one that his children could ride. For a hundred different reasons, people came to the Jockey Ground during carnival time, some for no better reason than the love of trading. I liked to trade with the fellows who were there to make money because for just a few dollars in cash, I could usually manage to make a good trade. During the rest of the year, horse trading of a fair degree was held at the mill on mill days, but even so, nothing could match the annual meeting at the Jockey Ground during the county fair.

My nephew, after trading at the tri-county fair for three weeks, had finally come up with a good-looking mule that seemed gentle enough but strong enough to handle work. On the way home we stopped to get a bite to eat, hitching our horses and the mule to a fence. When I turned around, this mule let me have it with both feet, right in the seat of my pants. It was a good thing that I was almost out of reach because he would have really sent me flying; as it was, I didn't ride very comfortably the rest of the way home. We later discovered that this mule was a kick-out that wouldn't work a lick. He went back to the trading ground the very next week.

Now that horses have become so scarce in the mountains and are no longer good, basic trade stuff, the mountain people have turned to other things for trading. The last time I was in the hills, the men still met every week near Middlesboro and Barbourville to trade guns and pistols and just about everything else you can think of: all kinds of tools, possum hound dogs, automobiles, sometimes even a good saddle horse as in the old days. Around the courthouse in Pineville, Kentucky, has grown a tradition among the retired men of knife trading which goes on almost every day.

The mountain tradition of trading is shown in the following lyrics that were added to an old English song.

> *When I was a little boy living by myself,*
> *All the meat and bread I got I laid it in the shelf.*
> *The rats and mice, they led me such a life,*
> *That I had to go to London to get me a little wife.*

Chorus: *Sing a ring tang rannigan,*
> *Jack straw fannigan,*
> *Feen fang fannigan,*
> *Sing a long way off, sing a long way home.*

> *Roads was muddy and the streets was narrow,*
> *And I had to bring her home in an old wheelbarrow.*
> *(Chorus)*

> *The wheelbarrow broke and my wife got a fall.*
> *Away went pretty wife, wheelbarrow, and all.*
> *(Chorus)*

> *I went to the river and I couldn't get across,*
> *And I paid five dollars for an old grey horse.*
> *(Chorus)*

> *The horse wouldn't pull and I swapped him to a bull,*
> *And the bull wouldn't beller and I swapped him to a heifer.*
> *(Chorus)*

The heifer wouldn't holler and I swapped her to a dollar.
The dollar wouldn't pass and I threw it in the grass,
And along came a bullfrog kicking up its...
Ring tang rannigan,
Jack straw fannigan,
Sing a fing fang fannigan,
Sing a long way off, sing a long way home.

Trading can be considered a mountain tradition, as reflected in many songs and stories. One tells of two fellows who were trying to trade chickens, one of them bringing Leghorn chickens, the other having Barred Rocks (Dominickers) to trade. As the men were wondering how to go about their trading, the fellow with the Leghorns suggested that the only fair method would be an even swap, a dozen Leghorns for a dozen Dominickers. The other fellow agreed that this was the only fair trade but added that since his Dominicker chickens were so much bigger, nine of them made a dozen.

A certain boy and girl wanted to get married but, not having any money between them, they had to ask the preacher to marry them on credit. The good man agreed that he would wait for his dollar, the going fee for marrying couples, but told them they would still have to buy a license. The boy and girl went to the county clerk's office, explained their problem, and asked the clerk if he would give them the license on credit. The clerk refused, saying that it was against the rules. They would have to come up with the two dollars before he would issue them a marriage license.

The couple arrived back home very downhearted. Old Grandma, trying to help, offered, "I've got some beeswax that you can trade." Old Grandpa added, "I saved all that tallow from the sheep I butchered. You can trade that in on the license too." So the next day the young couple went back to the county clerk's office and offered him the beeswax and tallow. The clerk agreed to the trade, but when he weighed up the wax and tallow, he told them that there was not enough to pay for the license; they would have to come up with something more. The two young folks then began to cry and pleaded with the clerk, "Can't we marry just as far as the wax and tallow goes?"

We must give the mountain merchants and traders credit. They had to keep abreast of the market prices outside the region in order to know what to expect for the goods they bartered, and in most cases, they couldn't be fooled. I would say that the bartering tradition held out longer in the mountains than anywhere else in the country.

One can see that life in the coal mining camps, with its good side and its bad, was never dull. Actually, the mining camp was a very closely knit, sociable community, more so than I have discovered any other place to be since

I moved away. If the people who ran the mines had cared about the local families as much as they did about profit (and everything else was secondary to that profit), if the miner had made a large enough wage to give his family a decent diet, if the houses had been sturdier — even if that had meant charging more rent — and if living conditions had been more sanitary, the coal mining camp would have been as fine a place to live as one might have hoped for.

10. Holiness People

I seldom go to church, except when I return to the hills where I was raised. Then I go often in that this is the mountain life, the custom I knew as I was growing up, and the sociability I have returned for. As I have mentioned, I was raised in the Missionary Baptist Church of which my father was a preacher, of which my brother Bill later became a preacher, and in which I served as a deacon for a number of years. When I was young, church services were held two or three times a week; women particularly would attend all of these.

Other denominations that arrived in the mountains later claim many followers, though. By 1900 the Presbyterian Church had begun sending missionaries into the mountains, primarily women who worked with the children and distributed clothing to the miners. From time to time they brought in a pastor of their faith to preach, but while the miners liked these missionaries well enough, not many converted to the Presbyterian faith.

One man who was planning to leave home for about a week made certain to give his wife some instructions as to how she should carry on in his absence. First he got out a gallon jug of moonshine, put it under the bed, and said to her, "See that whiskey, wife? If the Baptist preacher comes along, give him all that he wants to drink of that." Then he went outside and put two big fat chickens under the coop. "See them chickens, wife? If a Methodist preacher comes by, give him all he wants to eat of them chickens." Third, he pulled out a brand new pair of long stockings and said to his wife, "See them stockings, wife? If a Holy Roller preacher comes along, you put both of your legs in one of them stockings and be durn shore you keep them there."

Some say that the Holiness Church was not organized in the mountains until the 1920s, but I am certain that the denomination had already sprung up by 1900, perhaps even a good deal earlier. Holiness Church members are also referred to as Holy Rollers because of the ways they shout, speak in unknown tongues, fall to the floor, and roll around during church services.

The Holiness believe in three definite works of grace: that a man becomes saved, that with more prayer he becomes sanctified, and that with more faith and prayer he will be filled with the Holy Ghost. Once filled with the Spirit, that person will receive the gift of speaking in and interpreting tongues. In general, the Holiness people can be seen as seeking the same goals and praying for the same kind of grace as did the members of the older mountain churches; since many of the first Holiness Church members were the more emotional, former members of the more established Methodist and Baptist churches, their beliefs reasonably have much in common with those of the two other sects. Yet the Holiness believed they had found a cleaner, purer religion. They wouldn't dip snuff, chew tobacco, or smoke cigarettes, and they looked down on all forms of dancing. The only way they were more lenient was that they weren't as critical of divorce.

Because the Holiness Church is relatively young, its beliefs have never been too firmly established. As well, many of the earliest Holiness preachers disagreed on which portions of the Bible should be stressed and how certain points in scripture should be interpreted. When we remember that many of the founders of different church sects couldn't read too well, it is no wonder that so many different branches became active. If a man disagreed with his own pastor's interpretation of a certain Bible passage, he was quite likely simply to pull out and begin his own group. Once sects split like this, they were seldom joined entirely together again. I asked one Holiness preacher to tell me how many branches of Protestant Christianity exist today. He told me he believed there are about 800 unaffiliated denominations.

One branch of the Holiness Church, the Jesus Only Church, believes that there should be no God other than Jesus Christ. This church sprang up around 1935 and then had quite a few members from Bell County. I recorded one of their sermons for the Library of Congress in 1938.

Another interesting branch of the Holiness Church is the Snakehandlers. These people claim to be able, due to their faith, to pick up poisonous snakes as the Bible says, without being bitten. Many, of course, have been bitten by rattlesnakes and have died, though the church members as a whole attribute such deaths to lack of faith.

I held an interview with Harvey Valentine whom I have known all my life, both through the 1932 strike and later on Straight Creek where he lived after the strike was broken. As a minister, Harvey has pastored churches and has handled the snakes in many religious services. His brother, also a minister, was killed during one such ceremony after being bitten several times by a rattlesnake. Harvey has lived through it all, married twice and fathered fifteen children, and is a typical mountain man who loves his home. Harvey has a great deal of insight into the lives of mountain people, having performed at their marriages and baptizings and preached at their funerals. I turn to him to tell something of the Snakehandlers Church.

Valentine: "I am going to tell you how I got into serpent handling. My brother handled them and had been bitten over a hundred times, but it had not hurt him. Finally he was bitten down in Panesville, Alabama, and he died. He refused medical treatment, refused everything, just sat there in a big chair until he died.

"After that, I started serving the Lord and going to church, though I wouldn't go to a place where they had the serpents. One day, one of my boys went out to fix a place to have dinner — we were going to have dinner on the ground that evening — and he called for me to come. There was a copperhead snake lying there that he'd killed. The thought then came to me that surely the Lord didn't intend for a man to pick up something like that, knowing it was going to bite and hurt him bad. I turned around and started back up to the house.

"It seemed like something just dawned on me there, and that was the scripture which says, 'He who would save his life shall lose it, and you who lose your life for my sake and the gospels, the same shall find it.' So I went and hunted that scripture where Jesus says, 'Go ye unto all the world and preach the gospel to every creature, and he that believeth and is baptized shall be saved, and he that believeth not shall be damned.' And Jesus said, 'These signs shall follow them that follow me, and in my name shall they cast out devils, and they shall speak with new tongues. They shall take up serpents. They shall lay hands on the sick and they shall recover, and if drinking any deadly thing, it shall not hurt them.' So I began to pray and ask the Lord to make a way for me at some time to go somewhere they had the snakes and let me handle the worst ones there in His name. I prayed that way for about five weeks.

"One night after my oldest boy had come in from the Marine Corps and wanted to go to church, we went together. During the service the serpents were brought out: three copperheads and two rattlesnakes, a black rattler and a yellow rattler. Some women began handling these snakes and then put them back. I realized that this was what I had been praying for and so asked, 'Lord, if it is your will for people to handle these snakes, let one of them bring the serpents to me.' Well, there was one person across the building who hollered out, got up, and walked around the Bible stand. She threw the lid back on the box that held the snakes and reached in; with one hand she picked up one rattlesnake and with the other hand took up another. As she knocked the lid down on the box, I closed my eyes. She brought the snakes over to me and laid them both around my neck. I asked the Lord if that was what He meant when I prayed to Him, for some sister to bring the snakes to me. When I came to myself, I was standing with one rattlesnake in one hand, the other snake in the other.

"From that time on, I handled the snakes, for awhile anyway, until one night. I had gotten hold of a black rattlesnake and was holding it up, looking at its head, when the spirit moved me to get rid of the serpent. A woman took the snake out of my hand and put it straight back in the box. That has been about ten or eleven years ago and I have not handled any snakes since, even though I am still preaching. I am not against it.

"I know that nothing is impossible with God, but some people, it seems, just want to pick out a certain scripture and make a hobby out of it. So Jesus said to preach the word, in season and out, and rebuke without long suffering; so I think I handled all the snakes the Lord wanted me to handle right there. If I am ever in service when the Lord moves on me to handle them again, I will handle them again."

Garland: "What is the name of the church where you preach?"

Valentine: "The Church of the First Born, but I preach at one church on Tuesdays and Wednesdays, at another on Saturdays and Sundays."

Garland: "Is that a large church here in the mountains?"

Valentine: "It's not yet too big, just through the county, just here and there. The name of the church comes from scripture, the twenty-third verse of the twelfth chapter of Hebrews. The denomination doesn't mean anything anyway. Jesus told Peter, 'Thou art Peter and upon this rock I will build my church and the gates of Hell shall not prevail against it.' And Jesus is coming for his church. The people who have been born again and who held out faithful to the end, they are the ones who will be going back with Jesus. I never did go for denominations too much. I always try to go according to the word, and that is it."

Garland: "Does your church speak in tongues?"

Valentine: "Yes, they believe in the three works of grace, the Father and the Son and the Holy Ghost. Of course there are people who believe that Jesus is all of it, but to believe that is to believe that there is not God, and that would be making Jesus out to be a liar. For Jesus said, 'Why callest me good? There is no good except that there is God.' I do not dispute with other denominations too much because there are some in every denomination who are doing the very best they can. I think when He comes, He will find some of His people in every denomination."

Garland: "Most of the churches in the South are called fundamentalist, which means that they believe that every word in the Bible was sent from God. Does your church or do you believe this?"

Valentine: "Well, I am a great one for the New Testament because Jesus said that he who tries to justify himself by the Old Testament is a backslider already. I pretty much will go along with the new scripture right on down to the bottom."

Garland: "Do you believe that a man can backslide after receiving the three works of grace?"

Valentine: "Some people do not believe that you can backslide after receiving the three works of grace. I can only give you the scripture on it. Over there in the second chapter of Revelations, an angel of the Lord was speaking to a man and saying, 'Nevertheless, I have somewhat against thee because you have left your first love. Remember where you left it and go back and repent, or either I will come and remove the candlestick quickly.' We go to the twenty-second chapter of Revelations, the fourth verse, where the angel is talking to the church: 'And any man who adds one word to this prophecy, the plagues of this prophecy shall be added onto him, and any man who takes away one word, his name shall be taken out of the Lamb's Book of Life, and his part shall be taken out of the Holy City.' Looks to me like a man could get his name jerked out, couldn't he?"

In September of 1966, I made a complete recording of a service that took place at the Pentecostal Church of Believers, a Snakehandlers church, in Roth, Kentucky. After the people heard that I was Reverend Bill Garland's brother, they made me and my wife most welcome. I was given a place right up front to put my recording machine and, in fact, sat on the bench right next to the boxes of snakes. As long as the boxes were fastened shut, I had no worries.

The music here was made by two unamplified guitars, clangs, and tambourines. The lead singer, using a microphone that led to a speaker on the wall, sang "Amazing Grace" faster than I had ever heard it sung. He was also about the best foot-stomper I had ever seen, not just tapping with one foot, but managing to get his whole leg and one side of his rump going to the fast rhythm.

Many of their songs were the old traditional spirituals speeded up, but others were dance or jig tunes sung with Christian words to make them acceptable. It seemed the faster the music was, the better the congregation liked it, all clapping their hands and stomping their feet until the music worked into a crescendo. Many then began to shout, jump up and down, or gyrate, jerking their bodies, shoulders, and heads to the music. All of this was supposed to show the working of God upon them, since they will not act in this way — in fact, do not even believe in dancing — unless God moves them. I found, though, that unlike the old-time Quakers, these Holiness people began moving on very quickly once the music started. Others began to speak in tongues, just gibberish to me.

During this particular service, as the men and women sang at the tops of their voices and hollered the praises of their God, they gathered around a sick baby, laying their hands on him and praying to God to heal him. They prayed for God to send them all the Holy Ghost, testified to the wonderful things God had done for them, and then, opening the box near me, took out the snakes and passed them around the church.

The preacher's part is not as important in this mountain church as it is in most others. He gave a very rousing, emotional talk while the congregation shouted "Amen" and praises to God and Jesus. Several times during his talk, the preacher went off into the unknown tongue.

Some people who are considered sinning folk by the rest of the church members may attend these services for various reasons: to accompany a wife or husband who is a church member, to meet a girl and have the opportunity of walking her home from the service, or just to hear the music. The church members will set upon such a newcomer, begging and pleading with him to come to the front of the church and be prayed for, saying if he resists, that he is headed straight for Hell.

My wife and niece accompanied me to record this service and were set upon in just such a fashion. First one, then another of the Holiness people would come back to where the two of them were sitting and try to get them to come to the altar. My wife let them know that both she and my niece were Baptists, hoping that this answer would keep the people from bothering them further. But it did not have a bit of effect. My wife was told, a finger wagging in her face, that she was bound for Hell. She was highly insulted at this and told me that never again would she go back in that church. Someone claimed during the service that there was a devil in the house, maybe in reference to us. One good brother suggested that they throw the devil out the window, but evidently the other church members were content to leave any devils that might have been there to listen to the remainder of the service.

As one witnesses all of this, one wonders "why" about a number of things. I will never know why the Snakehandlers do not use nonpoisonous snakes for their ceremonies. Nor can I understand why they do not believe in doctors and will allow a person to die rather than call for medical help. Why should it be necessary to go to these extremes to show their faith? Why do some Holiness people have the desire to handle the snakes when members of other Holiness churches do not? Why does it become such a compelling desire? And why is this compulsion so much stronger when the people have been worked up into a frenzy by loud, fast music? But if we have all of these questions, it is because we are unbelievers and cannot understand.

I do not know whether it is entirely proper for me to express an opinion as to why these people differ from the more conservative church members, but from long observing and associating with Holiness people, I find that many of them are folks who truly like music, especially these fast-type songs. Going to the Holiness church satisfies their love of music and serves as an outlet for their need to dance. To those who would say that there is no such need for dancing, I would point out that people have been dancing, we are certain, since as far back as recorded history goes. There is no culture that does not have some form of dance.

This is not to say that the Holiness people are faking, that they are not Christians. I simply wish to explain why they hold such a fast and frenzied form of worship. I might add that as I recorded this particular service at Roth, there were some young boys outside the church house doing modern dances like the frug and the chicken.

Now, we must realize that for many years there have not been any dance parties to speak of in the mountains. I will be called to task for this statement by some, as there still is dancing at the road houses and at the hot spots along the highway, but very few mountain people go to these places unless they are out for business, looking for a prostitute, or taking some fling at what they consider high society. The old family-type, folksy dances really are no more; therefore, the churches provide a place where people can go pat a foot and enjoy fast music, people who would be going to folk dances and dancing the whole night through if such parties were still held.

Folk dancing has always rested on an unsteady foundation in the mountains, tolerated rather than sponsored by the majority of hill people. Most believed that dancing was carried on only by sinners, or at best lukewarm Christians, so it was condemned in most churches as an instrument of the devil, held up as a destroyer of the young, and declared a sop to the hellbent element of the community.

The old Regular Baptists and Hardshell Baptists, even the Methodist Church, realized that all people sinned a little, that young men especially would sow a few wild oats before settling down, and as a result these churches were fairly tolerant of folk dancing and parties. But the newer Holiness Church, as I have mentioned before, demanded that its members live without sin, just like Jesus Christ: no dancing, no parties, no snuff, no smoking, no cussing. When a fight or a killing occurred at a dance, the Holiness Church seized upon this to condemn further such parties, although the same kinds of violence often broke out among people going to or from church. Soon dance parties were forced to become hush-hush affairs, and gradually they died out altogether.

Once the Holiness Church opposed folk dancing, other church groups, like the Baptists who had once tolerated dance parties, joined in the crusade against all forms of folk culture, even going so far as to condemn folk songs and singing. They began to look with displeasure on the lovely folk songs and traditional ballads of the mountains unless the words were adapted to Christian themes. We see here a contradiction, I believe. The churches that were the most opposed to singing and dancing simply took over the music to suit their religious services.

The following is such a song, which has been sung in many forms throughout the mountains. Originally it was an old English ballad about the wife of a seaman who sings to her baby:

> *I have a letter from your sire, baby mine, baby mine.*
> *I have a letter from your sire, baby mine.*
> *It was written over the seas and forwarded unto me.*
> *And I'm as happy as I can be, baby mine, baby mine,*
> *I am happy as I can be, baby mine.*
>
> *I have a letter from your sire, baby mine, baby mine,*
> *Have a letter from your sire, baby mine.*
> *It was written over the sea and he's coming home to me,*
> *And I am as happy as I can be, baby mine, baby mine.*

As sung in the church, the same tune was used to tell the story of God's Bible. The "brothers" referred to are the apostles or writers of the New Testament.

> *I have a letter from my Father in my hand, in my hand,*
> *Written by my elder brothers, oh how grand, oh how grand.*
> *It was written over the sea and forwarded unto me,*
> *And I am as happy as I can be in this land, in this land.*
>
> *I am not afraid of dying in this land, in this land,*
> *But I often feel like crying in this land, in this land.*
> *Then I cried, "What shall I do?" for I had not read them through,*
> *And they made me all anew in this land, in this land.*
>
> *Death is called a dreadful monster in this land, in this land.*
> *When he calls I will not answer, oh how grand, oh how grand.*
> *He may come most any day, but they'll find old empty clay,*
> *And I wonder what they'll say in this land, in this land,*
> *And I wonder what they'll say in this land.*

There are very few mountain people who now know how to dance the old folk dances, who know of any dancing, for that matter, other than the twisting that their children see on television and imitate. It is up to people like Folkways Records to preserve the old folk dances, party songs, and games, all the many folk forms that are being lost. Maybe in the future, the descendants of the mountain people will want to know about such things. In any case, the Holiness Church, now one of the largest denominations in the mountains, will have to answer for what it has done to mountain traditions.

11. Shooting from the Solid

By the time the United States entered World War I, miners were fairly well organized, and in spite of the hard fight put up by the operators, coal mine workers were gaining better wages little by little. The eight-hour day was coming into effect and laws had been passed to prevent boys under age sixteen from entering the mines; nevertheless, these laws were not strictly adhered to by the companies.

The famine of orders which had brought a good deal of hardship to miners and their families earlier was no longer a problem once the war began. Coal was in great demand, jobs were plentiful, and wages began slowly to increase. For example, a mule driver's pay, which had been $1.94 per day, rose to $3.44. But at the same time, the cost of living as determined by prices at the company store was going up twice as much. Flour went from $1.95 to $2.40 per 24-pound sack, bacon from 20 cents to 40 cents per pound (this was not breakfast bacon but the old salt pork, fat and thick). Of course, coffee was rationed, as was sugar. So with better wages, many of the miners were no better off than before. When payday came, the miner usually had a "snake" on his statement.

As well as owning the miners' houses, the company also owned the only grocery store in the mining camp. The majority of these stores had no refrigeration, which meant that the miner's diet consisted mainly of beans, potatoes, salt pork, and some canned goods, though canned peaches and corn were so expensive that most miners could not afford to buy them. Miners ate a lot of bologna and canned salmon. I particularly liked boneless ham, something I never see anymore. In the spring of the year when vegetables like poke salat began to come up, people ate so many greens that almost everyone got sick with "bloody flux," dysentery actually. Each spring this sickness accounted for the deaths of many children who hadn't received enough milk to balance their diets.

Some coal operators allowed local farmers to peddle fresh meat and surplus produce in the camps, exchanging these goods for the miner's scrip. A farmer could then buy at the company store those goods he didn't raise himself.

The coal operators paid their men twice a month, generally every other Saturday, but between paydays they issued scrip against each miner's account. The miner's wife bought food at the company store just about every day because the miner seldom had enough credit at the company office for her to get scrip enough for more than one day's food. The coal companies usually hired one or two clerks to wait on people at the company store (back then there was no self-service). A woman would stand outside the counter and ask for the goods she wanted as the clerk collected the items and laid them on the counter. When she had requested all she wanted, or could afford, the clerk would count up the purchase and take from her that amount of scrip. Seldom was credit extended to anyone. If credit were advanced, it was done by the bookkeeper who kept his ledger in an office separate from the store proper.

The bookkeeper kept a record of each miner's tonnage in one column and of the amount of scrip drawn in another. Since house rent, the price of coal for the miner's family stove, doctor bills, and the miner's burial fee were charged each month against his tonnage, in addition to the scrip which had been issued and spent by the miner's wife, he often would receive no pay at all. Come payday, the bookkeeper would draw a curvy line through the record of two weeks' tonnage, a snake.

The companies' greatest problem at this time was transportation: there simply were not enough railroad cars, or gondolas, to haul away all the coal that was being mined and sold. Most often, the larger companies with their greater influence managed to acquire the gondolas, leaving the small operators with no possible way to move their coal out of the region.

With so many jobs opening up, child labor in the coalfields became more and more prevalent, in spite of laws prohibiting it. My older brother Richard became a trapper boy at age nine, meaning he opened and closed the trap door, used on the main haulway for ventilation, to let the mules and coal cars through. My brother Bill entered the mines at fourteen, my brother Bob at twelve. The family's needs were so great that these risks were taken, but I still cannot condone letting children so young into the mines.

In 1919, at age thirteen, I too had entered the mines on my own word that I was sixteen, thus legally eligible for work. Since I only weighed ninety pounds at the time, anyone could have judged that I wasn't sixteen, but because my work went in on my brother's number (my tonnage was added to his), the company was willing to overlook the illegality. The worst part of it was that the coal company officials seemed to believe they were doing me and my folks a favor by allowing me to work.

It was a shame to let a child with eyes as bad as mine (only 20/200 vision in my better eye) work in the coal mines. When I would first enter the mines, my eyes would take such a long time to adjust to the dark that for quite awhile I could see nothing. When I came out of the mine into the light, it was much worse; the light hurt my eyes so badly that I would be completely blind and would have just to stand in one place for awhile until I regained my sight. Always I was afraid that the foreman, on seeing this, would make me quit my job, but if he did notice, he said nothing. I eventually learned that by walking out of the mine instead of riding out, I could stop just inside the mine entrance, allowing my eyes to adjust more easily.

The first mining was done by the light of a lard oil lamp, resembling a little pitcher with a long pouring spout. A wick of cotton string hung out of the spout, the other end hanging down in the lamp which was filled with lard oil. This lamp made for the poorest of lighting and released an awful lot of smoke which, I believe, contributed to the black lung condition suffered by many miners.

Next in use were carbide lamps which burned gas made from carbide. The carbide was put in the lamp's bottom compartment, water was put in the top, and the two were fastened together by thread, as a jar lid is fastened to a jar. This lamp had a valve that regulated the amount of water which mixed with the carbide to create the gas. Once mixed, the resulting carbide gas rose through a small hole in a tube leading from the carbide compartment to the top-front of the lamp. At the top end of the tube was fastened a reflector into which was set a wheel. Inside the wheel was a flint with a little spring behind it. The rising carbide gas caused the wheel to turn quickly, sparking the flint and thus lighting the lamp. This device was far superior to the old lard oil lamp in that it gave off many times more light and, as well, it did not smoke. Also called an open lamp, the carbide lamp could be used in mines where there was a good deal of gas. Later it was replaced by the safer, battery-operated light. All of these lamps were and are worn on the miner's caps, attached by a hook.

There are several ways to mine coal under a mountain: the standard system, the long-wall system, the panel system, in addition to their many variations and combinations. The decision of which system to use depends on many things: the lay or pitch of the coal seam, the type of top and bottom in each seam, the amount of water in the mine, and the degree to which the mine was gaseous. I have chosen to describe the standard system in that it is generally considered the best mining plan, but many books have been written on each method.

There were a number of ways to shoot coal with the early, slow-acting black powder, different men having their own methods. In most cases though, entry drivers began by boring two holes in the middle of the solid face of coal. The first, the "cracker" or "breaker," was a short hole, only about three feet deep, that was bored on a sharp slant. If the coal pulled out as it should, the cracker would create a notch in the solid face. The second hole was bored about three feet deeper and was begun at a spot not too far away, as the purpose of the second shot was to blast the cracker a bit deeper. Now this second shot might not shoot all of the coal out, making it necessary to dig the remaining coal out with a pick. My brother Dick was the best at digging out a cracker that I ever saw.

A well-worked space, or "room," which was being shot from the solid would require that three or more shots be blasted on both sides of the cracker, loosening enough coal for a day's work. Usually the side shots, or "steps," were bored at distances three feet apart, though this might vary according to the height and the hardness of the coal.

The angled cracker shot resulted in a "V" or notch, as I have mentioned. The side shots next to the cracker would be bored at roughly the same angle. Succeeding side shots would be bored in such a manner that at their "points" (the deepest points of each hole bored) they would be one foot farther apart than at their "heels" (the spots where the holes are started in the coal face). In other words, holes bored for side shots gradually fanned away from the sharp angle produced by the cracker. In this way, the holes bored for shots closest to the sides, or "ribs," of a work space could be bored straight into the face of the coal. This method was safe yet allowed for the maximum amount of coal to be blasted from any work space.

Now I was a good coal shot, unlike my brother Bill. He knew what he intended to do but depended on his eyes to balance and line his holes. Since I didn't have the eyes to depend on, I did everything by measurement. I had only to work a few days in a room before I knew just how to regulate the distances between my shots.

If holes are bored too far apart at their depths, "too heavy on the point," the coal will be too heavily burdened, will not have room to move, and will not pull out cleanly. Sometimes this will cause a "windy," blowing out at the start of the hole and making a hell of a big wind. I have heard one of these windies coming, blowing timbers, powder cans, and any other debris it could pick up, and I have lain down to let the thing roll right over me. Mixing two kinds of powder, like dynamite and black powder, could also cause a windy. Since the dynamite is a much faster powder, it will go off first, cracking the coal a little; the slower black powder then will blow out. Obviously, these windies were very dangerous, could kill a man if he were close enough. On the other hand, if the points or depths were bored too "thin" or too close together, the shot would simply blow off at the point but leave the heel, the coal near the face, undisturbed and hard.

The powder was made up right on the job from ten-quart cans. We also had shooting paper which we rolled into cartridges an inch to an inch and a quarter around and anywhere from thirty to thirty-six inches long. We poured them full of powder, stuck in the fuses, and inserted the powder cartridges into the holes we'd bored, usually tamping in coal dust behind. With our lamps we lit the fuses, which burned for about four or five minutes before reaching the powder; sometimes we lit six or eight of these fuses in sequence, timed so that one would blast right after another.

The old black powder caused many explosions because it created a flame; dry dust in a coal mine will explode just like gas when ignited. In such a case, there will actually be three explosions, though they occur so close together, it is hard to distinguish one from another. A dust explosion will result in the mixing of dusts and gases; this mixture also will explode; an explosion of the smoke created by the first two will usually follow. For this reason, colite was later adopted in mines in that it doesn't create a flame. It is one of several "permissible powders" which have been used precisely because they lessen the chances of an explosion.

In order to keep the entries on center, the miners had to survey periodically, using center bobs on strings. One bob would be hung in the center of the entry, another hung down near the face or end of the entry. One miner would stand near the coal face and shine his light out toward the entry opening. Another miner stood behind the first string and sighted a line with both strings and the other miner's light to determine the middle of the entry near the face. This procedure let the miners know where to drill their holes in order to keep the entry on center to the end of the property.

The entry drivers, working in twos as buddies or partners, had to shoot down two or three feet of slate above the coal to create a working space high enough for the mules to walk in. A man tried to shoot this slate down as squarely as possible, using colite or dynamite; some entries could be shot down with only one hole, six feet deep, in the middle of the entry. Other types of top slate or sand rock required two shots, one on either side of the entry.

If the top were slate, it could be drilled with a ratchet machine, also called a Fort Wayne drill, which was very similar to a breast auger. The Fort Wayne drill had a threaded bar, a boxing, and a hand crank the miner turned, pressing the cutting bit, or auger, forward. If the top were sand rock, it would have to be drilled with hammer and steel.

Sometimes the main entry would hit a fault where the coal seam would shrink to only a foot or eighteen inches. If the top were sand rock, only the best entrymen could drive the entry. Uncle Alfred McFarland was one of these so-called hard rock men. This Negro man, whom everyone called Uncle Alf, was so good at his work that when I shook steel for him to drive, I was never afraid that he would miss the steel and hit me. If there had been a John Henry around, I think Uncle Alf could have given him a run for the title of "The Steel Drivingest Man Alive."

Often as my brothers and I were driving an entry, the top would change from slate to rock. We would have drilled thirty or forty feet in the very soft slate top with a breast auger and then would run into ten or fifteen feet of stone that was so hard we would have to pull out the hammer and steel. After about six inches of this very hard work, we would "sneeze the hole" by shooting a half stick of dynamite in the hole made by the hammer and steel. We could then drill about six inches more with the Fort Wayne drill before we would have to work again with the hammer and steel. Then we would sneeze the hole again. I can remember that my brothers and I worked an entire day, getting a hole only five feet deep in rock like this.

Over most coal seams are three to eight inches of what is called draw slate. Sometimes it will stay up, holding to the rest of the top, but other times it will pull loose and fall. A miner tests the slate above him by hitting it with the side of his pick and holding his other hand against it. If he can feel any vibration or if he hears a hollow sound, he or someone else will need to set a timber there to hold the slate up. A miner may also find round formations of slate in the top, called "kettle bottoms." Extending up two or three feet into the top, a kettle bottom might very well consist of a ton or two of slate which at any minute could turn loose and fall. Here too a miner must be careful to set his timbers, or he risks getting mashed.

When I was only about ten years old, my parents and I took the train, there being no road to speak of, to my oldest brother Bob's house for a visit. He was at that time working with my brother Dick in the mines at Chenoa. I remember seeing the men coming, carrying Bob home on a stretcher. Slate had fallen on him, dislocating his hip and shooting it back four inches. This accident made him a cripple for the rest of his life. The Workman's Compensation law had been passed finally, after the miners union's fighting for it for many years, but since Bob had not signed yet, he was not eligible for Workman's Compensation under the law. Immediately after he was injured, though, the company bookkeeper arrived to get his signature to insure that the coal company would not be held accountable. Eventually, Bob received $450 for his injury.

My father had been involved in a similar accident, a slate fall that mashed his head, leaving him blind for three years. At that time, before the Workman's Compensation law, he was threatened by the coal company; if he sued, neither he nor any of his sons would ever be allowed to work in any mine in Kentucky. The coal company could have followed through with this threat by putting all our names on a blacklist of so-called troublemakers. When they stood to profit, the operators were crooked both with their workers and with the government.

A space of coal six to eight feet deep was worked alongside the cross entries, at least six feet away from where the entry shots were being fired to prevent its being shot in. This space, called the "gob," held the slate or rock that had been shot down; shoveling the rock into it was called "gobbing slate." Mine timbers were set along the outer edges of these gobs. The miner tried to keep the pile as smooth as possible by placing larger blocks of slate on the outside of the pile. Once the entry had been driven far enough for another breakthrough to be turned off, slate from the gob piles would have to be loaded on cars, hauled outside, and dumped. Since the slate always contained a certain amount of oil, these dumping grounds eventually began to burn, some continuing to burn for years. I have known slate dumps to explode, throwing slate and rock in every direction. In later years, even today, the cinders taken from such burned-up slate piles, called "red dog," are put out on country roads.

The entry drivers were also responsible for the ventilation of the mines. Just as soon as the main entry had been driven about sixty feet underground, two airways were created, one on either side. One provided for the intake of fresh air, the other returned the air that had circulated throughout the mine back outside. Early mines used fire-heated furnaces. Air warmed by the furnace would naturally pull out of the mine, causing the other airway to draw fresh air in. It would again circulate throughout the mine and be pulled back out at the furnace-heated opening. Since this was not a very efficient method of ventilation, large fans soon came into use, either exhaust fans or pushing fans, whichever the mine company wanted. Along the airways as well there were booster fans to keep the air flowing.

To direct the circulation of air, brattices were constructed to divert the intake-current of fresh air to all working portions of the mine. At first, temporary brattices in the form of canvas curtains were hung across breakthroughs. Later, as the mine was driven farther, permanent brattices were constructed out of wood or, in some cases, concrete. The breakthrough which was nearest the heading would not be bratticed until the next breakthrough to the airway had been driven through, usually sixty feet away. This practice insured that the entry drivers at the main heading would never be more than 120 feet ahead of the air.

The cross entries which turned off the main entries used the same system of airways. This was a good system for ventilating the mines when it was properly maintained and when enough fans were actually in use to keep the air flowing. Still, many things could go wrong. A slate fall could tear out a brattice, allowing the air to cut across a breakthrough without completing its circuit. In this case, the working place above the torn brattice would be without any circulation of air, except for the slight circulation of fresh currents caused by the movement of cars being hauled back and forth. In any case, each mine hired one man whose sole responsibility was to build and maintain the brattices.

In addition, most mines require the installation of humidifiers, though they are needed much more often than they are actually used. In the winter and early spring especially, the air outside becomes dry, and the air currents circulating throughout the mine will carry off most of the moisture from the working place. When the coal dust dries out, it is much more likely to explode; therefore, especially in the winter months, humidifiers, often in the form of water sprayed across the air intake, needed to be installed to reduce the possibility of an explosion.

The cross entries in a mine are four hundred feet apart. Rooms in the coal mine are usually forty feet wide, each one having two sets of track laid about ten feet from both sides, or ribs. These rooms are continuations of the breakthroughs from the entries and turn off at about the same width as the breakthrough, thirty feet. After being driven about thirty feet, they are widened out to forty feet; also at this spot, a track switch-off is laid.

The room is worked or driven about two hundred feet from the cross entry. Then a breakthrough is cut through the twenty foot pillar which has been left to hold up the roof, this breakthrough leading into another room. For example, rooms on the left side of first right will cut through to rooms on the right side of second right. Once the two rooms have been connected, the pillar is mined back to the spot where the room widened from thirty to forty feet. The stumps, the coal left to hold up the roof where the rooms branch off, are much wider than pillars. They must be left to protect the airway from a roof fall, even though such falls are desirable and will certainly occur once the pillars have been dug out. This, the last work done in a coal mine, is called "robbing work."

When all the entries have been driven to the property lines, when all the rooms have been worked, and all the pillars worked back to the stumps, the robbing work begins. This means that the pillars which have held up the top but which also account for a good deal of unmined coal are pulled out, allowing the roof to fall. The robbing work begins closest to the heading in the rooms off the last cross entries. As the coal in the pillars is dug away with a pick, the weight of the mountain gradually begins to come down, causing the coal to become softer. A lick with a pick at the weakest spot in a remaining pillar will cause the coal to loosen up. In cracking, the pillar will often spit fine pieces of coal into a miner's face.

In robbing work it was especially important that the miner judge the top and bottom accurately. If the bottom was soft, the timbers which had been set about three feet apart to support the top would sink into the bottom without breaking. But if the bottom was hard, the timbers had to be set in two solid rows, only a foot apart. Even with these precautions, though, I have seen timbers a foot in width crushed or belly out when the bottom was hard. Once this begins to happen, you often hear a low rumbling. This sound means a miner better shove his coal car out, loaded or not, and make for the main entry, because the top is about to fall. When the top is soft, you may also hear a boom as the coal begins to heave out.

Sometimes two or more acres of coal may have been robbed before a general fall of this kind occurs. These falls mean that the coal in the top, usually a long way up, has fallen, causing cracks so high that in some cases, the surface of the ground above splits, sinking the water that is running down the mountain. I remember being in the mines during a fall like this and holding onto the rails while the wind lifted my body up and down, up and down.

After the smaller falls, which reach up only about ten feet, the top will come down against the coal. In cases like this, one must timber up well next to the fall and in a space about ten feet wide, continue to work back the stump or pillar. If the stumps became too hard to pick, the miners returned to shooting the coal or, in later years, to cutting the coal with machines. With a machine, this robbing work became even more dangerous because the noise produced made it difficult to hear the slate as it began to fall. And the company didn't want to risk damaging a valuable machine.

Since robbing work was so dangerous, it was usually performed by the most experienced miners. By digging coal with a pick, the miner doing the robbing work could usually make quite a bit more money than he could otherwise, though when the coal was very hard, he would not average much more than the other miners.

When all the side entries had been robbed back to first right and first left, the main entry itself would be robbed in the same way. Many times, though, the coal company managed to buy or lease land beyond the original property line, in which case the entries were driven farther. I have known mines to be ten, fifteen, or more miles underground. The length of the haulways makes these deeper mines much more difficult than the shallow mines, especially in the pumping out of water.

"Squeeze" or "creep" often results in mines where poor methods have been employed, when too much coal has been left in the mine for the top to fall normally, but simultaneously too much coal has been mined and removed for the top to stay intact. As a result, whole haulways may buckle and become useless, or stumps, pillars, and timbers may sink completely into a soft bottom so that the top and bottom will press together. The whole mine begins to move and shift so drastically that in the majority of cases, nothing can be done. I knew of one mine that lost 20 percent of the coal because poor planning had brought on a creep. If a mine is well managed, all the coal should be taken out. But sometimes good management and profits do not coincide. Besides, royalties are paid only on coal extracted from the mine, and punishments are not levied for coal lost underground.

The company owners gave the entry drivers advantages: a miner at this occupation would be given all the empty cars he needed, and if he wanted to go back at night and load out the slate he had shot down, the company would supply him with a mule driver for four hours. Such preference encouraged workers to drive the entries quickly, thus creating more rooms for men to work in. My brother Dick and I always tried to stay in entry work because we could earn more money and we could stand on our feet for part of the day rather than always working on our knees. Since we gained reputations as good entry drivers, usually we were assigned to this work.

I have worked in coal as low as twenty-eight inches and as high as forty inches, but most of my fourteen years in the mines were spent working on my knees. I also have scars along my backbone where I skinned myself on little pieces of coal sticking out of the top. God, the wonders of coal mining!

Hazel remembers that shortly after we were married, "It didn't take long for it to be brought very strongly to me what a miner's work was really like. Jim came home with a knee beginning to swell up and turn red and told me that this was the second time this had happened. The other knee had been in this condition three times, Jim told me. The coal seam was only thirty-six inches thick, so there was no way to work but on your knees. The hard rock bottom would bruise the knees plumb to the bone, and they would have to be lanced to let the puss out. This was one kind of surgery the local camp doctor would do. I made Jim a bandage out of padded cloth, about two inches thick, to wrap around his leg just below the swelled knee to keep the injured part from touching the bottom. He worked this way a month or more before the knee was well enough to stand working on. Jim told me that sometimes, when he would accidentally hit the sore knee against the bottom, he would get sick from the pain.

"Miners did not stay away from work for small injuries like this. If they could work, they worked. Crippled men worked, some with only one leg, some with only one arm. I knew of one man, Tom Brackett, who with only one arm and only a thumb left on his one hand, still worked in the mines. Some blind

men also worked there. Men who were sick with TB or cancer kept on the job until they could no longer get to the mines."

Constant work with a pick was very hard on a miner's hands. The skin between the first finger and thumb would get as calloused as shoe leather. Also, this work made a man's hands thick, stiff, fumbly, even years after he had quit work in the mines. So when anybody says that a miner can match a gun thug in gun play, he must be making a joke. A gun thug, who does nothing but handle a pistol, has all the advantage over a miner, who has spent his whole life at hard toil. A miner can shoot from a laying down rest, can fire well if he already has his pistol in his hand, may be able to shoot a shotgun, but if he tries to match a gun thug in a fair fight, the miner will get killed every time.

While all the men who work in the coal mines are commonly referred to as coal miners, the mining process involves many different types of work. In an old mine of one hundred workers, there would be not more than seventy-five coal diggers and loaders; the rest worked as "day men," meaning they were paid by the day rather than by the ton. Among this group were those who hauled the coal; those who laid the track; those who built the brattices to feed air up into the head of the mine where the diggers were working; and those who worked out on the tipple where the coal was weighed, shaken into sizes (block, egg, and nut), and dumped into the railroad gondolas; those who worked as blacksmiths, sharpening the miner's picks and breast augers; and those who built and repaired mine cars. Most every small company also had a wagon and a team of mules for the one man hired specifically as a mule driver. In addition to their tasks at the mine, mule drivers delivered coal to the miner's houses. (Each miner had to pay $4.50 for a wagon load of coal, the same amount that he had loaded for about 40 cents.)

The mule driver was responsible for getting coal cars to and from the mine. Miners pushed their own cars into the entry where the mule driver could hook up his team. Once the "gathering drivers," as they were called, left loaded wagons on the side tracks, the string team driver, who had a team of three mules harnessed one in front of another, hauled the loaded wagons away to the tipple.

Before a mule was taken into the mine, however, one eye was blindfolded with a piece of canvas attached to the bridle. Since mules' eyes focus separately, this meant that when the animal entered the mine and the blindfold was removed, the mule could see well out of the one eye which had become accustomed to the dark. Likewise, before the mule driver led his animal out of the mine, he would again blindfold one eye, leaving the canvas covering on until the mule reentered the mine. If he were driving a string team, he would only have to blindfold the first mule as the others would follow along.

The water in the mines softened the mules' hooves, so that periodically each mule had to have its shoes removed and had to be permitted to run free, sometimes for as long as six months, in order for its feet to harden again. The hard pulling required of these animals meant they had to be reshod often.

Mules worked very well in the mines, especially under the control of an experienced driver. Many mules suffered broken legs and had to be destroyed. Others became stubborn and mean, what I have called kick-outs. This stubbornness often resulted from poor treatment on the part of the mule drivers, some of whom used big, plaited whips, eight feet long, that could severely cut up a mule's rump.

The lead mule hardly ever had to be whipped, but when the driver felt like whipping the swing mule (the animal in the middle of the team) or the wheel mule (the one next to the coal car), he would fasten its tail to the steel rail. The lead mule would keep moving on, stretching the wheel mule out and holding back the team while the driver let go with his black snake whip. Once when I saw a mule driver beating his animal in this way, I was very pleased to see the tail chain break loose. That mule got the chance to let his driver have both feet right in the chest, sending the man back into the second coal car. Like most others of his trade, this mule driver was tough; I thought he was dead, but he climbed right out of that coal car only to beat the animal more.

Sometimes accidents occurred when a mule team became excited on the job, as happened to old Ollie Clark's team. Ollie, a Negro fellow, was a fine mule driver and handled his three-string team expertly, never resorting to the whip. Once down at the Castro mines, Ollie's three mules became excited by something and started back into the mine without him. He took after them but they wouldn't stop. One part of that mine that had been worked out and had filled with water had not been bratticed off properly. Only a plank or two lay across it. The three mules took off down there, fell into the water, and either could not or would not turn around. All three drowned.

I remember Ollie just sat down and cried. Those mules had always minded him just like babies, doing anything he wanted them to. I even saw him once come out of the mine with that string team pulling sixteen loaded cars of coal. The company didn't fire Ollie because neither the company officials nor anyone else could figure out what had caused those mules to run away. Everyone knew that it wasn't Ollie's fault. He hadn't been whipping the mules; he didn't need to.

The mule drivers held a countywide competition from time to time to judge who had his animals best under control. My brother Dick won several times with a mule he called Old Sue. Old Sue would come to Dick from just as far away as she could hear his voice and when Dick wanted her to, she would even climb right up and across a coal car. Once mechanization came to the mines, the mule driver's fine occupation was the first to become obsolete.

Some people say that men have a love for working in the coal mines; even one of my half-sister Molly's songs says, "That man has a lust for the mines." I do not believe this. I never went into the coal mines a day in my life that I didn't have a dread on my mind that I might never come out again. Any sensible mining man is aware of the dangers surrounding him, many of which are beyond his control. First of all, mining is done for profit; safety rates fairly low on the scale of musts.

My brother Dick and I worked together in a mine on Horse Creek in Clay County, Kentucky, shooting coal from the solid. Twice a day we would shoot the coal, at noon and in the evening just before leaving work. The miners took an hour for lunch, usually from 12:00 to 1:00, so that the smoke produced from the blasting could escape the mine before they returned. When we put off these coal shots, one of us had to stand right above the mouth of our working place to stop any miner from passing by, because sometimes pieces or even entire blocks of coal would fly all the way to the front of the opening.

We had stored our two gallon cans of black powder about 150 feet away from where we were shooting, what we believed was a safe distance from the blast. We lighted our fuses and ran out of the way, my brother moving through the trapdoor hung across the haulway. I stopped just around the corner to be out of the way of flying coal but also prepared to keep other miners from passing by until after the shots went off.

One of our shots made a blow-out; instead of blasting the coal out of the solid, it only made a small crack and blew fire out into the mine. Well, I thought my time was up. The flames rolled right to the mouth of the place, all around the two cans of black powder. I hollered for help and made for the trapdoor which my brother threw open for me. This move, of course, would have been useless had the cans of powder exploded, but luckily for Dick and me, they didn't. Later when we went back to the work place, we saw that the paper around the cans had been scorched — very close indeed.

Another incident occurred at a mine called Slick Lizard at Cary, Kentucky. This, by the way, was the first mine where I ever worked, earning 50 cents an hour. My two brothers and I were running a contract there, a fairly common practice whereby one or more miners contract with a coal operator to drive the entry, load the coal into gondolas, haul it, and do all of the "dead work" for an agreed amount per ton. Sometimes one or two other men would be working on such a contract with us, as in this case were my Uncle Dan Parten and his son Bob. Well, as lunchtime approached, we prepared to shoot. I readied six holes in the solid and one slate shot in the entry heading, the opening to the working place. Bob Parten, who had not been working long in the mines — what we call a "green horn" — for some unknown reason began hollering, "fire in the hole . . . fire in the hole!" I was about ready to light my shots and did not understand why he was calling out. As a result, I forgot what I was doing, as the miners would say, "forgot my ass." As I came out, I lighted the slate shot.

Once I found out this green horn had given a false fire call, I got so mad that I forgot about having lit the slate shot. I ran back under it to light the six coal shots, and then on my way back, began to light the slate shot, only then seeing and remembering that it was already lit. Well, be you me, I got as far away from it as fast as I could go, and had just run off far enough to escape being killed when the slate blast went off. Had it not been for the second or two I had to escape, I would have been dead sixty-one years ago. This story illustrates how the human mind in a time of stress can cause a man to hurry, to forget some detail that could cost him his life.

Under the constant dread of accident, one tries to stay alert. This caution in itself can often prevent an injury. I remember one instance when I had noticed that the top of an area I was mining was bad and so had set timbers alongside the track, next to the car I was loading. I either saw or heard something, probably the latter, and as I stopped to listen, I could hear the slate above me tearing loose. As quickly as I could, I jumped back next to the mine car when two tons of slate came crashing down. It fell so close to me that it smashed the carbide flask on my hip and caught my feet. Luckily, I was not hurt.

My brother Dick was not so lucky. He was killed by a fall of draw slate, two tons of it that broke his back and neck.

I have seen a man caught under slate like this, one of the most horrible things I have ever witnessed. The slate fall had not killed him but was mashing the life out of him. The pain was so great that be begged me to knock him in the head with a pick.

There was an old saying popular among mine foremen, almost to the point of being a tradition in the mines. In the morning as the foreman came around to the men at work, he called out, "Round and round. Get a move on. Kill a mule, we'll buy another. Kill a man, hire another." This wasn't meant maliciously, only as a jockeying expression, but the saying does testify to the ever-present dangers of the occupation and to the companies' lack of real concern.

12. Sparks and Dust

During the boom years of the First World War, huge changes were taking place in the coalfields, largely because the United States had assumed most of the coal orders that England and Germany previously had filled. In 1911, 18,000 tons of coal were mined in Harlan County, almost all of it by small, exploratory operations. The average coal output per man per ten-hour day was approximately three and one half tons. Ten years later, 3,000,000 tons were mined, and ten years after that 14,000,000 tons. These enormous leaps in production were due primarily to the advent of mechanization and the seizure of the coalfields by giant coal combines. To give some indication of the societal changes that resulted in the mountains, the population of Harlan County alone jumped from 10,000 to 64,000. The average tonnage per man per day rose from three and one half to seven and one half.

Union membership showed a marked increase; in fact, I remember my father's helping to set up many new locals of the UMW of A during these boom years. Once the union came to be recognized by the coal companies, many wage increases were won, workers were offered free transportation to the mines, some companies even built a few more outhouses and whitewashed the company shacks, others put in bathhouses where the miners could wash.

Some people claim that miners are a dirty people; this is nothing but filthy slander. Miners are the cleanest people there are in that they must bathe each day when they remove their mining clothes to wash off the coal dust. Dust does not only get into the miner's eyes and lungs but seeps into everything and must be washed off. But coal dust is not dirt, my friends; coal dust is clean. It will make a man very black, but again, that is not dirt but a color. Even if a man just puts on his mining clothes and does not work that day at all, as often happened, his work clothes alone will blacken his skin with coal dust. A miner changes underclothes daily, of course, but his outer clothing will last much longer if it's not washed as often.

No, the miner did not have a shower or a bathtub. In my day, many who lived in the coal camps had never washed in a regular bathtub. Not until I was twenty-one and went to Lexington to take the examination for mine foreman did I do so. In a hotel there called the Goose, the bathtub and I first got acquainted. It was in that same bathroom, while I was in the tub, that I saw my first cockroach. As far as I knew, there were no such bugs in the coal camp, though we had plenty of bedbugs.

The miner took his bath in a two- or three-bushel washtub, the same one his wife used to wash clothes in. The good woman would heat a kettle of water on the stove and when it got boiling hot would pour it in the tub, cooling the water temperature off somewhat with water from a bucket. After the window had been covered up, the man would stand over the washtub and wash, his head and face first, then his neck, arms, and shoulders. Usually he would dry these cleaned parts off with a towel before squatting down in the tub to finish his bath. There was an old saying about this kind of bathing: you wash as high as possible, then as low as possible, and then you wash old possible.

Additionally during these boom years, the Workman's Compensation law was passed by the state. The union also won some benefits for injured miners' families: a woman was awarded the great sum of $4,500 upon the death of her husband or $6,000 if her husband were totally disabled for life. Yet while the union made advances, the coal operators associations were busy consolidating their forces as well. The old plantation-type system began to disappear as larger companies bought and leased land away from the small, exploratory mine operators. More and more, the coal mines came to resemble highly organized factories.

The large operator was able to shove the small mine owner out mainly because he could afford the new machinery which was to change mining methods so radically during this period. Such large operations built their own small, coal-fired powerhouses and began to make their own electricity, stringing wire into the mines and buying motors with which to haul the coal. This mechanization of course, meant the end of several mining trades, most notably trapping, which could now be handled with automatic doors, and mule driving, replaced by motor men in much smaller numbers.

The first electricity used was 250 volt DC which, if a miner got into it, would give him quite a jolt. Since the motors were much lower than the mules had been, not as much top needed to be shot in the entries. If the coal were four feet thick, the miners didn't have to shoot any top at all but just ran the motorized cars into the loading area. At the same time, more wire had to be hung in the rooms and airways, a necessity which proved dangerous and complicated in the long run.

Soon motors were developed which could run on rechargeable banks of batteries, thus avoiding most wiring problems. These battery motors made it possible to put rubber wheels on cars and motors and move them anywhere necessary in the mine. Of course, such advances did away with many a track layer's job. At about four tons apiece, battery motors could not haul as many cars on a track; therefore, in most mines the battery-powered motors were used to gather loaded cars onto a side track. From there, a bigger motor that ran on a wire would haul loaded cars out onto the tipple and bring empties back.

In the transition from shooting coal from the solid to using cutting machines, some companies experimented with punching machines. Running on compressed air from the company's own compressors, the punching machine was pulled up on a board four feet wide and eight feet long. Under the back end of the board was a wooden horse about ten inches high. The man running the machine, wearing a clog or "scotch" on his left foot, would "scotch the wheel," meaning put a block beneath the wheel about a foot and a half from where the machine hit the coal. Using the punching machine, a man could cut approximately five feet deep and five feet wide, after which the board would have to be moved before the procedure began again. Another man, called the "hostler," sat beside the machine and shoveled out the loosened coal. On the average, the board could be repositioned eight times during the work day, in other words, eight "boards" could be cut, the size of the average room inside a mine. Once the punching machine had loosened the bottom coal, loaders would bore two holes, one in each corner of the face, and shoot down the rest.

Since it took two men to run these early machines, and because they could only loosen enough coal in a day for two or three loaders, the punching machines did not prove economical enough to gain wide use. They best suited miners working in gangs under individual contract. Some companies never did try the punching machines but converted directly from shooting coal with black powder to using the electrical coal-cutting machines.

A track layer was responsible for tramming the cutting machine near the coal face. There the machine man would judge whether the top were safe enough to cut under. If he found the working place stable, he would pull the machine into it.

The coal cutter was hauled up to the right-hand corner of the room, a jack was set against the top, and the machine man would cut six feet into the face, about one foot from the bottom. Then the front jack, a chain attached to its bottom, would be taken across to the left side of the room and set against the top. A second jack would be set against the top on the right side, behind the machine. The machine, once started, would feed itself across the room, cutting six feet deep until it reached the other side. After cutting across the room, the machine was pulled back onto its carriage, ready to be trammed to the next working space. The track layer might also, if the miner in this particular room had drilled his holes, insert the charges and shoot down the coal. Again, a hostler worked with the machine man, shoveling the dust away.

Many types of electric cutters were tried, some which could be used in high seams of coal, others which could take advantage of lower seams. Some were built to take advantage of those five or six-inch layers of "mother coal," a softer mixture of coal and dirt often found between layers of harder, purer coal. Machines were used that cut right into this softer dirt, which was then shoveled onto the gob. Mother coal used to be thrown away since it wouldn't burn, but these days it is often rinsed off, washing most of the dirt away, and sold. (Some companies have ripped off the government by loading up mother coal with the rest of a coal shipment and selling it to TVA.)

Arc wall machines, which were also employed, started in low, cut up to near the top, and then curved back down; however, these were not very popular. The bottom cutting machines were generally considered the best.

Electric machines were a big step forward in terms of the amount of coal a miner could load in a day. With only three men at work with the machine — the machine operator, the hostler, and the track layer — enough coal could be cut in a day for twenty or thirty miners to load. Nevertheless, these mechanical advancements entailed some drawbacks. First, the machines created enormous amounts of dust. When I was assigned as a track layer after one of these electric coal cutters, I remember, there was so much dust that many times I could not even see the machine. I could be away from work for a week and would still be coughing up coal dust. In my opinion, no man could work after one of these machines without getting black lung. Also, the machines necessitated more wiring in the mines, exactly what the battery-powered motors had been brought in to avoid.

Once I was working in a very deep mine at Kitts, Kentucky, where the men, as is customary, were riding into their working places in empty coal cars, when the motor ran into an electric wire that had been knocked down by a slate fall. Fire began to fly all over the place. My uncle started to jump out of the car while it was still moving, but I grabbed him. I knew that unless the flames hit us directly, we would at least be safer inside the car. We crouched inside until the breaker outside was broken, cutting off the electricity. The sparks and flames finally stopped.

A spark put off by one of these coal cutting machines could easily, and did in many cases, ignite gas in the mine, causing an explosion. Because of the pull against the top, such machines could also cause slate falls. Many men were injured tramming the machine from place to place.

Other machines introduced during the war years added to the efficiency of the coal mine operation: the electric drill bored the holes to be shot, electric pumps replaced the old siphoning system of removing water from the mines which had required that there be a greater drop than rise for the water to pull itself. But all of these machines had one purpose — to get the coal out using fewer and fewer miners. This purpose they accomplished.

By 1932, when I was blacklisted from the mines, many operators had begun to experiment with coal loading machines, though I was no longer mining when these came into full operation. Mining is so different now that if I went into the mines, I would be one of those green horns I have written about. I will turn to Tom Inman, a fine source of information, having operated most of the old and the modern machinery used underground. Tom has been totally disabled from a mining injury and is a black lung victim.

Inman: "I started working around the coal mines in 1934, outside at first, unloading slate, drying sand, and things like that. But I was still a member of the UMW of A. Everybody belonged to the same union. I went inside the mine to work when I was fifteen years old. Back then, you would sign that you were sixteen and then could go in as a chalk eye; this meant that you worked with some other fellow and that your coal went in on his number. A lot of more experienced miners liked to work these chalk eyes because since the miner himself paid the chalk eye, he could be sure to make some money on the younger man's tonnage.

"I worked with all kinds of coal cutting machines, but my first was a 35 B Jeffrey, a machine that cut the bottom. Later they came out with machines that you could tram, that were put on tracks. I have run the old Standards and Universals and the old chain saws that ran along a chain, and then later on cables. I remember when the permissable control boxes were put on the machines. The old control boxes made sparks, which was very dangerous. Many machine men got their eyes burned because of this. The sparks could also put off gas in the mines, causing an explosion. The permissable box was enclosed so that no sparks could get out. Now, these old bottom cutting machines have become illegal because of the sparks they make. Those 11 B Sullivans that came out with permissable control boxes, they could be used. About all of the bottom machines, like the 35, have been taken out of the mines.

"As for shooting coal, air is the safest thing that you can use. They set up an air machine on the outside that would build up a 14,000 pound pressure. This air was piped into every working place. Electric drills had come into use which were much faster than the old method of auger drilling. You attached your own pipe onto the air pipe that brought the pressurized air into your working place, the explosion would occur, and the coal would be shot down.

The same pipes could be used over and over again; you just needed to reload them. Shooting with air, since it made only a little dust (and that you could fan out in a few minutes), was much better on your health.

"Later, the Joy Company came out with another cutting machine that you could use to cut across the bottom, then up the side, or any way you wanted. You could cut a pound plug out if you wanted to. Still we would have to shoot the coal down, and so most of the time we used this machine to cut across the bottom. But if I was cutting a breakthrough to another working place, I would cut with it up the side and then pry the coal down with a bar.

"I also used the arc wall machines. They circle-cut while staying on the track. I ran one of them at Page, West Virginia. The next machines ran on rubber tires, no track. With these you didn't circle-cut, but you could cut a square or any other shape you wanted to make. They also had belt lines, or pan lines, for the coal to run on and their own dusters, not like the old bottom machines where someone had to shovel all the dust out of the machine's way. But it seemed these cutters only made that much more dust. Many times I have turned my machine off and walked around to the face of the coal to see where my cutter bar was. Any man who worked on a machine, ran a motor, or cupelled after a motor had to have a good spotlight to be able to see. A lot of times, too, those machines would get hot; the oil smoke and dust would mix and bring on what was called 'miner's asthma.' You can take note of it: take all the machine men and hostlers after machines and the motor men and the cupellers — they simply all have black lung. And it does not take them long to get it either.

"In using the belt to move the coal out, we went ahead and cut, then timbered the place, and then shot down the coal. After this, the belt, which could be used for ninety feet, was brought in. They had what was called a piggyback loader which was on a plate that slipped right under the coal. The piggyback had arms on it that raked the coal into the belt. Then the belt carried the coal out of the working place.

"Also the Joy Company, I believe, came out with what was called the 'duck-bill.' This was a shaker pan without a chain in it but with a lip in the front. As you came back with it, the lip would catch the coal and just shake it. Some called these machines 'hootenannies'; others just referred to them as 'shakers.' They worked all right but weren't used very long.

"Since about 1950, in this part of the country, they have been using pins to hold up the top; this was done even earlier in West Virginia. Used to be that a lot of men were killed by what they called 'rib rolls,' where the slate rock would loosen and fall off the sides of the haulways. Now that doesn't come down. It's pinned, buddy. That fastens the loose slate to the solid slate above it.

"Nowadays there are not as many timbers used as in the old mines, though they still follow the continuous miner with timbers. These machines cut both ways; they will cut across the working place and then just jump under the coal and cut back. They have two cutting heads, like augers, running counter to each other, and they take all the coal out as they go. I've worked around these machines, but I've never worked one myself. I can't because they're hydraulic. The coal passes on back to the belt and goes on out of the mines. But every time a continuous miner moves forward, timbers are set. This is done until the working place is driven as far as it's supposed to go.

"They hardly ever lay track in the mines anymore; just when they have a really long way to tram the coal, they might. But most of the mines today just have belts that bring the coal all the way out to the tipple and pour off into the railroad gondolas. Except maybe down in Clay County, there aren't any more little old-fashioned mines left that I know of."

When I first worked in the coal mines, shooting coal from the solid, my average tonnage was three and a half per day, for which I received about one dollar per ton. This sounds like a reasonable wage for those days until you realize that back then, miners worked an average of 154 days per year. Many things happened that would prevent a man from putting in a day's work; often there were no orders to fill. In any case, once the coal cutting machines came into use, output more than doubled. At the same time, however, a miner's pay sank to 40 cents per ton, less than half the former pay rate. So who did the machinery help? Not the miners, I'm sure.

One concession gained by the UMW of A during the first years of my membership was portal-to-portal pay. The union wrote a clause in the contract stating that a miner was to be paid a minimum amount of money for each day that he showed up at work, even if the mines weren't running because of something beyond the miner's control. Before this, anyone who was not a day man would not be paid anything except for the tonnage he loaded, regardless of how many hours he might have spent in the mine working.

A good coal loader could make far more on a normal work day than he could in accepting the portal-to-portal, which, it should be remembered, was a minimum. Still it was difficult to get some miners to work hard, to make $20, when they could get $13 for portal-to-portal.

Tom Inman explains this: "When many of the miners got hip, they would only load one or two cars and then get their minimum pay. My crew always made better money, though, never falling back on that fixed portal-to-portal. I think that establishing the minimum was a good thing, but I don't believe that it should have been paid unless a man loaded a reasonable amount of coal or unless he'd been knocked off work by a breakdown in the company's equipment or a slate fall. Then after he had loaded a reasonable amount of coal, the portal-to-portal could have been added. If a man found his work place fallen in, he still was supposed to move to another room and load at least one car before receiving his portal-to-portal.

"Since I ran the coal cutting machine and was paid more for being the gang leader, it was my responsibility to see that all the loaders on my run had a place to load, if they wanted one. In later years, the portal-to-portal system was discontinued, but something similar was written into the contract: a man would be paid seven dollars just for showing up, even if he just went into the mine and came right back out again."

Some say that this portal-to-portal system forced smaller coal operators to close down their mines. Many mine owners tried to get around this clause in the contract by giving gangs of men individual contracts to do all of the work, including putting the coal in the gondolas. Gang work's real effect was to cut out the miners who were low producers, especially many of the older miners. It also contributed to and sped up mechanization.

Mule drivers, trappers, and many others were out of work suddenly with the advent of machinery. They simply accepted the introduction of machinery until one day, they found their jobs were no longer needed and they would have to leave the mountains. Since they knew no other trade, it was hard for them to find work. Many ended up later on the WPA; for quite awhile, mountain men went to the cities for work but most of them ended up on home relief, especially in the '30s.

The machine men, however, were swiftly becoming the aristocrats of labor in the mines. They did work longer hours, and I guess their jobs were the most unhealthy of any in the mines, but since they were in such great demand, they could make more than twice as much money as the ordinary miner. The companies began to humor them, letting them have quite a bit to say about who would get the best working places; in fact, many times machine men had more influence with the companies than did the foreman. Once I saw this change I realized, I suppose for the first time, that mining would soon be a highly skilled occupation. In my later years as a miner, I saw the division of labor become more and more pronounced; men who were better at carpentry work were used exclusively to build brattices for ventilation, others were designated as special track men, others worked every day outside as tipple men, weighing the coal and dumping it into the coal cars. All were UMW of A members.

The only thing holding back an even more extensive use of machinery was its enormous expense. The newer mine fields in Harlan County were opened up by big companies — the Peabody mines at Black Mountain, the Chevrolet mines, U.S. Steel's captive mines — that could afford building more machines to do the work and hiring fewer miners.

A lot of the small companies preferred not to use the new machinery.

Things were going fairly well for the small operator during these years, two hundred to five hundred tons of coal being produced per day. To lay out the money for modern machinery meant putting the coal company deeply into debt, a debt that seemed unnecessary at the time. C.R. Coleman, the small operator I worked for, never wanted to buy machinery. He was happy enough just having his women and maintaining the good relationship he held with most of us who worked for him. By the 1930s, "Mosey" Coleman, as we called him, and the entire system of small exploratory mining would be swallowed up. This trend began during the boom years and accelerated with the introduction of machinery.

Some may agree with the coal operators, that the plight of the Appalachian coal miner is not their fault, that using machinery rather than men is a sign of progress. But if this were the case, why did those same operators later hire gun thugs to threaten the miner and his family? Why did the operators not join miners in going to the state and federal governments to demand that new jobs be created? The huge companies took away men's jobs, jobs that were the only trades these men knew, by buying machines that could only be afforded because of the money the companies had made from the miner's labor.

In the early days of mining, when the coal operators did not have any orders and were forced to shut down, they at least let the miners live on in their company houses until work could be found elsewhere. An operator might even carry some of the men for awhile in hopes of gaining orders to fill. Maybe this was a restoration of the old slave system, but it was a hell of a lot better than the big, fascist financial combines which tried and almost succeeded in taking over the mountains and turning them into a Hitler-type society. Even after the Wagner Act, the big operators still tried to fight the federal government. Who were the traitors of our democratic form of government? Not the mountain people.

It seems that one owner of a large mining operation who had actually seen a coal miner was staying with his family at a hotel near the mine. Since his wife and daughter had never laid eyes on any of his workers, this boss ordered his foremen to have two or three miners sent up to the hotel. When the men arrived, the father called out, "Come on out here, wife. Come out, daughter. The miners are here." At this the daughter answered, "Hitch them up there, Dad. I will be out in a minute or two." Just then, the operator's wife came around the corner, carrying something in her hand. "I brought this for the miners," she said to her husband. "Here is some hay for them to eat while they're waiting."

13. Out-scab the Scabs, 1923–1924

The relatively calm and prosperous period of the first coal boom could not and did not last too long. In 1920, once Germany and England began to recover from the effects of World War I and at the same time to regain many of their coal markets, the demand for Kentucky coal slacked off. This slight depression didn't last long; in fact, by late in 1922 coal orders had picked up again. But the operators had received a scare. Most mine owners became harder to deal with; others even tried to back out of contracts with the union. The operators seemed to be probing for any weaknesses they could find in the miners' organization.

Some would ask us to believe that the mountain people had been so isolated from the mainstream of American political life that they knew nothing about political parties and organizations. Nothing could be further from the truth. I have mentioned already the early efforts at union organization under the Knights of Labor, but it should also be known that the mountain people have a long tradition of support for third parties. In 1917, Eugene Debs received a heavy vote for president among miners; I cast my first ballot in 1923 for Bob La Follette on the Farmer-Labor party ballot.

My friend Tilman Cadle remembers: "One governor of Tennessee would not send in the militia to break a strike. The Kentucky miners took heed of this and said, 'Well, we'll elect a Democrat for governor of Kentucky since the Democratic governor next door seems to be in sympathy with us.' But once they did help to get a Democrat elected, this man proceeded to send the militia in on them. A lot of miners wanted to vote for Eugene V. Debs, but the politicians would keep hammering on the idea that a vote for a Socialist was a waste. Many miners would answer, 'Well, I have been wasting my vote all these many years, so I might as well vote for the man.' Over half the people in the mountains are ashamed to admit that they are either Democrat or

Republican, so they just say, 'I vote for the man.'" When we think of American political thought and American unions, let us remember that in neither case were Kentucky mountain people behind the door.

By 1920, though I had only worked in the mines for a year, I was an active member of the United Mine Workers and one of its locally elected officers. At this time, most mine workers in my camp were union members and, in terms of the wildcat strikes we held over local grievances, we were meeting with C.R. "Mosey" Coleman, our owner/operator, with fair success. On the national level, however, the union had some serious problems. The greatest of these was District 19's status as a provisional district.

In a full-fledged district, rank-and-file members elect their own district officials, while for provisional districts the national organization appoints officers. I believe that in 1920, only four UMW of A districts could elect their own officers. Provisional districts were and are simply a method of muzzling the rank and file, and they clearly reflect John L. Lewis's tyranny over the union. Tilman Cadle says that District 19 was at one time before 1920 a real district but became indebted to the national organization and was taken over. I'm not certain about this.

The union's other major problem resulted from the different districts', by way of the national organization, settling on contracts with different expiration dates. This practice was definitely a sacrifice Lewis made in accordance with his belief that one had to sacrifice something to get a contract with the coal operators. If the operators in District 19 asked for a contract to go into effect May first, Lewis would undoubtedly have suggested June first if that were the day that the Ohio district's contract expired. But at this suggestion, the operators would threaten not to go along with the UMW of A in any way. Eventually, Lewis would back down on the issue of the contract date in order to gain recognition of the union, a 10 percent increase in wages, or some other concession. But when there are two districts, perhaps more, all with U.S. Steel mines, if Kentucky goes out on strike after the contract expires, U.S. Steel's orders can be filled easily enough in Ohio. Even in Kentucky alone, District 23 (Western Kentucky) would in some cases continue working when we in District 19 were out on strike, or we would be working while the Western Kentucky miners were out. This was no way to run a union and win, but it was a way for Lewis to maintain his good salary and to keep his own men in office.

Tilman Cadle: "I would say that in about 1922, the UMW of A began to lose ground. There were a number of strikes from 1922 to 1924 which weren't at all supported by the national union. Professional strikebreakers and the state militia both contributed to the failure of these strikes. I have been told that the UMW of A organized one nonunion mine during these years where the workers were getting 38 cents per ton. The union made a contract for them to get 32 cents per ton. When the miners wanted to know why they were getting less with the union than they had without it, they were told, 'We have to out-scab the scabs.'"

"Out-scab the scabs" was a phrase used so often that it became almost a slogan of Lewis and his national organization. Likewise Lewis and the national UMW of A contended that no one could run a strike successfully in a time of recession. As evidenced by the 1977 coal strike, the rank-and-file miners have never agreed with either of these theories; they believe that if wages are cut, you throw out your water and go home. Even so, the Lewis theories discouraged the miners and exposed just those types of organizational weaknesses that the operators sought to exploit.

In 1923, I had gotten so tired of working as a coal miner that I decided to take the little money I had saved, move up to Cary hollow, and start up a moonshine still.

Once I moved, I found that there was a bunch of men cutting cross ties up where I had planned to set up making whiskey; I was afraid they would turn me in, so I turned to farming, about fifteen acres of corn and a garden patch. Well, that one year broke me from farming.

While I was living on that little mountain farm, the miners at old Straight Creek, a mile and a half below where I lived, went out on strike. These miners had heard that the UMW of A members in the Ohio district had been given a raise.

The Liberty Coal Company, as was a fairly common practice, brought in prostitutes to accommodate the strikebreakers, setting four such women up in one of the coal camp houses. Four old miners decided on direct action in this case. They went over the mountain, and finding the house where the prostitutes were staying, they started shooting into the place. One of these women, whom they called Big Six, was shot in the buttocks. The operators, of course, called the sheriff, but when he got there, not only had the men put their guns away, but the women had left the camp running.

This same coal company also offered free transportation to men willing to work in the Straight Creek mine, neglecting to tell such miners that a strike was going on. Even though many men had traveled from far away in hopes of finding work, the majority of them refused to, once they arrived and realized they would be breaking the strike. Those who had enough money took the train right back home; those who didn't worked just long enough to earn the money for the fare. The companies were especially prone to try this trick on Negro miners, but to the honor of the black mining men, very few Negro miners ever scabbed or broke a strike. Many of them would choose instead to walk back home, even if this were one hundred miles or more away.

The UMW of A had a no-discrimination clause in its obligation — "I will never discriminate against a fellow worker on account of creed, color, or nationality." Many Negroes were elected to local union offices. And inside the mines, everyone was treated equally, except in those few mines where the bosses tried to be tougher on the Negro workers than on the whites, giving whites the easier jobs and better working places.

But once the work day ended, blacks and whites were separated, living in different coal camps, attending different churches and schools. My father did preach occasionally at the so-called colored church and would invite black preachers to his white church as well, but this was unusual. Mixed marriages, even mixed dances, were virtually unheard of, but as one would expect, some mixing was done on the sly. Sometimes the white boys would try to make time with the black girls.

Such an instance led to a race riot in Cary in 1923. Girt Roark, a young white boy from a large family, engaged a young Negro man in a shoot-out over a black girl they had both been going to see. It could have gone either way, since both of the boys were shooting, but Roark was shot and killed. When old man Roark (one of the fellows who had raided the prostitutes' house) heard that his son was dead, he simply went berserk and began shooting at every black person he saw. Many other local whites joined in, these being that show-off kind of people who are always ready, right or wrong, to jump on the underdog.

When the blacks poured into the town square to ask for help, the law refused and simply let these people, many of whom had lived in Cary all their lives, be driven out. My own feelings and those of my family were all in sympathy with the Negroes, but we were definitely in the minority. All we could do was help secretly. I slipped to Uncle Alf McFarland's and hid three of his children in my home until he could get them away.

This was a sad day. I had known many of these people all my life. I had had them as customers when I sold newspapers, I had sold them blackberries, I had worked with them, I had gone with my mother to see their babies. Given only two days to get out of Cary, these people had to leave everything they had. Alf McFarland, for example, had three cows and nine head of hogs running out and was not even given time to gather the animals up and sell them. When he asked me to take the stock, I told him that I didn't have enough money to pay for the animals, but he said "Jim, I would rather you had them than anyone else. Give me what you can." I handed him all the cash I had, $216, though the stock was worth much more than that.

Within a week, all of the blacks in Cary had gone, leaving all that they owned behind. Though a few black miners still work at Scotia and at other mines along that left fork of Straight Creek, I don't think any blacks have lived there since this riot. They may buy at the stores up there, but understandably, they choose to live elsewhere.

Another incident of this kind involved an old black man in Pineville. Uncle Ben, as we called him, was about seventy-five years old and lived by himself, gathering scraps from the local groceries to feed to his hogs. One night two white prostitutes forced their way into his home, and a white man who wanted to get the old fellow in trouble called the police to report that Ben was entertaining white women. When the police charged into his house, they found Uncle Ben sitting before the fire and the white women in his bed. He stood up and called out, "Praise God, you have come. Will you get these women out of my bed? I've tried to get them to leave here but they won't go." But the police proceeded to arrest the old man and take him to jail. As soon as they could raise bond money, some friends had him brought home again.

When word got to me that the white fellow who had called the police was getting together a lynch mob to take poor Uncle Ben out and hang him, I didn't waste any time. I told Ben's two sons-in-law to arm themselves and come over to his house, and I found about fifteen white men to bring their guns and join us. Everyone was ready to shoot should that be necessary. Well, since we hadn't hidden the fact that we all were going to protect Uncle Ben, the lynch mob never showed up to carry out their threat. The deputy sheriff did come around, though, to ask what we were doing; we just said that we were going skunk hunting. He knew what we meant. Finally, the case against Uncle Ben was dropped, but we continued to stand guard at his house for about two weeks nonetheless.

What have I learned about race relations from these experiences? I am convinced that if working people had been left to their own devices, both Negroes and whites would have ignored race distinctions long ago. In the South there would have been far more interracial marriages. Would this have been bad? I don't think so, just as long as the marriages took place because of decisions the people themselves had made. It certainly would be far better than the system which the white rich have tried to maintain — what they call "sowing their wild oats in black soil."

During times of a strike, the mountain farmers gave us steady miners a hard time. They made most of their livings from farming but would come to the mines in the winter to earn a little extra money. The coal operators realized this and knew that a wage cut in the late fall or winter, while it might incite the steady miners, would not discourage a farmer who had come in to make any wage offered. These small farmers didn't consider their working under such circumstances scabbing; in fact, many of them didn't know what the term meant. For the most part they were sharecroppers, as my father had been, who had not raised enough to produce a solid surplus. Once their crops were laid by, the mines offered them a chance to sustain themselves.

Even so, when these farmers, many of whom were our friends, came in prepared to take away our jobs, we could not allow them to. We would try to convince them that their working was taking the bread right out of the miners' mouths. Some farmers would join the union and pay dues while they worked as miners; these we could handle. But others refused to join, and they were simply not permitted to work.

The companies couldn't run the mines with only these green horn farmers on the job. They required some experienced miners to keep the operation moving and to keep the green horns from killing themselves or injuring others. To handle the small farmers who refused to join the union, the steady miners left on the job worked many schemes: first, green horns were given the lowest-paying jobs and second, since mining is piece work, each man receiving pay only for the tons of coal he loads, we made certain that if any man had an empty car, it would be one of these farmers. Their track, for some reason or another, would not get laid; slate would get pulled onto their track. There were many things that could be done short of striking, which is always a last resort. No steady miner wants to go on strike for he knows he'll suffer more than anyone.

Since the small farmers generally were the local moonshiners and since their markets were the coal mining communities nearby, we often would tell a scabbing farmer we'd indict him for selling whiskey or even bust up his still if he didn't join the union. This plan proved very effective, but it wasn't used unless all other ploys failed, it being against every mountain man's principles to inform on anyone. Usually just the threat of indictment could stop a man from scabbing. The only drawback was that we would lose our whiskey supplier and would have to find another.

These farmers, most of them, were good people, but their problems were a bit different from those of the industrial worker; therefore, some of them had to be convinced of the union's importance, of the importance of sticking together. Once they were starved off their little farms, as happened to most of them, and found that they had to make a living mining twelve rather than six months a year, they became good union men.

There are different types of strikebreakers, as any union man or woman knows. One is the poor miner with a large family who has to choose between seeing his family starve and working during a strike. This is the hardest decision he will ever be called on to make. On the one hand, the company will offer him a steady job and the best working place in the mine if he continues to work, while on the other hand, the operator will threaten to blacklist him and have his family thrown out in the road if he does not work. The union, if organized at his mine, can only promise better wages if the strike is won. Many a good man was driven to scab — to starve babies, especially if they are your own, is a hard thing to do. Many a good man, too, I'm sure, went to an early grave because of this conflict, for no man ever feels like a man again after he has scabbed for the operators.

But all miners, both those who had kept working out of necessity and those out on strike, hated the professional strikebreakers. While these men, following strikes across mine fields, would be paid large sums of money, they never stayed on after the strike was settled. Even if they wanted to keep working, the operators would not allow them to stay since even the operators realized such men could not be trusted. Some of the scabs were young local drunks, stupid boys who would do anything for a bottle of whiskey. The company would get them drunk and put them to work; sometimes it would be two or three days before these fellows even realized they were breaking a strike.

I recall one such instance when two local toughs woke up from their drunken stupors and discovered what had happened. That night after midnight, they slipped back up to the mine, up high on the mountainside where a long string of loaded cars was sitting. They took the blocks from under the wheels and turned the whole string of mine cars over the hill, tearing up the tipple and the incline both.

In other cases, striking miners took direct action to punish professional scabs. I remember when local miners disarmed one of them, gave him a cowbell, and sent him off across the mountain. Every time he would stop ringing the bell, the strikers would shoot at the spot where they had last heard a ring. A friend of mine still has the pistol that they took from this particular strikebreaker and calls it, "the pistol I traded for a cowbell."

Since I was not too directly involved in the 1923 strike at Straight Creek, I asked Myrtle Garland, a distant relative on the Lucas side of my family, to discuss her memories of the period with me. Myrtle's husband, Jess Garland, is also a distant cousin on the Garland side of the family. Myrtle, born in Laurel County, Kentucky, moved to the Straight Creek mining camp with her family at age ten.

Myrtle Garland: "By the time we moved to Straight Creek, my father, Julius Spivey, was not able to work. My two older brothers worked and my mother, Serina Lucas Spivey, always kept at least two boarders in order to help feed the family: my two older brothers, myself, my three younger brothers, and my father.

"Once my dad died, I couldn't get to school much. My mother took in washing and hoed corn to get food for us children. I would have to stay at home and do the housework.

"I married in 1918 to Jess Garland and we lived together for fifty-three years. There were nine children born to our home; we lost two children and we raised seven. My husband has been dead for five years now. He had retired and was drawing a miner's union pension when he died.

"We lived at Straight Creek, Kentucky, during the miners union strike of 1923 and '24 when they sent men from the militia in with all kinds of guns to run the union men out. At that time, we just had two children, one and four years old. They both had pneumonia, fever, measles, and whooping cough. While we sat in our dark house with them, I could hear our sick children trying to get their breath; even when I went out on the porch or on the steps of our house, I could hear them. When my husband would make a light, someone outside would holler at us to turn it out, so we had to sit there in the darkness. The militia shot over our house until the mountains were set on fire.

"Well, finally we had to leave there. The union chartered thirty-five boxcars to move thirty-five families of union men away to Molus, Kentucky, in Harlan County. This was a mining camp that was empty for some reason. The union had either bought or leased those houses for the union men and their families to live in. We lived there just a few months.

"I went to Pineville to stay with my mother who was sick. I stayed with her until she died six weeks later. Seventeen days after that, my third baby was born. It was a wonder that I carried it to its time after all we went through in the strike.

"Then we moved back to the mining camp at Arjay, Kentucky. Jess worked there, but they seemed always to give him the worst working places, maybe because of his stand as a union man. Anyway, he worked in water holes, would come home wet to his waist every day. We did well to get one dollar a day in company scrip since he was loading coal for 20 cents a ton. Some days I was denied scrip altogether even though my husband was at work.

"We just moved from one mining camp to another, trying to find something better, even if it was just a dry place to work in. Jess had gone to work in the mines at Wilton, Kentucky, when he was fourteen years old and he worked in the mines all his life until he got old and retired. He worked in all kinds of mines, all over three counties. After we moved here to Dorton Branch, he would have to walk fifteen miles to get back to his job. No bus ran on Sunday."

Jim: "When the militia was there at Straight Creek, did any of the women suffer because of it?"

Myrtle: "Oh yes. When they would start in shooting, people would be running and screaming, though I don't know whether any were killed or not. The young men in the militia would get liquored up on moonshine and even have shooting matches at each other, but us mining people kept away from them.

"My sister-in-law Mary Sinkhorn lost her baby because she was scared so bad. She was at my house, though this was against the orders of the militia — you weren't supposed to have any visitors. She told me she felt the baby die, and three days later the baby was born dead. She had to have a midwife since she couldn't get a doctor."

Jim: "Did your husband work any on the side?"

Myrtle: "Yes, he ran a barber shop on Saturday, would take the metal company scrip. He did this for a long time, which was a big help, because his mine wages were hardly enough to live on.

"We lived across the road from some people who were of a different nationality, Hungarian, I think. My husband had a large black moustache, really impressive. With his sparkling brown eyes, he looked like a German general or something. One day the woman from across the road asked me, 'Lady, would your husband be American?'

"I said, 'I guess so. He was born and raised here.' When I told Jess about this, he cut that moustache right off."

Jim: "How about milk or baby food in the company store?"

Myrtle: "They had no milk or baby food in the company store so there was no way to get milk unless you could get it from a neighbor who had a cow. There was no refrigeration in the store, not even ice."

Jim: "Do you remember there at Glendon how the babies and all the people had that bloody flux in the spring?"

Myrtle: "Yes, one of my neighbors' whole family was down with the flux. All three of their children had it. They were almost starved to death. Two of the little children died. My sister's husband had made her some plank shelves to put canned fruit on. She took those planks and made a casket for one of those babies."

Jim: "Who paid for the company doctor?"

Myrtle: "The company would generally furnish the doctor with a house (I don't know whether they charged rent or not), but the miner paid him. Each man's pay was cut a certain amount by the company to pay the doctor. Still, this didn't cover childbirth or operations. There was no drug store in the mining camp. The doctor would just make up the powders he wanted you to take from his little bag. He also had pills in little bottles."

Jim: "As a general rule, did the doctors seem to be in favor of the miners or the operators?"

Myrtle: "It was awfully hard to get the doctors to turn in reports of accidents if the injuries weren't awfully bad. I know my husband had his great toe broken in the mines. He had a terrible time and couldn't work because of this. Since he had to work on his knees, there was no way to keep him from hurting the toe, but he could not get the doctor to turn in a notice that he couldn't work. I don't know the reason why the coal companies fought so hard against a miner who was injured getting a settlement. At that time, we had the Workman's Compensation law, and the state paid you for the accident. But I've been told that the more accidents the companies had at their mines, the more they had to pay for coverage by Workman's Compensation."

Jim: "Back in those days, was there any way for working people to get into the hospital?"

Myrtle: "Not for a long time. But if a miner was mashed up bad in the mines, they would take him to the hospital. No one sick was taken to the hospital; I never was in a hospital. All my children were born at home, and everyone else had their children in their homes. Later the miners had a hospital in Pineville and in case of a really bad sickness, if there was room for them, people could go."

Jim: "How long did women stay in bed after childbirth?"

Myrtle: "Oh, I only stayed two or three days and then was up waiting on the rest of them. But many women didn't move from the bed until after nine days. It was so nice; after a woman had a baby in the coal camp, the neighbor women would bring as good food as they had and see that the mother and baby were properly taken care of. I have had neighbor women come do my washing and ironing free for two or three days after I delivered a child. Those days are gone forever. I know I miss them a lot."

The 1923 strike was both a shock and a surprise to me, this being the first time I had ever encountered the state militia, a group that later I was to encounter many times, in the course of many strikes. It was composed mainly of young boys, fellows who for no reason were fond of shooting their guns off. At old Straight Creek, this got so out of hand that soon their gunfire had literally set the mountains ablaze. Some of their gunfire went all the way over the mountain and came down in Arjay on the left fork of Straight Creek, four miles away. Striking miners and their families were afraid to put out the mountain fires, believing that they might be shot.

Alfred Hensley, the local Baptist minister, even feared going to his own church. When he went to the militia captain to complain about the violence, the captain assured him, "If you're afraid, I'll send a couple of my men with you."

"Oh no," said Hensley, "it's just your men that I'm afraid of!"

To justify their violence, the militia and the coal companies claimed there were armed miners in the mountains, hiding out with the intention of firing. This was a lie. There was no show of arms on the part of the miners, though they were indeed mad enough to do almost anything.

Down at the Straight Creek train depot, one miner, my cousin Dave, in fact, hit a gunman with a brick and was immediately arrested by the militia boys who swore to court-martial him. Though I was young, only eighteen, I attended a meeting on the left fork of Straight Creek of fifty or sixty miners who had heard of this. One man after another said that if Dave were hanged, they would die with him. And I assure you they meant it. Many of them were in tears of frustration. Before they could prepare to take any action, though, my Aunt Serina Spivey swore out a fictitious warrant against Dave in federal court for selling whiskey. By this time the National Guard had replaced the militia. With the civil warrant, Sheriff Greene could take Dave lawfully out of the militia's hands.

The men of the National Guard behaved better than the militia, but they were still company men. They disarmed the miners, at the same time allowing the scabs to keep their weapons. The company guards were never disarmed because the county sheriff, a man beholdened to the coal operators, appointed them all deputies. Though in this strike, as in many others, the governor of Kentucky swore by all that was holy that the Guard was neutral, this same pattern always took hold: if a miner shot a company guard, he was shooting a deputy sheriff, but if a company thug shot a miner, he was defending himself against a man resisting arrest. The only real difference in this strike was that the miners were all dispossessed. As Myrtle Garland describes, the union managed to find its men houses at Molus. Even though the mines weren't running there, the families at least had a place to stay. The company proceeded to fill the houses at Straight Creek with strikebreakers and scabs.

As always happened once the militia was brought in, the miners lost the strike; the union, too, was forced out of this part of Straight Creek. But while neither this strike nor most others during this period were successful as far as winning concessions was concerned, they all helped to keep the honesty and morale of the miners alive. The years 1923 and 1924 were the beginning of the union's decline in the places where I worked. In most cases, the miners reacted to failures such as the Straight Creek strike not with stronger organizations but with individual or small-group direct action.

14. Hard Times at Coleman's Mine, 1924–1928

Come all you miners from down the line,
I'll tell you all my troubles at Coleman's mine.
It's hard times at Coleman's mine, it's hard times, poor boy.

Every day in the early morn
You will hear Tom Swonner blowing that horn.
Well, it's hard times at Coleman's mine, it's hard times, poor boy.

If it blows only twice you can go back to sleep.
But if it blows five times, from the bed you gotta leap.
It's hard times at Coleman's mines, it's hard times, poor boy.

Go to the drift mouth as fast as you can run,
Or that man trip will done be gone.
Well, it's hard times at Coleman's mines, it's hard times, poor boy.

Well, I work like a dog, but darn it all,
I just can't make a dollar a'tall.
It's hard times at Coleman's mines, it's hard times, poor boy.

Wife goes to the store, she goes in a flirt.
Miss Minnie says, "Is you man at work?"
Well, it's hard times at Coleman's mines, it's hard times, poor boy.

Wife goes to the office, she goes in a flip.
Miss Minnie says, "You can't get no scrip."
It's hard times at Coleman's mines, it's hard times, poor boy.

There is old George Jones, he is a skinny old man.
Every time we buy meat we buy his old hand.
Well, it's hard times at Coleman's mines, it's hard times, poor boy.

Here is old Mosey Coleman. He is the worst one of all.
Said, "You could get rich if you half work at all."
Well, it's hard times at Coleman's mines, it's hard times, poor boy.

Well, my back is getting swayed and my belly getting thin.
There is going to be a meeting but I don't know when.
Well, it's hard times at Coleman's mines, it's hard times, poor boy.

"Hard Times at Coleman's Mine" by Jim Garland

When the union met in 1924 to make a new contract, less than half of the working coal miners were enrolled. I didn't know any of those men in the delegation sent to negotiate the contract; I cannot even say whether they were elected or not. I do know that, recognizing that union leadership was dwindling, the operators played hard in the negotiations, finally agreeing to a contract that was worse than no contract at all.

After the delegates returned, local number 3241 at Blanche, Kentucky, of which I was financial secretary, tabled the contract. We saw that the miners had been given no concessions and that, in fact, the national organization had forfeited many of our rights: we had lost union representation; we lost any right to decide whether we would have new help in the union or not; we were denied the right to charge initiation fees of new men coming into the mines. The new contract led even more miners to desert the union.

Harlan County locals had by this time all but quit paying union dues. Because the workers in Harlan were moved around much more often and because the mining operations there were more likely to be owned by one of the large combines — U.S. Steel, Peabody, and the like — the union there had never been as strong as in Bell County. Too, many more people were coming into Harlan County from Pennsylvania and West Virginia especially. A good number of Hungarian miners and Poles also entered Harlan County during the 1920s. There were three hundred White Russians taken on at Lynch. In contrast, the Bell and Knox County miners were for the most part native and stationary workers.

Working without a contract, we at the Fox Ridge mine at Blanche still held wildcat strikes over local disputes. C.R. Coleman, the owner/operator of Fox Ridge, would usually deal fairly with us once we had thrown our water out, set up a strike committee, and gone to him with our grievances. Mosey acted just like a little slave driver, except he didn't have a whip. Actually he was content to live on in the big house with his Negro cook, the only black person left up Straight Creek after the Cary race riot.

In 1925, at age twenty, I married my wife Hazel. She was thirteen. I had $16 to buy the license and pay the preacher, but my lack of money really didn't matter as I had never been without a family. With Hazel, though, it had been different.

"*I was born in Pineville and raised on Stinking Creek by my grandparents. My own mother worked six, sometimes seven days a week and could not take care of me. I always thought of my grandma as my mother; my real mother seemed more like a sister to me.*

"*My grandfather was of the old school and did not think a girl needed to have much education, so I didn't get to school very much. In the first place, the little single-roomed schoolhouse was three or four miles from our home, which was too far for me to walk as a young girl. For these reasons I did not get a very early start toward an education. I wanted to go to school, though, and when I grew big enough, I went on my own initiative, finishing about four years of common school.*

"*We had three hundred acres of farmland and were better off than the many who had forty acres or less; they could have no surplus stock to sell. We also had some meadowland that produced good hay to feed our work mule and cattle. My grandpa never had to work out for other people like so many of the small farmers did, partly because all his children worked until they married off or moved away to take other jobs. The small farmers and sharecroppers would have to leave their families and go to public works some place. Some went to the cities, but most went to the coal mines and would come home to farm on weekends.*

"*When I was thirteen, my grandma died. My grandfather, who was by that time a very old man, wanted to marry again, to a rather young woman he'd met. This woman didn't like me, didn't want me around, so I was put out on my own. Since there wasn't any work where I was raised for a girl my age, I began to visit my relatives and help out with whatever they needed done. I remember hearing my aunts and uncles grumble about how hard times were, and I knew I was taking food right out of their children's mouths. I tried to eat very little. My mother didn't come for me, and I guess I just took for granted that she didn't want to be bothered with me, though I never actually knew how she felt about this.*

"*Finally, a man named Messer, the husband of one of my cousins, came to where I was staying and offered to let me move in with his family. He said he would buy me some clothes if I would help his wife around the house and take his little girl, one of two children, to school. I agreed, not knowing what I was getting into.*

"*He had shot and killed a man and was expecting at any time to be killed by some member of this dead man's family; in fact, he was off his rocker. He slept with two pistols under his pillow and a shotgun beside his bed. All through the night, he would wake up and begin hollering, grab his pistols and rush out looking for some imaginary assassin. The mules would make a little noise in the barn that would set him off; a rooster could crow and make him sure that someone had come up to the house to kill him. He and his wife were always quarreling. I was afraid to go to sleep at night for fear that he'd start shooting and kill me by mistake. I decided that I couldn't stay there, and one morning, putting on the three dresses I owned, one on top of another, I left the house to take their little girl to school. When school turned out, I asked another girl to walk the child home.*

"I walked back up to Laurel Branch to my uncle's house, even though I knew I wasn't welcome there. When I arrived, I found everything was in a torn-up state of affairs. My grandfather was going ahead with his plan to marry, and his children were all up in the air about it. Of course, I didn't have any say in the matter. I did find out that my grandfather had agreed to deed one hundred acres of the farm to his youngest son if the son would not raise too much trouble about the marriage, despite the fact that the farm had come to the family through my grandmother. My mother heard nothing about this agreement.

"In any case, it had been a good thing that I had left Messer's house because a few weeks later, that man went crazy and killed his wife, my cousin. The neighbors found her dead and the little baby, only six or seven months old, crawling over its dead mother. I thanked my lucky stars, for if I had been there, I surely would have been killed too.

"The sister of the young woman my grandfather was to marry came over to my uncle's house from the mining camp and asked me to go back with her. This I did, expecting to get a job of some kind there. Once I arrived, I found that I had two cousins living in the camp. I stayed with one of them awhile, but was pestered so badly by the younger brother of my cousin's wife that I felt I had to leave. I then went to stay with my other cousin's family but found I didn't like that any better. I thought about trying to go to my mother in Corbin, Kentucky, but couldn't bring myself to go. I was a small girl, I had never been in a city, and I was afraid of being left alone there. My grandma had taught me not to trust anybody, least of all boys, and to tell the truth, I was having a hard time keeping the boys away.

"I did get acquainted with a girl about my age and later met her brother, who was about six years older than me. He and I began walking to church together. He was a miner who was supporting his sister and his mother and seemed to be different from the other boys. One thing, he was older and didn't try to mess around. We hit it off quite well. I liked his folks; they were friendly with me, and I felt welcome when I was in their home. This was Jim.

"Jim and I had not been going together very long when we began to think

we were in love with each other. But we had one problem: we both knew I was too young to get married. Jim offered to take me to my mother if I wished to go, but still I couldn't bring myself to move to Corbin. We talked marriage over many times and thought that the best idea was to wait three years, even though this seemed like a lifetime. If you had lived in a mining camp during those years, you would have understood my worries. The greatest sport in the camps seemed to be trying to take another boy's girl. This was many times worse when the girl did not have parents to protect her.

"After several experiences where I had to virtually fight the boys, Jim said, 'Well, if you are sure, just come on home. I will go get the license on payday and we will get married.' Jim's mother said it was ok by her for me to come stay with their family until we were married. When payday came, Jim only drew $16. Out of that he paid for my wedding dress, paid the preacher, and bought the license, to which I forged my grandfather's name. We became Mr. and Mrs. Jim Garland.

"Yes, I was young, too young, and we knew it. If there had been a better way, we would have waited, but we did what had to be done. We were married for fifty-three years. If I was to do this over, I do not doubt for a moment that I would do the same thing I did then.

"Jim was the only support his mother and sister had since his older brother had married, but Jim's mother still felt that the house we shared was very much hers. Jim was an easygoing boy and had always let his mom and sister do whatever they wanted with the money he earned. I guess they were a little peeved that now he had a wife. The four of us lived together until his sister Sarah married. His mother went to live with her and her husband. Then we had our own home, such as it was — two little rooms stuck on the hillside above the mine's tram road. This was really the first time I had ever had a home."

1925 was also the year I decided to apply for a mine foreman's certificate. In order to be issued one, a man would usually have to receive a recommendation from his local operator, a rather crooked system that resulted in many unqualified men's gaining considerable control of mining operations. Mosey Coleman told me that I couldn't earn a certificate without such a recommendation from him, but since I was interested in mining and in the coal company I worked for, I decided at least to try to get one.

A miner with his operator's recommendation in hand was still required to take the State Board of Examiner's tests at the University of Kentucky in Lexington. Without the recommendation, you had to be exceptionally smart, as well as experienced, to score highly enough on the exam to be certified. If you had at least five years of experience in the mines and scored at least 75 percent on the test, you would be issued a second-class certificate. To become a licensed first-class foreman, you needed in addition to have worked at least three years in a mine classified as gaseous (a mine with at least one and two-thirds percentage of gas by volume in the air).

Since I didn't have Coleman's recommendation, hadn't in fact asked him for one outright for fear that he would deny me, I went to another man nearby, a small-time coal operator named Custer Bailey. Being a friend of the family, Bailey agreed to give me the recommendation I needed. Once I had received my second-class mine foreman's certificate, I showed it to Mosey. And sure enough, "By God, Jim," he said, "you should have asked me."

As mine operations became larger and more mechanized, foremen and assistant foremen assumed greater responsibilities. They were to see that the miners all did their jobs as efficiently as possible — and they were charged with enforcing safe mining practices, too, except when those practices interfered with the production of coal. Many foremen were also expected to ferret out and fire union men who might cause trouble. Some cutbosses, because they measured the slate for which each miner was paid, made a practice of cheating the men out of their deserved pay.

An Italian miner's wife had given birth to a baby boy, so as was generally done, the miner took a few days off from work to celebrate the occasion with his friends. When he came back on the job, the foreman jumped all over him and demanded to know what the devil he meant by staying off of work. The miner answered, "My wife, she hahva de baby, Boss." But the foreman insisted that was no reason to stay away from work for three days.

Hoping to appease him, the Italian answered, "I name him for you, Boss. I name him for you."

"But how could you name a baby after me?" asked the foreman, annoyed. "You don't even know my name!"

"Oh yes, Boss," said the miner, "I name him for you. I call him Son Ne Bitch. Everybody call you dat."

Wilson Spivey, 87, was an assistant mine foreman for the Peabody Coal Company shortly before the 1931 strike and worked as foreman also at Cary and Blanche, Kentucky. He can describe some of the pressures the mine foreman worked under.

Spivey: "I went to work in the coal mines at eleven years old; my first day's pay was 45 cents for nine hours of work. In 1925 I bought a farm (my family lived there when I worked at Black Mountain) but I kept on working in the coal mines until twenty years ago when I retired.

"As foreman, I measured the slate that the miners had gobbed. They paid the miners scarcely anything for all that work. Some of this draw slate was dark, some was light. If the miner got any of the dark slate in his car of coal, he was bawled out and docked so much pay, his coal car might be set off on a side track until he had picked all the slate out, or he might even have to spend a day picking slate out of the coal at the tipple for no pay. If he said anything about this, he would probably be let go. So all miners had to be very careful not to let any of this dark slate fall into their cars of coal.

"The company didn't want the foreman to include the removal of this dark slate when he measured. The miner, who might be your next-door neighbor, of course wanted the full number of inches counted toward his pay. This left the foreman between a rock and a hard place.

"I always believed in a good safety policy, in keeping the mines well timbered, and I was strict about this. Many miners would take the chance to get their coal loaded before they'd timber up. I wouldn't stand for this and the union backed me. I have let men go for being careless, but I never had a miner killed in the part of the mine where I was cutboss or mine foreman. I am very glad of that."

During the years after I received my mine foreman's certificate, we at Blanche continued as union members, holding wildcat strikes and paying dues to the national union. In 1926 I was elected president of my local, an office in which I served for three years.

Since at that time no welfare or unemployment compensation system existed, a local union president, in addition to his other duties, was responsible for insuring that the sick or injured men in his local would have enough money. The company rarely allowed any man's family credit because once the injured miner was able to work again, he might just move to another mine. I took around the paper for sick miners, and all who wanted to would sign for an amount to be deducted from their pay, added onto the account of the injured man.

I might also mention here the miner's burial fund, created out of monthly pay deductions of usually one dollar. This money was to pay for the casket, suit, and burial of the miner or anyone else in his immediate family. There was no charge made for the cemetery plots; the companies donated pieces of poor land, land unfit for farming that wasn't located above coal.

In the old days, neighbors washed and dressed the corpse (embalming was rare) and laid it out in a casket, which in most cases had been handmade by someone in the community. A custom much like the Irish wake, called "sitting up with the corpse," came with the mountain settlers and in many cases is still practiced. The casket is placed in one room and the people attending it will sit in a room adjacent. If the home has only one room, the casket will be placed in

Mining in Eastern Kentucky, ca. 1915

Theodore Dreiser and Aunt Molly Jackson, Pineville, 1931

Aunt Molly Jackson and Sherwood Anderson, New York, 1932

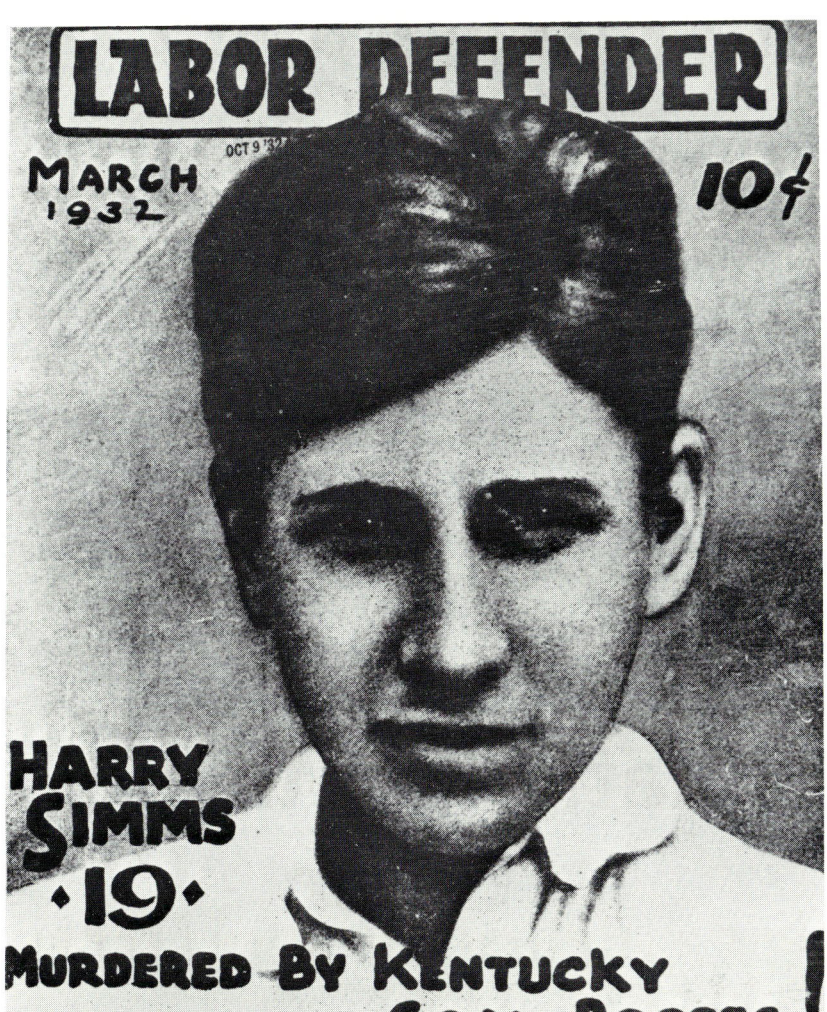

Drive Out the Scab-Herding U. M. W. A.!

Defeat the Strike-Breaking Attempts of This Tool of the Operators!

The past ten days have seen two new developments in the attempts of the operators to break the strike. On the one hand the terror against the strikers has been greatly increased. Harry Simms has been murdered. Almost all local strike leaders are either in jail or have warrants issued against them. All strikers meetings — even local meetings of the NMU — are barred in Bell and Harlan Counties. If the operators' plans go through, the strike is to be crushed by the most ruthless and brutal terror in the history of American Labor struggles.

THE UMWA — TOOL OF THE OPERATORS

At the same time the operators are now preparing to use much more than before their most reliable strike breaking instrument — the corrupt and discredited United Mine Workers of America. The UMWA is coming into the Kentucky strike field, not at the request of the miners, but at the orders of the coal operators. The operators have ordered this "company union," which they own body and soul, into the strike area for one reason only — to smash the strike and send us back to the mines under worse conditions than ever before.

Far from concealing this the UMWA leaders themselves openly admit that they are going into the strike field at the request of the operators and at the request of the same "law" that has murdered Harry Simms and is today engaged in beating, jailing, and shooting strikers and strike leaders. They state openly that their purpose is not to organize the miners for struggle against starvation, but to smash our fighting union the National Miners Union, and break our strike.

UMWA ENDORSED BY BLAIR AND BROUGHTON

One of the chief scab-herders of the UMWA, James M. Shellhorse, in a statement to Knoxville newspapers last week declared:

"Sheriff Blair of Harlan County and Sheriff Broughton of Bell County are both distinctly friendly to the United Mine Workers of America. I carry letters with me from both sheriffs and Mayor Brooks of Pineville, giving me absolute freedom to carry on my work in these counties. I, as one member of the United Mine Workers of America approve of the attitude of the law enforcement agencies of Bell and Harlan Counties in driving the Red movement out of Kentucky."

In the same statement Shellhorse does his bit to starve us back to work by urging that no one shall give aid to the Workers International Relief, which is today supplying aid to the strikers.

UMWA BOASTS OF ITS STRIKE BREAKING

In other words, the UMWA, through the mouth of this rat, Shellhorse, boasts that it is working hand-in-glove with those who have murdered Harry Simms, who have beaten-up and half killed scores of our comrades, who are now engaged in railroading our strike leaders to long terms in prison. With this statement the UMWA stands exposed as the worst enemy of the strike, working side by side with the thugs, whose hands are red with the blood of our comrades, to break the strike.

Let no striker, let no miner, forget this: The UMWA is openly an agent of the coal operators. The UMWA is lined up openly with our worst enemies. The UMWA has but one purpose, one reason for existence, to smash our strike and force us back to work with our demands lost.

Our demands can only be won if the strike breaking attempts of the UMWA are defeated, if the scab-herding UMWA is driven from the coal fields.

Strikers and Miners Still at Work:

Refuse to Allow the Scab-Herding UMWA Officials to Speak at Mass Meetings!

Demand that all aid going into the Strike Fields shall be Distributed to Strikers and not to Scabs!

Demand that all Aid shall be distributed through your own Relief Committees to make sure that it is used to strengthen the Strike and Not to Weaken It!

Expose the UMWA to Every Miner as the Open Strike-Breaking Tool of the Coal Operators!

DRIVE THE SCAB-HERDING UMWA OUT OF THE COAL FIELDS!

FORWARD WITH UNITED RANKS IN OUR STRIKE FOR 50c MACHINE COAL, A CHECKWEIGHMAN ON EVERY TIPPLE, THE RECOGNITION OF OUR MINE COMMITTEES, THE RELEASE OF ALL STRIKE PRISONERS, AND AN END TO GUN THUG RULE!

SUPPORT AND BUILD THE FIGHTING UNION OF ALL MINE WORKERS—THE NATIONAL MINERS UNION!

CENTRAL STRIKE COMMITTEE
KY.-TENN. MINERS STRIKE

Box 73 — Pineville, Ky.

NATIONAL MINERS UNION
KENTUCKY DISTRICT

Jim and Hazel Garland, 1933

Jim Garland and daughter Margaret, 1934

Jim Garland and his Kentucky Mountain Singers, at New York World's Fair, 1938. *L. to r.:* Dorothy Burton, Sarah Gunning, Jim, Hazel Garland, Mamie Quackenbush (Jim's niece), Jimmie Garland (in front).

Above: Jim Garland at Newport Folk Festival, 1963.
Right: Sarah Gunning at Newport Folk Festival, 1964.

Faith Folknick and Jim Garland at Smithsonian Festival of American Folklife, Washington, D.C., Summer, 1974

Jim Garland and sister Sarah singing for Rounder Records, 1974

Jim Garland at coal tipple on Straight Creek, 1978

the corner. Friends, neighbors, and relatives will stay with the corpse, drinking coffee, talking, and singing until time for the burial.

The neighbors who have opened the grave will also serve as pallbearers at the funeral ceremony. After the coffin has been opened so all who desire to may take a last look, one or more preachers will preach the sermon at the graveside. Most everyone in the camp will attend the service.

If the deceased has been a particularly strong union man, miners will carry his casket, and the mines will not run on the day of the burial. Each miner has a union badge, one side bearing the red, white, and blue, the emblem of the clasping hands with the eagle on top and fringe on the bottom; this is worn in parades. Miners wear the other side of the badge, black and inscribed with "in memorium," at funerals. During such a ceremony, after the ministers have made their sermons, the miners throw sprigs of myrtle into the grave, lower the casket, and stand around the grave together.

One good thing about the coal mining camps — there were always enough friends to dig one's grave and arrange for one's burial. In cities where I have lived, the funeral is often performed by strangers; even the minister hired for the service may not know the deceased. At the funeral of my sister Aunt Molly Jackson, a woman well known as a singer and a songwriter, a minister was brought in who had never met her.

The mountain gravesites, while worthless spots of land, needed to be located in dry places because the mountain man or woman abhors a wet grave. Now most of the coal camp cemeteries are overgrown with thickets, brambles, and vines. There is no one left to keep them cleaned out. It seems to me that the government, which gives away so much, could afford to maintain these old graveyards where people who worked all their lives to build what we now have lie buried. Why not give some of these people who are on welfare the job of cleaning these local graveyards? This would not take anyone's job away and would show some respect for those who have passed on. I believe that our elected officials could legislate this humanitarian act. Regardless of what we think of our foreparents, they are us; we are them. We are part of their bodies and part of us is lying up on those overgrown knolls in very bad condition.

In the early 1920s, the miners had remained law-abiding Christian people. They were not willing to recognize that their county and state governments were cooperating with the coal operators and that the operators, rather than being the miners' benefactors, would defend the interests of property and private wealth over even the human right to live. As the coal associations gained more and more power and as the competition for contracts with the Great Lakes became more fierce, however, the miners began to realize that their county officials were enforcers of company policies.

Injunctions were taken out that forbade known union men to step off the public highway and that prohibited more than two of them from meeting together. If we failed to obey such injunctions, we were threatened with arrest. After several court orders of this kind were made public, the average miner's regard for the law became so low that he didn't even recognize federal judges.

In Tennessee professional strikebreakers were baptized in the name of John L. Lewis. Company sucks were stripped naked and whipped with switches in the presence of women. One particularly effective tactic was used later at Ross, Kentucky, when a group of scabs and gun thugs approached a picket line that had been set up by the local women. These women grabbed the gun thugs and stripped them naked while some of the local men took off through a cornfield after the strikebreakers. After four women had managed to hold down one of the gun thugs, my sister Molly took his pistol and shoved the barrel right up his rectum. Never did this particular thug show his face there again; even when I met up with him years later, he told me this had taught him a lesson he could never forget.

Once the sheriff arrived with a large force of deputies to make arrests, the women declared that all or none of them would go to jail. Since many of these women had babies at their breasts and others were pregnant, the sheriff just said something about requiring the women to come to the jail later — nothing was ever done. No one, in fact, was jailed after this incident, and the people won their strike.

April was a black month in 1926. My brother was killed working with me in the mines. Even though he was quite a bit older than I, we had always been very close, Dick's having taught me much that I knew about mining. Dick had a fine sense of humor and loved to gamble; sometimes he would borrow a stake from me to play on when he was broke. He was also a strong union man.

Dick's eye had been hurt in one mining accident, putting him off work for several months. He was supposed to get a little compensation for his injury but they kept holding back his money. Until the check came for his eye, Dick decided to board with me and Hazel and to go work at Coleman's with our brother Bob and me, the three of us working the entry and the airway. Along the side of the entry, we had taken out enough coal to make room for the slate we shot down. It was in this place that the ton of slate fell on Dick and killed him.

This broke me and Hazel up pretty bad. Baptized by my brother Bill, we joined the Baptist church and I became a strict church member, taking a position as deacon and teaching Sunday school.

Hazel recalls these hard times: "Bad things seem to come in bunches. When Jim's brother Bob, his wife Mary Jane, Jim, and I were all being baptized, Jim's sister Sarah got in a fight with another teenaged girl and cut the girl thirteen times around the back of the head with a penknife. They arrested

Sarah and took her to jail; some people thought the other girl would die, but luckily Sarah had not hit a vital spot. This had us all torn up again. How Jim's mother stood all this, I will never know. Well, Jim and his brothers got an attorney for Sarah, and the mine operator went her bond so Sarah could leave the jail. Sarah finally got out of this trouble because Jim's lawyer kept putting off the trial. After awhile, when the girl she had cut up went bad and no longer appeared against Sarah, the judge threw the case out of court. Even so, all this cost Jim $500 in lawyer's fees and other expenses. That was big money back then.

"Along in 1926 and 1927, Jim began to worry about the union. He would worry because an awful lot of miners were turning in their books and quitting the union. Jim went to several mines and made speeches, trying to get the men to hold onto their charters and books awhile longer. Although our local there at Blanche was one of the strongest in the district, Jim said it got harder and harder to get the men to come to union meetings and to serve as officers. They seemed not to trust the district anymore."

I recall then that a Baptist minister came to have supper with my wife, my mother, and me. During the meal, he spoke to us about the Ku Klux Klan, a group which as he explained opposed the Catholics, the Jews, the Yellow, and the Negro. He encouraged me to join. That night at the little local church, I saw for the first time the Klansmen dressed up in robes, their faces covered, and later I attended one of their meetings.

There a speaker told us a story about an Italian who had washed his socks in the spring that the road crew had to drink out of. His running commentary threw off on the Jews in all kinds of dirty stories. He told of a young girl whose fingers were pressed in a vise by Catholics, and he recounted what he thought were funny stories about Negroes.

After the meeting the Baptist preacher asked if I wanted to join the Klan. I told him that were I to join such a group, I would be a liar, for my union had an obligation not to discriminate against a fellow worker because of creed, color, or nationality. I assured him that I would point this out to all the men in my local. As a result, the Klan never caught hold at all on my part of Straight Creek. (I mention this because many have denied that the Protestant churches were used as bases from which to organize the KKK.)

Injunctions, scattered wildcat strikes, growing disillusionment with the UMW of A, direct action, all this characterized the months around the Lewis/Brophy election in 1926. By this time, number 3421, of which I was still president, was the only active local remaining in District 19. The others had become disgusted with Lewis's theory of no strikes during a recession and with the defeating results of contracts that expired during different months and so had turned in their charters.

During the discussions in our local concerning the election of a national president, I remember that a blind man from Pennsylvania came by selling rubbers and flints for miners' lamps. We voted to buy sixty-six sets, one for each man in the local, and were continuing our talk of the election when this blind man interrupted. "Don't have too much confidence in Lewis," he advised and then left us.

We knew that Lewis was a tyrant, that he had surrounded himself with handpicked men, and that the rank and file was deserting the union. Though I didn't know much about Brophy, a Pennsylvania man, I and the others in my local decided that if he had enough nerve to run against Lewis, we would all vote for him. And we did. Still, even though we were the only local left active, Lewis won by a fairly large majority in District 19. I feel fairly sure that the district officials like Turnblazer (who had always been a union suck, brown-nosing Lewis, and the field organizers voted the dead locals. Someone certainly did. We had been the only local paying dues and had affiliated separately with the AF of L, paying a capital tax to the American Federation as well, but this election was to put an end to our local too. In 1928 when I could find no one interested in serving in any local office, I turned in our books and moved to Harlan County.

15. Bloody Harlan

My wife Hazel and I moved into Harlan County where I went to work for the Peabody Coal Company at Black Mountain. Until I could get enough tonnage on my account, the company would not rent me a house in Black Mountain itself, so Hazel and I lived four miles away in the free town of Evarts, a town not owned by any company. I ran into added trouble securing a home for us in Black Mountain as a result of my leaving work for two weeks to look for employment elsewhere. When I returned to Evarts, I found that the Peabody Company had never officially discharged me and that consequently the account of my tonnage had sunk very far below the average. Childers, the local UMW of A field organizer, confirmed this. To build up my account, I had my brother's son Robert "Popeye" Garland come into the mines unofficially to work on my number and the next month . . . "Oh yeah, Mr. Garland, you can have a house."

My wife Hazel remembers some of the advantages to living in Black Mountain, and some of the disadvantages, too. "They had a bathhouse for the miners so the men could take showers before they came home. This made life much better for miners and their wives. They had the best company store I had ever seen, refrigeration so they could keep milk and a much larger variety of food stuff. The houses at Black Mountain were better than most mining camp houses. They were built from one by four lumber, tongued and grooved; it was called cealing. It was nailed to studs both on the outside and on the inside. Most of the Black Mountain houses had four rooms heated by a coal grate. There were not many wells to get water from, though, so I had to carry water quite a long way. Of course, the toilets were the outside privy sort, one toilet for each two houses. They set between the rows of houses. The toilets had long wooden boxes, set in the bottom to catch the manure, that were taken out and emptied once a month. This was done at night, and the stink those nights kept most people awake. We called them 'the sugar wagon.' The manure was dumped down below the mining camp and no effort was made to cover it up or fence the children out. Jim's little nephew was playing one night and ran right in to the manure; he came home in terrible shape. There was no effort to keep the flies out of the toilets, so the maggots were always in there. There were very few screen doors; none at all were furnished by the company."

Once Hazel and I moved into Black Mountain itself, I realized that for the working man, things had come to an awful pass. For the first and only time in my years coal mining, I took a job as foreman. One of my jobs was to measure the draw slate which runs in seams five to fourteen inches over the coal and which had to be removed and thrown back onto the gob pile — hard and heavy work. For removing a space of draw slate an inch thick, thirty feet wide, and a yard long, a miner was to be paid seven cents. I was careful to give each man credit for exactly what I measured on my tape, but the cutboss who had worked there before had evidently been cheating all the miners in his measurements. I saw within a few days that all the reckonings I had made were being remeasured. Rather than waiting to be fired, I told the operator that I wanted to resign as cutboss and go back to coal-loading work, even though as cutboss I had made $225 in one month and could only make about $125 a month loading coal. I saw that I wasn't cut out to be a mine foreman.

I also remember when casting my vote at Black Mountain in the 1930 elections, the mine superintendent's son-in-law came right into the booth to check how I would mark my ballot. I cast my vote to suit him, but when he turned his back to leave, I marked a vote for the opposing candidate too, thus disqualifying my ballot.

A new regulation had been made that required a miner to set a safety timber directly in front of his car. I was always careful to follow these rules, to protect my job, of course, but more importantly to insure my own safety. One day I was working the coal face on an uphill grade. In order to get my car near the solid, I had to run my motor down a hill, cut the motor off, and then throw a scotch under the car when it had rolled near enough the coal face. On one such trip, I knocked out my safety timber, having so little control over the motor, just when the cutboss came in.

"You've got most of your timbers placed better than anyone else on the run," he said, "but your safety timber's not up." I explained to him what had happened. "Well, that timber's not up now," he answered, "What do you think I ought to do about it?" I told him, "Do whatever you want to, buddy. That's your business. I'm just doing my job." I was fired.

I went to Childers, the UMW's field representative, to complain, but he was unwilling to act: "If you're fired, you're fired." I've often thought about my having resigned as cutboss only three weeks previous to this incident, after I had seen how the company was gypping its coal loaders. In any case, Hazel and I moved again, this time to Kitts, about twenty miles down below Evarts, and I went to work for the Whitfield Coal Company. This was 1930; the Great Depression had hit the entire nation.

Again, because Tilman Cadle and I went through the 1932 strike together, Tilman's having served on many strike committees and worked to organize miners under a number of different auspices, I include his comments here as a second opinion on what happened in the 1930s in the coalfields.

Garland: "What happened in this region when the Depression hit the country?"

Cadle: "Well, the mines were hard hit; there is no denying that. Many mines closed down completely. Others were working only two or three days per week. The miners' wages were cut, and their families, already on the brink of starvation, saw that prospect coming closer and closer. There were a few wildcat strikes, or rather work stoppages, because of the wage cuts. These led some coal operators to start lock-outs, meaning the miners could no longer live in company houses. If the companies were forced to shut the mines down because of the famine of orders, the miners had to be allowed to remain in their homes until the mines started working again. But if the company could induce a strike by cutting pay so low that the miners would not work, then the operator could say, 'Get out of my houses,' claiming a strike when in fact they were just engaged in a lock-out."

Garland: "Do you recall the Harlan County Coal Operators Association?"

Cadle: "Yes, I guess that was one of the most powerful organizations in the country. They managed a strike-breaking fund for Harlan County: each operator paid so much per ton of coal mined to the association, and the money was used to hire gun thugs and to pay for other expenses of breaking strikes. This made the smaller operators dependent on the large international cartels like General Motors and U.S. Steel and kept the small mine owners from making separate settlements with the union.

"There was a great lot of competition for the lake trade between the Harlan County and Cumberland Valley associations. The one that secured the orders with the lakes could work its mines in the summer, and the one that did not would have to cut way back to just a few days per week or shut down altogether. Some of the large mines like Lynch were run by U.S. Steel and known as captive mines. Since they used their own coal, they could run anyway."

Garland: "Did these captive mines pay a higher wage than most?"

Cadle: "Yes, they did."

Garland: "How about civil rights in the captive mining camps?"

Cadle: "At Lynch, since there were no roads to speak of, people all came in on the train. Gun thugs would meet every train that came through, and if a stranger got off, they would ask him where he was going, who he was. If he said he was looking for work, they would show him the personnel office, but if the man didn't get a job, the same thugs would tell the stranger they didn't want to see him after the next train left. If a relative came to visit, the Lynch miner would have to report this to the office and explain who the visitor was and how long he planned to stay."

Garland: "Even though the captive mines there at Lynch paid eight dollars and a penny per day, the miners there lost money on the clean-up system. A worker had to stay in the mines until his working place was cleaned up, no matter how long this took. Also, if he were unable to report for work, he had better be sick, or he went out into the public road.

"At least the company store there had refrigeration so that the miners' babies could drink the milk they needed; in fact this was probably the best company store in the mine fields. In 1932, when I was a witness before the Senate Subcommittee on Labor, the Red Cross came in with charts showing that the children at Lynch were overweight. One of the miners there, Bolter Smith, went off his rocker and began to swear and rave, to call the Red Cross representatives names, swearing that Lynch could not be used as an example of how people were living in the mountains. La Guardia had to dismiss the hearing at this point to avoid a riot. This claim made by the Red Cross was understandable once you realized that its local officers were, for the most part, the wives and daughters of the coal operators and of the petty county officials who were owned by the operators. I never knew of a single Red Cross official's being a miner, a miner's wife or daughter. The classes were divided there."

Cadle: "The worst thing was that the mine operators, big corporations, were taking money and resources out of the state and putting very little back in. What money was channeled back was in the form of better machinery; this only put more miners out of work.

"Some companies worked a few days each week, some resorted to dumping coal on the ground to allow a few miners to live on until the winter when coal sold better all over the country. Some people just 'starved by,' as we called it. I don't think they themselves knew how they managed. Some of the women, especially the Negro women, would go down to the closest towns to get the better-off people's laundry, bring it home, wash it, and iron it. The black women were very good at taking care of their families when their men were out of work.

"In the early months of 1931, the men had just about come to the end of their ropes and began to talk union again. This was not the national UMW of A or District 19 officials who were trying to organize the miners, but a man by the name of W.B. Jones. He seemed to take the leadership, and the miners showed signs of an organization: they began to hold mass meetings in Harlan County and to march out of the hollows into Harlan town and Evarts. They said that the choice was either to work and starve or starve and strike and so they chose to strike for better working conditions."

Garland: "What did the UMW of A officials do about this new attitude on the part of the miners?"

Cadle: "The officials of the United Mine Workers would have nothing to do with the organizing of the strike that followed. I remember attending several of these mass meetings where the men were hoping to see Turnblazer, the District 19 president, in attendance. But he never would come. Some little field-worker was always sent to represent the union; Bob Childers was one of them. The miners kept asking for Turnblazer and, never getting an answer, were becoming more and more critical of the UMW. Childers got kindly hot about the miners' keeping on asking for Turnblazer and finally said, 'Well, I'll tell you where he is. He is just where Jesus was when the people kept asking for him; when they found him, Jesus was talking with the wise men. That is where Turnblazer is, down in Frankfort talking with the wise men.' "

I had heard of some activity up around Black Mountain but at that time, I didn't know what it was all about. I figured that this was just another wildcat strike, probably over "booms."

When mining under a sandrock top in a room with a rock bottom, once enough coal has been removed, the sandrock won't sink normally. All at once the top will come down hard, ten, fifteen, maybe twenty tons of it, crushing to death any miner who happens to be below. Later a method was devised to try to remedy this: drilling deep holes in the coal and shooting with dynamite to create resistance.

During the year I worked at Kitts in 1930, the operators had reduced wages for loading coal to 40 cents a ton and cut the pay for all other mining occupations correspondingly. The mine at Kitts was running only two or three days a week. I was busy, though; my wife had typhoid fever. She was down for about two or three weeks, then up for a week, then down sick again. When I wasn't working, I was taking care of her.

We at Kitts were slow to hear of Jones's organizing. Bell County was not involved at all, probably because that's where the District 19 headquarters were located; Lawrence "Peggy" Dwyer, the UMW national representative, was in Pineville and Turnblazer was in Jellico, just over the Tennessee border.

Once Jones's people spread to Harlan town, though, I did hear about them. Jones spoke in Harlan, and the next morning there were over thirty-five of the company's dependable stooges there, in addition to armed deputy sheriffs, appointed by Harlan County Sheriff John Henry Blair to intimidate the miners. Soon after this meeting, a secret defense corps was organized. My brother-in-law, Sarah's husband, was picked but I was not; the organization needed men who could leave home for long periods of time, if necessary, without being missed, and since Hazel was still very ill with typhoid fever, I was needed at home. At Kitts, the situation was gearing up for a confrontation. Out of the two hundred who worked there in the Whitfield mines, thirty-five men were made deputy sheriffs. They carried guns right into the mines to work and became known as "would-be gun thugs."

Hazel remembers the story of a run-in we had with one of these thugs. "After we moved from Black Mountain to Kitts, we still returned to the Black Mountain camp often because Jim's sister still lived up there. During one of our visits, a neighbor of hers got his eyes burned with the electric cable on the coal-cutting machine he'd been running. He asked us if we would drive him down to the hospital at mine No. 31 to have the doctor look at him. He was in great pain. We drove him down, and when we were about halfway back to the house, a gun thug pulled us over and began cussing us, saying that the man we had with us in the car was drunk. We tried to explain, but the thug wouldn't listen. Finally he cooled down enough for us to get him to look at the man's eyes, and since the thug knew the injured man, he let us go. But he didn't say 'I'm sorry,' or anything.

"This gun thug was Jim Daniels, one of the men who was killed at Evarts in 1931. He was kicking a Negro man when he got his: someone shot his head off with a shot gun blast. He was a mean man. He even dispossessed his own mother from a company house.

"We lived about one year at Kitts. The mine there wasn't running steady, only about three days each week. Jim and his uncle, who also worked there, would walk in the mines, two miles deep, on the days that the mines didn't run. By preparing things in their work place, they could manage to load more coal on days when the mines did run. Sometimes when they were off work, we would all go fishing in the creek there at Kitts; it wasn't very polluted then. In all, we had lots of fun that summer.

"Jim and his uncle liked to make their own pick handles so one Sunday they went into the mountains and cut down a small hickory tree, about eight inches through. They cut about six feet of it into pick-handle length and brought it home to work on. Well, lo and behold, old man Whitfield, the mine owner, was in the mountains that day and found that the tree had been cut. He went ranting and a'raving, trying to find out who had done the cutting, and if he'd found out, they both would have lost their jobs for sure. That tree probably was worth less than a dollar.

"I came down with typhoid fever while we lived at Kitts and I almost died. I'd been vaccinated against the fever but I took it anyway. The doctor said I had had the germ before I got shot. I was down in bed for six weeks, and part of the time I was out of my head. Jim was trying to work and take care of me at the same time, and I'm sure he had a time of it. I would start chilling, and he would put hot pressing irons at my feet and back. When the chill would break, I would start burning up, and he would have to start rubbing me down with rubbing alcohol until I stopped being hot. Sometimes he would have to do this several times a night. His aunt looked after me and gave me medicine until Jim came home from work. Everyone thought I wasn't going to make it, but somehow I pulled through."

My Uncle Jim Elliot and I happened to be in Pineville on March first visiting relatives when we heard of a UMW of A meeting to be held that very night. Though not many leaflets had been sent out, an awful lot of men from Harlan had come down to find out if the UMW planned to regroup. Joe Burton told us about the meeting once we arrived in Pineville. I asked my uncle what he thought about our going ahead to it. "Might as well," he said, but I was very suspicious. I had gone from being one of the stronger UMW of A advocates in District 19 to being a disillusioned man. Turnblazer, Dwyer, Lewis, none of them liked me, and I didn't trust them either. They were handing out false papers contending that certain miners had been blacklisted (of course, any man out of work wants some reason to hold onto), as if to say, "let's you and me go bumming," but they weren't doing much to help workers organize or gain any concessions from the operators.

Dwyer even claimed that Jones's union had put the small operators out of business. He was lying through his teeth; he knew better. Competition among the coal companies themselves had busted up the small exploratory mines. Those that out of economic necessity or choice kept using the old mining methods went under, but Peabody and U.S. Steel, they didn't go broke, because they were making money at the expense of the small mine owner. Too, since the newer methods of mining produced more slack coal (finely ground coal), while the old method of shooting coal from the solid produced more block coal, the type of coal priced in the contracts was crucial. These days, slack coal is the most expensive, but in the '30s it was the cheapest. For example, during the strike of 1932, slack coal sold for $1.76 per ton while block coal was selling for five or six dollars. Once the large companies managed to have contracts based on slack coal, the small operators naturally went under. The older mining practices that produced more block coal were simply not economical enough if the rates were to be determined according to machine-produced slack.

My uncle and I did decide to attend the UMW meeting, held inside the theater in Pineville. As we were walking in, we spotted the foreman from Kitts, Petrie, who was obviously stationed at the door to check if any of his men were there. He had always been good enough to us both because he approved of our hard work; as we walked in, he spoke to us briefly.

There were many speeches delivered that night, but the only one that I remember well is Phil Murray's; he seemed the only one who stood up and discussed honestly why the UMW could not make a contract. Otherwise, I believe that the UMW that night committed its cruelest act — asking the men there to give up $10 to join the union again. Anyone there, had he been any man at all, would have bought ten dollars worth of milk for his child before giving that money to any organization. Most of the men went home disgusted.

Sure enough, when my uncle and I reported for work the next Monday, March 3, we weren't allow to enter the Whitfield mine. We sat outside the mine opening for two or three hours until finally our tools came out on one of the mine cars. At the time, I considered myself lucky not to have been killed.

I owned a car, but I didn't have a dime for gasoline to move it. I left it in a garage there at Kitts, and Uncle Jim Elliot and I, leaving our wives at home, walked fifty miles out of Harlan County and into Bell to the home of some relatives on Straight Creek. There we borrowed enough money to return for our wives.

As I was leaving Kitts with Hazel, I could tell that the operators were already scared of Jones and his organization. The Peabody mine at Black Mountain, which had been the first center of Jones's organization, had by springtime fired almost everyone. A good number of these men had migrated to Wallins Creek, formerly a Ford company town. Some IWW literature had come into Harlan County (I got hold of a red song book), though this material might very well have been planted by the coal companies.

Actually Jones's union never was a union in any strict sense but a mass of unrecognized people acting under Jones's leadership. These miners wanted the UMW of A to lead them against the wage cut, but the formal union had offered them little encouragement. Even without the support of the national organization though, Jones's people held a number of wildcat strikes, some successful, most unsuccessful.

In the early spring of 1931, wages were cut again, to 32 cents per ton. A checkweighman was no longer permitted to weigh the miners' coal in determining each man's pay; instead, the companies reverted to the less accurate system of measuring. As Tilman Cadle explains, "Before we had an organization, they didn't weigh the coal but just paid each man by the car. Once organized, the union made one of its first demands that the coal be weighed, and where the union was strong enough, the company allowed a checkweighman." Each miner took so many hundred pounds from his number and credited that amount to the checkweighman for his services. As my experience at Black Mountain, one month as cutboss, should indicate, the miner was decidedly at a disadvantage when his foreman's measuring determined his pay.

By this time, most of the miners were broke, and more and more of the

Harlan men were joining defense committees or strike groups under Jones. The unemployed men, most of them blacklisted and thus ineligible for work anywhere in the region, gravitated toward Evarts where Jones had located his headquarters.

On May 5, the Peabody Company was bringing a truckload of scabs up to Black Mountain from Harlan. Since the only road to the mine ran through Evarts, the miners of Jones's self-appointed union were there prepared. Most of them were armed, for by this time there was no other way to hold a picket. The thugs were armed as well, not only with pistols and shotguns and high-powered rifles but with machine guns. And to top it off, they wore deputy sheriff's badges — such odds.

Many people ask me why the miners didn't kill all the gun thugs, pointing out that the miners held such a majority. First, you must remember that those hired men did nothing but gun-thugging and that the miners' hands, stiff from working, were slow and clumsy with a pistol. But even if a miner tried to fight fairly, even if he succeeded, he would lose in court. Any miner who shot a gunman deputy had only a ghost of a chance for an acquittal.

But this day, in spite of their disadvantages, the miners fought, resulting in what to this day is known as the "Battle of Evarts." Two carloads of gun thugs drove up the road through Evarts and met the picket line. They jumped on one of the Negro pickets and started to beat him when all hell broke loose. Both sides began firing. When the shooting was over, the gunmen all lay dead. The leading thug, Jim Daniels, had had his head blown off. The miners proceeded to strip the company cars of machine guns.

Tilman Cadle: "Turnblazer of the UMW of A had been in Frankfort making a deal with Governor Sampson to send in troops. Sheriff John Henry Blair of Harlan County was also calling for the state militia to break the strike, but the governor didn't want to send troops in. He said he was afraid that if he ordered those young boys in while the miners were armed, it would cause a lot of people to get killed."

However, the state militia was called in immediately after the violence at Evarts. Before the night could fall, before the troops arrived, the UMW of A leaders were busy riding throughout the county, pleading with miners not to fight with the militia. They spread the enormous lie that the troops had been ordered in only to keep the peace and that no scabs would enter Harlan County. This was all poppycock; there never was such a thing as a neutral militia.

When the troops entered Harlan, the men put away their guns and went to welcome them. At that time the old captain gave a speech saying, "If you fellows want to shoot anyone, shoot one of my boys here. They will give you back as good as you can give." Even though Turnblazer's arrangement with the governor had called for disarming both miners and company gunmen, the militia only carried out half the agreement. Mainly because J.H. Blair, who was paid off by the operators, had deputized most of the thugs and a good number of strikebreakers too, the state troops only arrested miners; two or three houses in each camp were raided until soon, most of the miners' weapons had been confiscated. The ablest leaders, those who had taken the most active roles in Jones's attempt at an organization, were all thrown in jail on any trumped-up charge that the operators' officials could think of. Some were charged with crimes they'd never heard of, like criminal syndicalism. If the county officials could level no such charge, a peace warrant would do nicely.

The strike was lost, leaving thousands of miners blacklisted as never before. Previously, the companies had each compiled a list of known union men; under this system, many miners just changed their names and secured new jobs. After the violence at Evarts, however, the only way for a man to get work was to present a letter of recommendation from his last employer. This system was airtight.

The strike had become just a little too rugged for the pantywaisted leaders of the UMW of A. Disowning both the strike and the men in Jones's following, they left the miners to their own devices. Most of the mining men were broke. Many of them had never been out of the state, had no education, and most had no other trade to which they could turn.

In the spring of 1931, after being fired from Kitts, I was working not in Harlan County but in Bell County — at the worst job I ever had. Hazel and I had rented a private house from one of the landowners in a little mine camp named Castro, just outside Cary on Straight Creek. I met an Irishman there who told me he had encountered "a bit of a lad who called this place 'Poor Do,' and he was an intelligent little fellow too." As a matter of fact, that name fit the place like a glove. I could only make about $2 a day and had to spend half that on carbide and powder to shoot my coal loose. This mine was exceptionally primitive for those times, using black powder to blast and mules to haul. In the six months I worked there, from April until August of 1931, I couldn't get ahead enough even to buy my wife a pair of $2 slippers. When she lost the heel of her shoe, I had to whittle another one out of wood. Those were the roughest times we ever had.

16. Grabbing at Straws: The National Miners Union

After I had been working at Poor Do for three months, one day in July, I came out of the mine for my lunch hour and ran into Charley Reed. He was carrying a sack of flour and some bacon. The other working men and I, knowing that Charley was unemployed, were extremely curious about where he'd gotten the groceries. But it was Reed who started up the conversation. He told us enthusiastically that someone was organizing a new union to better the living conditions of the miners.

Many of us were skeptical; it sounded too good to be true. Some man said right out loud, "No damned body gives a damn about coal miners or their families." But Charley wasn't giving up so easily. "If you don't believe me," he said, "just look at this food they gave me." Evidently Reed had been given quite a pep talk by someone. He told us, "They're trying to help the unemployed guys. They're going to organize the National Miners Union."

I, for one, knew Charley, knew that he had been a good union man in days gone by. Always one to carry a gun in the earlier strike troubles, he had been accused of shooting a biscuit out of a scab's mouth in one strike. Part of me was grabbing at straws; I was impressed by what he had to say and so went to his house that night to talk further. I was looking for something, some way that conditions might be improved for the miners and their families. Having such a hard time feeding just my wife Hazel and myself, I didn't know what in this wide world a man with a large family could be doing to stay alive.

Charley talked and talked, but I stayed suspicious. Reed told me that a man and woman had given him the food, saying that a group called the National Miners Union was willing to start organizing the miners in Bell, in Knox, in Harlan, and in East Tennessee, any place where miners believed they needed an organization. Obviously, these people had trusted Charley in that they had told him about their headquarters in Pittsburgh, Pennsylvania, and revealed that they had already organized some mines in Eastern Ohio. According to Charley, these folks were anxious to organize at any mine where the UMW of A either had pulled out or had refused to lead any strikes.

Tilman Cadle, also one of the first Kentucky miners to learn of the NMU, adds, "Miners in other districts had already begun to organize another union. In fact, there were two new unions springing up: one, the Progressive Miners Union in Illinois, and the other, the National Miners Union in Pennsylvania and Eastern Ohio. The NMU held a convention in Pittsburgh, and invited the miners of Kentucky to send delegates. A few Kentucky miners were sent. When they returned, they reported that the NMU was an independent union controlled by rank-and-file members. Soon after this, Kentucky miners began to join the organization."

But I was more cautious than some and wanted to know more. I had lost one job because I had attended the Pineville meeting of the UMW. Anyway, I had a job and Charley didn't at this time. As I figured it, he had nothing to lose. But the more I thought, the more I realized that I, too, had very little to lose. Charley Reed said he was going to arrange a meeting at Arjay, leaving me, in the meantime, to hold my own counsel and ponder what he had said.

Working or not, the people were on the brink of starvation. When the mines at Poor Do shut down for a week in late July, the men came to me and asked that I head a committee to go into the towns nearby and beg food for those families who had nothing. This I did. Our committee also asked the county judge if he would issue food vouchers against county moneys. He answered that while it was possible to issue such vouchers, no merchant would accept them, knowing that the county itself was broke and couldn't honor them. In any case, I finally convinced the judge to give us ten $3 vouchers. But before he handed them over to our committee, he insisted on first calling the local coal operator to make certain we weren't striking. I had to ask him what in the name of God the mine's being on strike had to do with babies who had no milk. Beyond this, though, I didn't press him too much; I was afraid he might refuse us even the small stipend he'd already offered and signed.

When we took the vouchers to the store to be redeemed, the manager hemmed and hawed about taking them. But when he saw that the miners were nearing the point where they might help themselves to far more than thirty dollars' worth of groceries, he agreed to honor the county vouchers.

You might think that under these circumstances ten families alone would have kept this food to themselves, but the feeling of the community there was that all the groceries should be divided among everyone. That night the food was parceled out at my house. Some of the packages included nothing more than a quart of flour and a coffee cup of hog lard. Those with bigger families got bigger shares, and we made sure that people with babies at home all got a few cans of condensed milk.

The lay-off lasted only one week before we went back to our wonderful jobs at Poor Do, making at most $1.50 per week. I kept hearing about the

NMU and thinking about it, until one day in August I heard that a meeting of unemployed miners was to be held at Arjay and that I was invited.

There were no formal organizers there, just Charley Reed heading up the meeting and about twenty miners sitting right out on the hill. Harvey Valentine and his brothers Lee and Snookie were among them. Many of the men were unemployed, though I don't think they had all been blacklisted. Some were guys who simply didn't want to work, who survived just through their art of getting by (you've always got some of those). In contrast with the $10 that Phil Murray had asked of miners who wanted to rejoin the UMW, the National Miners Union's initiation fee was only 25 cents per week, and that was asked only of miners who were still working. At the Arjay meeting, an organizing committee was set up, and we learned of a strong unit of the NMU at Wallins Creek in Harlan. Those miners, many of whom had been part of Jones's group, had already contacted the NMU and had drawn outside organizers; they also had sent delegates to the Pittsburgh meeting. After our meeting in Arjay, the NMU decided to contact us through Charley Reed.

Shortly after this, in September, Hazel and I moved about one mile farther up the creek to Glendon where I found a better job and house. In the meantime, unemployed miners were beginning to organize locally for the NMU and were making quite a bit of headway among working miners.

Food remained our first problem. Harvey Valentine remembers, "The coal companies kept so little in the stores that when the miners could get scrip, there was nothing to buy. This situation led to many work stoppages. Everyone was in debt to the coal companies because they paid miners so little for the coal. I can remember when a truckload of food was brought in from town, the miners' wives were almost driven to fight over what little there was. When Charley Nick, a miner who had a large family, came into the store to get some food, the store clerk said, 'Charley, everything is gone. All we have in the store is a little pepper and salt.' And Charley asked, 'Do you have any rope? A man might as well hang himself as starve to death working if he can't get anything to cook for his family.'"

As the NMU gradually gained membership, with women and men organizing together for the first time, the Workers International Relief began to gather and distribute food and clothing for those out of work. At least if you had to have a pair of shoes, you would be sent some from the union warehouse. Soup kitchens were set up for community cooking and meals, most notably at Wallins Creek and at the Missionary Baptist church in Arjay; it should be said, however, that the Missionary and Primitive Baptist churches were not the only ones to let their buildings be used for such purposes. Some of the Holiness churches also took part in these soup kitchens and later lent a hand in the strike.

Gun thugs in Harlan County burned down one soup kitchen and killed

Mr. Julius Baldwin, who was in charge of running it. They also beat up a minister who had become involved in the organization — Jim Grace.

The NMU had as its base several thousand blacklisted miners, most of whom had at one time been strong members of the United Mine Workers but who felt betrayed by the UMW of A. Whether or not this sentiment was justified is for people to decide for themselves; far be it from me to try at this late date to point a finger of accusation at the UMW, for it did so much in later years to better the miners' wages. In any case, these men with no jobs were willing to do all they could to organize a strike. If that took the formation of a new union, well and good.

By the fall of 1931, most camps on the left fork of Straight Creek had NMU locals. The new union had also gained the support of most ministers in the area. One would have to have lived in the mountains to realize the importance of the churches' support to the NMU's initial success.

As Hazel describes the labor conditions at Glendon: "The miners at Glendon had several wildcat strikes in 1931. The first was because they thought they were not getting what their coal cars weighed and elected to have a checkweighman. This was a legal requirement; when the miners wanted a checkweighman, the company was supposed to allow one to be hired at the miners' expense. But the company did not want this, so they came to the tipple and ordered the checkweighman off their property. When the miners heard about this, they took a vote on the spot and decided to dump their water out and return home. The wildcat strike lasted about two weeks. The man elected as checkweighman told the miners after all of this that he wouldn't accept the job anymore anyway, because he didn't want to have to shoot a company gun thug or get shot. So the miners voted to return to work.

"They had been back for about a week or ten days in November when the company announced a ten-cents-per-ton cut. This was not a 10 percent cut, as the miners were only getting 40 cents per ton in the first place. The day workers were to get a like amount of wage cut, about 25 percent. This was an awful blow. At least half the miners were already in debt to the company and could only get as much company scrip as the company wanted them to have. Anyone who spoke up against the company was not allowed to have any scrip. Of course, the miners came out on strike against the wage cut. Jim was elected chairman of the strike committee because we had no children and could talk back to the company a bit better."

Perry, Ross and Cary, also owned by the Federal Coal Corporation, were likewise planning wage cuts. I was on the strike committee that each day answered the operator's call for a meeting. But at each of those meetings, we were told that we could only have our jobs back if we were willing to work under the wage cut. I pointed out to Jim Humes, the operator, that thirty-five babies had already died that year from bloody flux due to poor diets and that another wage cut would come right out of the miners' bellies. When he just laughed at this, I walked out.

Hazel has this to add: "This strike lasted three months before the larger general strike even began on January 1, 1932. In fact, Glendon was held up as an example to other miners as to how they should organize themselves. The National Miners Union, by October, was leading the strike at Glendon through local miners. The strike committee, of which Jim was chairman, would have settled the strike at any time the company would agree to rescind the wage cut and let all the miners return to work. Some of the miners did try to go back to work, but those who had stayed out marched around the camp, telling the ones who were scabbing they had three days to leave the area.

"Well, this was just what the coal operators wanted. They seized on this as an excuse to ask the federal judge at London, Kentucky, for an injunction against all the striking miners. The scabs swore out warrants against all the men left on strike. Only a few of the leaders were arrested. Jim's brother, who as a minister had tried to keep the strikers from beating the scabs up, was arrested; another Baptist preacher who was trying to scab swore out the warrant. The injunction forbade the miners to set foot on company property and forbade the miners to congregate in groups larger than two."

In spite of the injunction, I worked daily to organize miners. Daring county officials to jail us, we walked all over company property to arrange weekly meetings. Four or five of the NMU women from Knoxville began to attend these meetings, helping especially in organizing the miners' wives into auxiliaries, something the UMW had never done. Soon the women's auxiliary elected a president, a secretary, and other officers along the same lines as the men's organization, though during the strike, the two groups more or less melded together.

Many of the mountain women, once called upon, showed enormous interest, particularly in distributing clothes and doing other relief work. But some of these women were hard for me to handle. Many who had never owned any real clothes of their own, who had always shared with relatives, would go down to Knoxville where the articles were sorted with the idea of outfitting themselves. I got pretty disgusted with this. Some of the women, on the other hand, were fine and serious union folks. They had to use a trial-and-error method in forming their organization, but truly, many of the wildcat strikes late in 1931 and during 1932 were led more by women than by men.

It was the women's responsibility to plan the mass meetings to whip up enthusiasm. Perhaps because of their hand in these rallies, these girls believed that we should strike the whole creek. We who had been through two or three strikes thought this was a mistake, that the NMU could never deliver enough food for all the families of men who would be out of work, but everyone voted for the strike.

Even though the NMU was not recognized by the companies, we had built organizations throughout the camps along Straight Creek, all except Cary. We never could organize Cary, partially because they had a yellow dog, or company-directed union. The Cary mine had also hired a killer, literally taken a man from the penitentiary and deputized him. This stupid thug had killed several people and ended up shot in the head himself after he attacked the daughter of a scab miner.

After we went out on strike in November, things began to happen fast along Straight Creek. From the newly formed Knoxville NMU headquarters, the WIR continued to distribute food and clothing, despite the attacks made on the soup kitchens. The International Labor Defense came into Harlan County and offered to pick up some of the court cases of jailed miners, like the Jones case, legal battles which the UMW had refused to become involved with. Some accepted the aid of the ILD; others did not.

The soup kitchens on Straight Creek and at Wallins Creek were still feeding folks. We sent people into Knox, Harlan, and Leslie counties with the only truck we had and filled it up with pumpkins, potatoes, whatever the farmers would give us. Many farmers contributed gallons of milk. Bakeries in Pineville, Barbourville, and Middlesboro gave us day-old bread. Too, some miners' wives had stored surpluses of fruit they had picked off the hills in the summer months and canned.

There were some newborn twins in the coal camp I used to talk about continually when asking for food in other towns. On one such trip when we went down into Knox County with a small truck, the little farmers there gave us potatoes, cabbages, and whatever else they could spare. Through all of this, my confidence received a real boost to see how the people divided the little they had — sharing their nothing, you might say. It made me think there might be hope yet.

I was staying pretty close to the Straight Creek strike, becoming more and more involved as it progressed, until my house was practically being used as a district headquarters. Frank Borich, the NMU president in Pittsburgh, reported that 10,000 miners had gone out, 4,000 of whom were blacklisted men, but actually the only blacklisted men were those who had taken part in Jones's organization and those who were actively at work organizing for the NMU. Many other unemployed miners claimed to have been blacklisted to avoid the shame of unemployment.

The NMU leadership did not consist of hundreds of men, for among miners, as in any other occupational group, few have any real leadership abilities. I would say that during this strike, only about 10 percent of the miners were very active. Another 50 or 60 percent passively accepted the strike, constantly growling that nothing was being done yet doing nothing themselves; like any union, we had a certain amount of dissension. But those people who claim that the NMU was nothing more than a tool for the Communist party are simply talking though their hats. The NMU was a bona fide union: its officials were voted in by miners, and the Straight Creek strike, in addition to the later, larger activity, was instigated and voted on by Kentucky miners.

By mid-November, wind was picking up, especially in Harlan County; much of this resistance was provoked by Peggy Dwyer. He, Turnblazer, and Childers had been the Jones organization's worst enemies, more effective even than coal companies, and they became the worst enemies of the NMU as well. They had known about the NMU organizations in Ohio and Pennsylvania even before the rank-and-file Kentucky miners found out about them. The UMW leadership also knew that the Trade Union Unity League had a recognized union in Illinois. And though the UMW national was still unwilling to take part in the Kentucky miners' struggle, its officials were determined that no other organization would fill the void. As Tilman Cadle attests, "The officials of the UMW of A were just as bad about red-baiting the miners and the organizers of the strike as the coal operators were. They accused everyone of being a Communist."

Copies of the *Daily Worker* floating around Harlan and Bell counties during November only aggravated this situation. Ben Shahn, writing from jail somewhere, contributed material; another man wrote an expose on conditions in the mine fields. But probably what hurt us the most was a cartoon that appeared about this time of the Bell County sheriff. The artist had pictured the man from behind, nothing but a big, wide bottom with two pistols strapped to either side. Actually, Floyd, as we called him, was at that time trying to maintain a neutral stand, so this cartoon made him madder than a wet hen. He demanded that someone retract the statement and apologize for this rendering of him. Trying to calm him down, I told him, "Floyd, there isn't any way to retract that. Anyway, that shouldn't bother you; it's the office of sheriff that the cartoonist is attacking. And those guys, under our system of government, can draw anything they want to."

November also saw the Theodore Dreiser Committee's entry into the coalfields. Dreiser and his group of writers had come from New York to conduct interviews and to evaluate the miners' situation. During one of their meetings, held at the Arjay Baptist church soup kitchen, my sister Aunt Molly Jackson sang a song she had just recently made up; she called it "The Hungry Ragged Blues." The Dreiser people were so impressed by her that they thought she was just about the whole Kentucky strike. In fact, she had done very little in the strike aside from going down into Knox County a time or two to solicit vegetables for the community kitchen.

The Dreiser people had not long been in Bell County when thugs from Harlan arrived in trucks complete with mounted machine guns. Floyd, to his credit, ordered these hired gunmen out of Bell County. But in spite of efforts to dispel the tension, the thugs gave the Dreiser group a hard time. They tried to trump up an adultery charge against Dreiser involving his young secretary; however, Dreiser assured them that for twenty years, he had been an impotent man.

More and more organizers were being sent into Kentucky from NMU headquarters in Pittsburgh, and more and more chapters of the union were cropping up throughout Harlan and Bell until it began to look as if the whole district would go out on strike. On the night of December 13, we held a meeting at our new headquarters in Pineville, a hall we had rented on the second floor of a certain Pineville restaurant located right next to the bridge. I came down representing the Glendon mine, which was already on strike. John Harvey, a writer from the *Daily Worker*, was there, as were Harry Jackson, an NMU representative from Pittsburgh; Vince Kemenovitch, an organizer from Pennsylvania; and a man named Joe, an organizer from New York. Of the Kentucky men, Charley Reed came, as did Tilman Cadle and several of the boys from Harlan town and Wallins Creek.

Also at this meeting was a young kid in a stocking cap, rough shoes and cord pants who was introduced to us as Harry Simms. Just up from Birmingham, Alabama, Harry was going to work with the young fellows in the union. I was to learn later that Simms was deeply involved with the Young Communist League. It is enough to say here that Harry and I hit it off immediately; soon he was staying at my house and we were organizing together.

At this December thirteenth meeting, we discussed the possibility of a districtwide strike with the organization we had managed to build up by that time. We realized that our forces were not very strong, that our main strength of membership was among unemployed miners, so we needed to determine whether we would have to organize a good deal more for any further strike activity to succeed. The men who were working generally favored further organization, while most of the unemployed miners hoped for large numbers of spontaneous strikes to pull out other mines where we had as yet no support. They, of course, hoped that through the strike they would be accepted back into the mines. Other blacklisted men had joined us just for the meager aid the WIR had been able to gather in support of the Straight Creek strike. They, in fact all of us, reasoned that if the strike grew to include most of the district, far more aid would be brought in.

The vote of this gathering, the district organizing committee, was overwhelmingly to go ahead with a strike, but to concentrate on as wide an organizing campaign as was possible in the remainder of the year. After the vote, no one questioned the decision, even those who had thought the large-scale strike might be a mistake. When I was nominated as a member of the strike committee, I protested, saying that only the best men in the district should serve. But when miner after miner, many of whom I did not know, rose to speak in my favor, I could not refuse.

We divided up the district into different sections: Straight Creek was one section, Brush Creek in Knox county was another, Harlan, Middlesboro, Fourmile, a Jellico section over in Tennessee, and others. To each we assigned a district committeeman who was responsible for leading meetings with the men and women in his area and for retaining speakers; sometimes Harry Jackson or Harry Simms would be called in to address these section groups, or sometimes the meetings would have to make do with Tilman or me. Tilman and Tom Curtz were the assigned section men at Middlesboro. They, and all other section organizers, were free to bring anyone from their area to the district meetings in Pineville to show people interested in the union how the organization planned and worked. It was all aboveboard.

One of our projects subsequent to this December thirteenth meeting was to set up a mass meeting at Arjay. In addition to spreading the news by word of mouth, we wanted to make up some leaflets to distribute. The NMU had managed to loan me a mimeograph machine, and I cut the stencil on the circuit court clerk's, R.E. Wilson, typewriter. R.E. was one of those politicians who was always running for one office or another, but one thing I must say for him — he took up the side of the union all the way through the strike. Never did he speak aggressively in favor of us, because he wasn't prepared to be arrested; he was the type of supporter who takes one step forward and then one step back with comments like, "Say what you want to — we'll get a reprisal." His wife, on the other hand, was an outspoken supporter of the NMU. During debates the operators held among themselves in Arjay, all of them sitting around smoking cigarettes and chewing tobacco, she would stand up and give them hell. "There ain't no sense in it," she would say, "children starving and people having to work for a couple of dollars a day." As I remember, Mrs. Wilson was the person who gave me access to the county typewriter; in any case, I'm sure that R.E. wasn't aware I was working up leaflets with his equipment. These pamphlets did little more than tell folks the time and location of the meeting, with the addition, "no scabs or sell-outs invited."

At the Arjay meeting, with Doris Parks, Harry Jackson, Clarina Michelson from the New York needle trades, and others from the NMU national in attendance, my nineteen-year-old wife Hazel got up to express herself for the first time at a union meeting. The gist of her speech was that the two of us had suffered enough and we were tired of it, that if we were not able to get by, just the two of us, she wondered what the heck could be happening to people with five or six children. My brother Bill, who had been instrumental in setting up the women's auxiliary, especially along Straight Creek, also gave a speech as did I. My point was, "I don't give a damn what you call your union." People were already calling us names they themselves didn't understand; even some of the working people were calling us the Communist party. If you had at this time said to a group of average mountain men, "I'm a Communist," they more than likely would have answered, "I'm a Baptist" or "I'm a Mason."

Even before the general strike, relief work was tough, as Hazel describes: "The state militia was still in Harlan County and was continuing to search the miners' homes for any weapons. Without warrants of any kind, they or the gun thugs would stop men on the street, on any public road, and search them. The farmers of Minnesota had sent two boxcar loads of Irish potatoes into Wallins Creek in Harlan County; the potatoes had been left in a warehouse there.

"Jim and Ford Bundy, another man who was on the relief committee, went up to Wallins Creek to get the pickup loaded with potatoes. It seems they had been tipped off to watch out for the militia. When they crossed over the little bridge into Wallins Creek, they just turned down alongside the creek, left the truck there, and split up, since they figured the militia would be looking for two men together. Well, Jim stepped around a corner and ran his belly right into the barrel of a submachine gun held by a young militia man. Jim said this young guy looked up, just as surprised as he was. Jim just took one step to the side and went on up the street.

"When he got up to the soup kitchen, he was told that the militia men were looking for him and Ford Bundy. In fact, the state troops were turning away anyone who tried to get any of those potatoes. Jim and Ford waited awhile and then had a local man go bring their pickup to the back of the warehouse. Several men with No. 4 coal shovels quickly loaded up the truck, and Jim and Ford started back to Straight Creek. They were so afraid that the thugs or militia might be right behind them that they turned toward Harlan town, figuring that the narrow, two-lane road would make it hard for the thugs to follow. They went about a mile and then turned back toward home. I guess the thugs had left Wallins Creek for the day."

You must remember that I was a religious man at this time, a deacon of the church, and that most of my family was quite religious. But when a person gets involved, truly involved, in a labor struggle, it's hard to keep his religious beliefs primary, mainly because he gets so damn mad. And I was mad. I was burned up and hitting out in every direction even though I didn't know actually where to hit. So I hit at the first thing that I could see, and that was the coal operators I was working for. It wasn't that I was fighting for higher wages; I was just trying to fight against further cuts in a starving situation.

When I later was brought before a Senate subcommittee and asked if I were a Communist, I said, "I don't know whether I am or not, but I sure as hell am going to find out." Harry Simms said to me, "Jim, remember everything has a material base." And that was the one comment that got me thinking about the bases of my religion and the bases of my politics. It led me at that time, 1931, to believe in the Communist party as the organization that might change things for the mountain people.

17. Won't the Bosses Be Surprised

In these weeks before the general strike, which had been called for January first, things began to get rough. Union people were harassed and arrested; some were beaten and others were shot at. Although I didn't consider myself a fighting man, I began to carry a pistol those nights when I had to pass through Cary, where the yellow-dog union was still holding on. With my .38 special cocked in my hand, I knew that if fired on in the dark, I could shoot back in a flash.

Through the efforts of the National Miners Union, the Communist party, and other liberal organizations, news of the miners' plight was slowly being brought to the American people outside the mountains. The farmers of Minnesota sent us potatoes which the gun thugs tried to prevent us from receiving. Colleges and universities throughout the country began to discuss the trouble in Bloody Harlan and Bell County, Kentucky. Even large newspapers like the *New York Times* began to take notice and print stories. This attention, of course, infuriated the operators and the local press, too. For all the non-Kentucky NMU participants, our opposition resorted to a new label, "New York Reds." Those described by this title were considered to be just as evil as Reds of the Russian variety.

The opposition's battle cry — that the National Miners Union posed a Communist threat in Kentucky — made us realize that this strike was going to be different from previous ones, more of a political struggle than simply a battle for better wages. I honestly do not believe that this ideological battle was the union's intent, but such an awareness among the miners could not be suppressed as long as local newspapermen, like Herndon Evans of the *Pineville Sun,* printed stories of "Russian Rednecks."

In planning the December thirteenth organizational meeting in Pineville, the NMU had invited the press and anyone else interested to attend. Evans came to the meeting, not knowing that we had tricked him into it, hoping to achieve an open acquisition of the press. Herndon had denied all the reports that the Daily Worker, *in addition to the* Courier Journal, Cincinnati Post, *and* Knoxville Journal, *had printed concerning the horrible conditions in Eastern Kentucky. During the meeting I made sure to point Herndon out: "This here is the editor of the* Pineville Sun, *about the yellowest little sheet that's ever been printed in the mountains of Kentucky. He knows he's lying. He doesn't do it out of ignorance, because he's a smart man. He knows those people up there are hungry. Herndon, you say they have plenty to eat — well, go up there and look in the stores. See if they've got anything for the miners to eat, even if the miners had money to spend on food. Anybody with eyes can see they don't have food in the stores. Anybody can see the babies being carried to the graveyards and buried, dead from bloody flux. I told him, "You can remember me, Jim Garland. The Red and the Redneck."*

The night before the strike, we took a large group of supporters from Pineville and the left fork of Straight Creek up to Kettle Island on the right fork for a mass meeting. About two hundred people showed up. I addressed the gathering right in front of the company store. I remember that during the meeting, a cross was lit above us on the hillside. One deputy sheriff who was a union member deputized our whole group. When we rushed up the hill, we found the company bookkeeper and weighman who, of course, denied having set the cross on fire. We knew they had done it though, to threaten any attempted strike action.

Later, when the strike was under way, Kettle Island did not pull out 100 percent, but most of the miners had indeed been convinced to join our cause. Yes, the miners wanted food to survive and were prepared to throw their water out and stay home until they could get it.

On January 1, 1932, more mines actually closed than we had expected. This date was the high point of our organization. Though we had never had a strong base of support along Brush Creek in Knox County, Brush Creek came out. The same was true of old Straight Creek and the right fork. But perhaps due to that meeting we had held the night before, many of those mines — Coleman and Sullerson just to name two — participated in the strike. All the mines on the left fork, except Cary, shut down completely. Fourmile came out; Lee Hollow came out. We couldn't strike at Wallins Creek, an NMU stronghold, because we had no mine there to strike.

This actually was not a strike in the true sense of the word, I suppose. It amounted more to a work stoppage, the miners having found that working to make a living was no longer profitable. I believe that had we strengthened our organization further before calling the general strike, had we planned for relief sufficient to support striking miners over a considerable length of time, more mines would have shut down. The blacklisted miners who formed the core of our organization were under the honest opinion that working miners would come out and that then the blacklisted man could win back his job. But we simply could not promise relief for long enough to convince many men to leave their employment.

In general, the miners were far more militant than the National Miners Union. Many mountain men wanted to really start in, taking everything they could find from the stores, be they company stores or anyone else's, and some miners did, in fact, begin to steal from any source of food they could find. The union, however, counseled patience.

On January 4, the NMU headquarters by the river in Pineville was raided and nine of the outside organizers (among them Doris Parks, Vince Kemenovitch, John Harvey, and Clarina Michelson) were arrested. Jackson and Harry Simms, probably because he looked like a harmless boy, got away. I was not in town that day and so was not taken to jail. Anyway, the operators and their friends in the country and circuit courts were much more interested in arresting the outside organizers.

To the dismay of the operators, this act only gained sympathizers for the NMU. The arrests of women, many of whom had worked through the WIR to distribute food and clothing, incensed many miners who had before taken a dispassionate view of the strike. Men gathered in Pineville, angry groups speaking in defense of motherhood and womanhood.

Meanwhile Tilman Cadle had found us a new meeting place, a farmhouse over the Tennessee border, where we went to discuss what to do about our people in jail. This meeting was interrupted by a scout; he had heard the police and gun thugs in Pineville discussing plans to take our people out of jail that night, drive them up on the mountain, and beat them up. Well, I had come to the point where I was ready to believe just about anything bad. The chips really seemed to be down.

We all decided to make a major effort to prevent this if we could, even if it meant shooting. We had bought some pistols earlier at a pawn shop in Knoxville, and this looked like the moment we would be called upon to use them. There was no doubt that the gun thugs had more and better weapons, but we figured that, should this come to a battle, the element of surprise might be on our side.

The meeting chose a committee of three volunteers to go to jail and demand that we at least be allowed to speak with our supporters. My eyes being too poor to make me much help in night shooting, I volunteered along with another man and his wife.

Of course, we were not at all certain that our people hadn't already been taken from the jail, but we moved as quickly as possible. There were only four roads out of Pineville: the two main roads north and south, another road up Straight Creek and a fourth up Clear Creek. Our forces split into four groups to check these outroads, the majority of the men standing by on the south road headed up Log Mountain since the police had chosen this place before to beat up troublemakers. Whoever detected any indication of the thugs' escort was to fire a shot and then run like hell.

Our group of three arrived at the jail about 1:00 a.m. and demanded at least to hear our friends' voices. The jailer tried to assure us that the nine were safely asleep, but I explained that we'd been sent by the strikers precisely to find out whether our people were indeed safe and that he'd be saving himself a lot of trouble by letting us speak to them. Grumbling something, he decided at last to admit us into the jail.

First we talked with the men in the larger compound, and then moved around to the smaller jail where the women had been locked up. I called out to Clarina Michelson, asking if everything was all right. She answered me, "It is now that we know our friends are on the job." She told me that the jailed women, their beds piled against the door, had not slept a wink; they, too, had heard through the grapevine of the plan to remove them from their cells. I assured her, "You girls go to bed and sleep soundly. There will be no union people ridden anywhere tonight, but there may be a hell of a lot of killing if anyone tries it." I never did discover whether that scout's report had been accurate or not, but in any case, no one tried that night to remove our people from the Pineville jail.

In all these scares, plots, and counterplots for and against the union, our best carrier was my wife, Hazel. After we got her a little .32 Colt pistol, she went just about anyplace we needed her. Only nineteen years old, she was so small, looked so much like a kid, that the operators and thugs must have assumed she couldn't be doing anything important. The NMU, however, soon realized Hazel's effectiveness in bringing other young women onto the union's side. Soon, NMU officials began to split us up, sending her to make speeches in one locale and having me speak in another.

Relief supplies were running low, sending many striking miners back to work, Fourmile and Lee Hollow, in particular. We decided to send out letters to all the coal operators, offering to settle with them individually in hopes of getting some men back to work under better conditions. But the coal operators' organization being much stronger than ours, all of them refused to talk settlement. Many wrote scathing letters to Bill Meeks, our district president, calling him every foul name they could think of. He weakened under these insults — I'm sure he was scared — so the union began to put more and more responsibility on me. The NMU rented a little apartment for Hazel and me in Pineville and moved us in. As Hazel remembers it, "When we moved there, Harry Simms came to live at our house and so did a writer from New York. We didn't know it at the time, but he was writing a play called *In New Kentucky* and was using Jim and me as his subjects. In any case, our house became the local headquarters of the union. We had the beds full and would take turns sleeping in them; we had as many as thirty people sleeping there in one night, in the beds and on the floors." That didn't cause much of a problem, though, since we didn't do much sleeping during these weeks anyway.

The Red Scare propaganda against us increased throughout January, abetted by the press. About the same time that Hazel and I relocated in Pineville, the trial of the NMU women took place there. These hearings attracted the serious attention of both our union members and our opposition. It was during this meeting that Doris Parks was questioned concerning her religious views. In defense of herself, she answered, "I believe in the religion of the workers. These workers have relied on your religion for bread and butter, and now they are starving. How can you ask them again to believe in religion?" Once Herndon Evans reproduced this statement in the *Pineville Sun* and called Doris Parks and the entire NMU atheistic, we lost more than half our members. The local papers continued to hammer on the religious theme to such an extent that, I believe, this issue bruised us more than had any other.

Those of us who remained were determined to hold as much of the organization as possible. By February, I had become secretary of the union. Part of my duty was to assume the unwanted task of dishing out our little bit of expense money to the local section organizers. Often I would have to tell one man that he would need to do without any funds at all so that an organizer who had farther to travel could get back home. I am happy to say that no one truly blamed me for my decisions, I think because I took time to explain why funds were so short. The section organizers knew that I gave each of them more money than I took for myself. Still, this situation did nothing for the morale of the people. You feel so helpless, knowing how much a certain thing needs doing, when just a little bit of money can make the difference between success and failure, but when that little bit cannot be found. This knowledge, however, was to make a better speaker out of me when later I traveled north to collect money for the Kentucky miners.

Earlier, I showed how the old English ballad "I have a letter from your sire, baby mine" was transformed by the mountain churches into a hymn about the gospels. I should mention that this same tune came out on a record in 1920 as the story of a young girl and boy. This version of the song was sung much faster; in fact it had almost been brought up to jig time. Here is a portion of its lyrics:

> Well, I am going round this world, babe o'mine,
> I am going around this world, babe o'mine,
> I am going around this world with a lonesome mountain girl,
> I am going around this world, babe o'mine, babe o'mine,
> I am going around this world, babe o'mine, babe o'mine,
> I am going around this world, babe o'mine.

In 1932, my youngest sister (Sarah Ogan was her name at that time; now she is Sarah Gunning) was in the midst of the same tough mine strike that Hazel and I were so dedicated to. Sarah's husband was a striking miner and one of their babies had died, we thought because it had not gotten enough milk to drink. Sarah took this same tune and made a labor song of it, a fine song which Woody Guthrie later recorded. My sister called it "I'm Going to Organize, Baby Mine."

> Well, I'm gonna organize, baby mine,
> Well, I'm gonna organize, baby mine,
> Well, I guess you'll be surprised, but I'm gonna organize,
> And I'm gonna organize, baby mine.
>
> Won't the bosses be surprised, baby mine,
> Won't the bosses be surprised, baby mine,
> Won't the bosses be surprised when they find me organized,
> Well, I'm gonna organize, baby mine.
>
> See the miner's children and wives, baby mine,
> See the miner's children and wives, baby mine,
> See the miner's children and wives, I'm compelled to save their lives,
> And I'm gonna organize, baby mine.
>
> I will write you a letter, baby mine,
> I'm gonna write you a letter, baby mine,
> I'm gonna write you a letter when conditions they get better,
> But I'm gonna organize, baby mine.

You can see here how a song changed from a ballad to a spiritual, back to a love ballad, and then to a labor song — four transitions. Sometimes the changes occur in reverse order; for example, a spiritual might be changed to a love ballad and then, perhaps, even to a swing or rock tune.

A similar transformation occurred with "The Old Ship of Zion," originally a sailor's song which was sung as a repeater by the men working on the railroad. It too adapted, the second version that I know of being a spiritual, part of which follows here:

> It is the good ol' Ship of Zion, when she comes,
> It is the good ol' Ship of Zion, when she comes,

It is the good ol' Ship of Zion, the good ol' Ship of Zion,
The good ol' Ship of Zion when she comes.

Oh, how will you know her when she comes,
How will you know her when she comes,
How will you know her, oh, how will you know her,
Oh, how will you know her when she comes?

We will know her by her captain when she comes,
We will know her by her captain when she comes,
We will know her by her captain, we will know her by her captain,
We will know her by her captain when she comes.

And who is her captain when she comes,
And who is her captain when she comes,
Oh, who is her captain, who is her captain,
Who is her captain when she comes?

King Jesus is her captain when she comes,
King Jesus is her captain when she comes,
King Jesus is her captain, King Jesus is her captain,
King Jesus is her captain when she comes.

The next adaptation of this song that I know of concerns a sorry guy who got a young girl pregnant. Here is how the lyrics adapted to this new theme:

We will see his little baby when it comes,
We'll see his little baby when it comes,
We'll see his little baby, we'll see his little baby,
We will see his little baby when it he-hi-ho-hi-hums.

And how'll we know it's his little baby when it comes,
How'll we know it's his baby when it comes,
How'll we know hit's his baby,
How'll we know hit's his baby,
How'll we know hit's his baby when it comes?

We'll know it by its black curly hair when it comes,
We'll know it by its black curly hair when it comes,
We'll know it by its curly hair, know it by its curly hair,
We'll know it by its curly hair when it he-hi-ho-hi-hums.

Of course, the most popular version of this song as we sing it today is "She'll be coming around the mountain, when she comes"; thus this tune provides another example of how the old ballads became spirituals and, later, *jig/folk songs. As you might have guessed, this tune was used in strike troubles.*

> *We'll join that picket line, one and all,*
> *We'll join that picket line, one and all,*
> *We'll join that picket line when the union gives a call,*
> *We'll join that picket line, one and all.*
>
> *Why will you join that picket line, one and all,*
> *Why will you join the picket line, one and all,*
> *Why will you join the picket line, join the picket line,*
> *Why will you join the picket line, one and all?*
>
> *We're getting tired of starving, one and all,*
> *We're getting tired of starving, one and all,*
> *We're getting tired of starving,*
> *We're getting tired of starving,*
> *We're getting tired of starving, one and all.*

We used this song a good deal on the picket line. Because of its question-and-answer form, any grievance could be substituted as a punch line and new verses could easily be made up on the spot. Too, this song definitely has a work rhythm and is therefore good for marching; it fits well with unionization.

When the coal operators had gotten that injunction prohibiting union men from stepping off the highway, we found that our best defense was mass disregard. The mass voice of the people is much stronger than any injunction by a single judge. You may say, "Well, it isn't right to break the laws of the land." But we were not at all sure that the law of the land said anything to prevent us from stepping off the state highway. I will agree that a man should be able to bar people from coming onto his private property, but the question is when the coal company furnishes your house, your food, your garden if you have one, and if you therefore are on the company's property when you go to get your mail at the company store, the land can no longer be considered private. This is public property. And the only way for us to fight an injunction which we knew was wrong, which denied every right our foreparents set forth to live by in this country, was to disregard it.

In the course of such fights, songs expressed people's feelings in a manner that allowed them to stand together. The IWW used them, the National Miners Union used them, as did the UMW of A. A song like "Hold the fort for we are coming, Christians be strong," became, "Hold the fort for we are coming, union men be strong." Rather than walking up to a gun thug and saying, "You're a bastard," which might have resulted in a shooting, we could express our anger much more easily in unison with song lyrics.

I had been put in charge of the Brush Creek section in Knox County. The last week of January, Harry Jackson and I decided to hold a meeting there with delegates from Brush Creek's four mines. One mine had shut down, but the other three were running. We hoped that by bringing all of these miners together, the employed and the unemployed, and by taking up all problems, we might be able to settle Brush Creek and gain some support for the rest of the district. Relief money continued to shrink, and more and more miners coming off work needed food. Some of us knew by this time that calling the strike had been a mistake, but we stuck by our guns as best we could.

As were most NMU gatherings, this gathering on Brush Creek was an open meeting, but by this point in the strike we were worried the company thugs might show up and cause trouble. Two gun thugs, Davis and Miller, did enter the Brush Creek meeting, but they didn't try anything, maybe because one of our delegates was keeping a double-barreled shotgun pointed in their direction. Harry Simms and I had hidden pistols under our clothes.

At this meeting I heard for the first time the definition of a gun thug. An old miner rose and spieled it off for us: "A gun thug is a thing that is a cross between a devil and a zebra. He has a yellow stripe up his back that he gets from his father, the devil. Around his body he has two stripes made by his gun belts, and he gets these from his mother, the zebra. On his breast he carries the star of law and order, but in his gun belts he carries the guns of damnation and hell. He is so low that whale shit looks like a cloud in the sky compared to him. He would fuck his mother, suck his brother, and eat his sister's afterbirth. He is the ninety-ninth son of a bitch and a bastard — this makes him 100 percent scab." The thugs sitting there listened without saying a word. Evidently, this was what they had been told to do, and having few brains themselves, they always did what they were told.

As for the business of the meeting, we settled a few minor hassles concerning whether or not the sub-locals should be allotted a share of the relief. I was to get out a leaflet announcing the mass meeting we intended to hold in February. Most important of all, the meeting showed us that the strike on Brush Creek was going very well. We set a Saturday date for the mass meeting, at which I was to be in charge. For some reason, the delegates thought that I would make a better speaker than Joe Weber, a New York propagandist who had been the leader of our district; I guess by this time, the men up on Brush Creek all knew me and felt they could trust my word. I wasn't known to promise things that we couldn't accomplish. The miners called this "telling it like it is."

The day of the mass meeting, as usual, I left Greasy Creek where I was staying with my niece Pauline Inman and traveled across the mountain on foot down to Brush Creek. As I came across the hill, I ran into twenty or so miners, all good union men I knew I could depend on. We had already developed a defense plan to be employed whenever an organizer put himself in a dangerous situation; still these men were waiting on the hillside expressly to meet me with a warning. They had heard that the thugs were determined to break up our meeting, and that I would likely be beat up or shot; they all wanted to know what I proposed to do.

I said, "Well, fellows, what are you going to do? It's your mass meeting. I'm only the speaker, so it's up to you what I do from here. If you think I am going up there all by myself to get beat up or killed, you have another thing a'coming. I will go if you fellows are willing to take your guns and pistols and defend me at the mass meeting. What I want you to do is decide if it's worth fighting for. Of course, if we weaken now, we might as well quit. If we don't hold this meeting, or at least try to hold it, they have us whipped. So you decide. I am not a brave fool, but I can make my body do whatever my brains say for it to do." Well, they decided that we should go ahead with our plan and hold the meeting.

Truly, I very much doubted that I would live through this strike. I was scared. I had been left holding the bag, so to speak, up in Harlan a short time before this and had only been saved from a beating because of my wife's courage (and due to the southern man's inbred respect for pretty young women). Three men who had the day before robbed one of our relief trucks threw shot guns down on me while another man, drunk, stepped down off the porch where they all were standing. He proceeded to cuss me. I'm sure he meant to beat me up while the three on the porch kept me covered with their guns. At this point, my wife came forward and laid her hand on the man's arm, saying, "What have you got against him? He never did anything to you." In his drunkenness, the man just looked at Hazel stupidly and then walked away.

We decided that no matter what happened at the meeting, I was to go on speaking. When and if the thugs arrived, they would have to come to the speaker's stand to get me. Our people were to crowd close around the stand so that when the thugs took me down off it, our group could grab them. If any thug put up too much of a fight, our people had instructions to hit him over the head with a pistol, shooting only as a last resort. We knew that since the thugs would be wearing deputy sheriff's badges, we could too simply be framed for killing a law officer. If no gunfire ensued, we could only be jailed for resisting arrest. We planned to strip any thugs naked, whip them with switches, and put them down on the railroad tracks. After a disgrace like this, the thugs would never bother us again. I wish I could say we whipped some gun thugs that day, but the truth is that the so-called deputies got so drunk building up their courage that they never made it to the meeting.

It was a great success. In addition to the miners present there, people had ridden in from little farms five and ten miles away. The small farmers, many of whom had put in some time at the mines, were just as interested in the outcome of this strike as were the miners.

Some opposition arose during the meeting from a small group that had come, no doubt, to heckle me. Believing they had some information that would stump me, they asked that I read aloud a message they'd received from Washington in response to the question, "Is the National Miners Union connected in any way with the Communist party?" I announced this group's request and asked everyone to stay, as I was going to read their note from Washington and a letter of my own at the end of the meeting. This took care of them. The other miners demanded that the opposition group stay quiet while we conducted business.

I spoke, promising no easy way but again offering publicly to settle with the coal operators on Brush Creek if they would only rescind the wage cut and let the miners go back to work. Thus far, the opertors had not responded. I didn't promise any easy win but said that we would do everything possible to feed the miners if they stayed out on strike. After my speech, I received many good wishes and a big hand.

Then I turned to the opposition. I announced that I, too, had sent a question to Washington regarding the NMU, but a question of a different sort. I had written to inquire about the legality of the National Miners Union. We had had experience with the United Mine Workers of America and had learned what it legally could do for us and what it could not do. I read aloud the response that the Department of Labor had sent me. It stated that the NMU was under the same legal constraints and entitled to the same freedoms as the UMW of A. Any act or measure taken legally by the United Mine Workers was by the same token legal if taken by the NMU.

To answer the opposition group's question, I agreed publicly that yes, it was true that the Communist party supported the National Miners Union, but I added that had the Democratic or Republican parties been asked likewise if they supported the NMU, they too would have responded, "yes," for all political parties claim to support all labor unions. They would be foolish to say anything else. I added, "The friends who support us are not so important right now as are those who are against us. We need all the help we can get, wherever it comes from. I don't ask anyone when they join the NMU if they are Communist, Democrat, or Republican, because their politics are none of my business." The meeting accepted this as a reasonable defense of the NMU, although we knew that neither the NMU nor the UMW of A had any legality as far as the coal operators were concerned.

Though the thugs had not disrupted our meeting, once they sobered up they did act in a way that is hard for some people to believe; nevertheless, this is true and quite a lesson of the cruelty of men. An old gentleman, about sixty-five or seventy years old, had introduced me at the mass meeting and delivered a short speech. After the meeting dispersed, a whole gang of thugs, including the mine superintendent, caught up with him and dragged him up to the mine office. There they took turns kicking and beating him. Finally, he told them, "I am not only a union man but a Scottish Rights Mason as well." At this point, the mine superintendent, probably being a Mason himself, let the man go. The old fellow, bloody as a stuck pig, crawled five miles down the road to a miner's house. The newspapers carried nothing of this outrage.

The first week of February, the First Baptist Church in Pineville called all the local preachers together, trying to convince them that the NMU was a Communist conspiracy. The county clerk rose and read some of the Young Communist League's pamphlets, claiming them to be union literature. At the front of the courthouse, I tried to gather a group and respond to these lies, but the police pulled me off the courthouse steps. The miners there followed me to our Pineville meeting hall where I explained what the YCL was and assured them that it was not one and the same with the NMU. In spite of our protests, this kind of red-baiting persisted.

Once we heard that the Waldo Frank Committee was coming to Bell County, we began to make plans to meet with its members. We knew that the strike needed support from outside the state and had, thus far, received very little help from any quarter. Times were hard all over the country, not only in Kentucky. Farmers were losing their farms by foreclosure and tax sales; in the cities people were standing in bread lines and men were selling apples on the street corners. It was a terrible year. Trains passing through the mountains were loaded down with people hoboing, both men and women, moving anywhere they might find work. But during these rough months, I didn't see any coal operators starving; all the while, the miners' bellies got thinner and thinner.

We assigned our strongest people to sections in and around Pineville to insure as large a turnout as possible for the Waldo Frank Committee. Even though Brush Creek was my section, Harry Simms was to take charge of getting people from this area into Pineville. The reasons for this switch were that Harry had been organizing the young people on Brush Creek and had just held a highly successful youth conference there. Though I wasn't at this meeting, I heard they had discussed the possibility of organizing gun clubs the night before the Frank Committee arrived in Bell County. Also, we believed that Harry could best lead these young people to Pineville. They would have to walk at least ten miles to get out of the mouth of Brush Creek and up toward Pineville. Only the younger folks could march that far.

18. In the Footsteps of Harry Simms

On February 10, the Waldo Frank Committee came into Pineville, bringing food to hand out to the miners. Since Harry took the Brush Creek section, and because I was already staying with Pauline and her family on Greasy Creek, I was to be responsible for hauling people from Greasy Creek to Pineville. I drove back and forth four or five times that day, bringing carloads of people in, mostly women, dropping them below the courthouse and returning to pick up more people for the demonstration.

Hazel was at our house in Pineville. She remembers, "I was getting ready to go up to town myself when the word came to me that Harry Simms had been shot on Brush Creek and that they were looking for Jim. I started to leave the house when about five thugs stopped me, wanting to know where Jim was. I said I didn't know. They started talking rough and then began to tear all my things out of the closets and dresser drawers. They found Jim's mine foreman's certificate, and one said to another, 'What do you know about a man with one of these going after a bunch of damn Reds?' I don't know why they didn't arrest me then; I think they had to go back to their leaders and ask if they should, because they had no warrant and no order to search our house."

As I drove into Pineville for the sixth time that day with another group of demonstrators, I saw Hazel in the road outside of town flagging me down. I stopped the car. My wife told me, "They've shot Harry. He's up at the Barbourville Hospital. And they're looking for you. They've come and raided the house, turned everything upside down. You better get out."

I told my load of people they'd have to walk the rest of the way, and like a damned fool, I turned the car around without taking Hazel with me. Frank Borich's wife was in the car with me; in fact, she had come on several trips back and forth from Greasy Creek just for the ride, taking up a seat that could have been filled by another miner who needed to get to Pineville. When Hazel told me that I had better leave, I just did, never thinking that she might be thrown in jail. She hadn't told them anything concerning my activities or whereabouts that day, but even so, they had not dared to arrest her. Even the thugs were shy about harassing the local women without orders from upstairs. I should have known though that the thugs would go back, get such permission, and arrest my wife.

I drove immediately to Barbourville and went in to see Harry. I could tell that he'd been badly shot, but no one would say how serious the wound actually was. Acting as if it were funny, Harry told me briefly what had happened: the thug had not said a thing, only shot him. Local people had put him on a handcar that ran on the railroad track and brought him to the Barbourville Hospital. Once there, he had been forced to sit outside on a rock because no one would stand for the hospital bill. Finally the father of one of the thugs responsible, Davis's daddy, agreed to stand for the bill and Harry was admitted. He'd been shot through the liver.

When I came out of the hospital, Davis's father asked me, "That's Joe Weber in there, ain't it?"

"Hell no, that's not Joe Weber," I told him. "That's Harry Simms, a nineteen-year-old boy, they've shot." At this, Davis seemed badly perturbed. He turned around and ran.

It was obvious from this comment that the thugs were after Joe Weber, the district organizer, and that I would have been their next choice, being the section organizer. Now Harry, they didn't even know who he was, unless someone tipped them off. But to this day, I do not know who told the thugs about the youth group marching to Pineville from up Brush Creek.

I drove on to Knoxville where I thought I would be safe, only to hear that Hazel had been arrested and jailed in Pineville. Here is Hazel's own account.

"I had not been home but a few minutes when the thugs came back, told me to get in their car, and took me to jail — the first and only time I have ever been in jail. They told me of no charges against me and said if I would tell them where Jim was, I could leave. I refused to answer any questions without my attorney, so they sent for lawyer Stone. He told me that I didn't have to say anything if I didn't want to, so I only said, 'Jim was always at home until you drove him away. I don't know where he is.' They kept me in jail three days and nights. It wasn't so bad, or rather, I didn't have any time to consider my plight. They would take me out every day, and Walter Smith, the rotten county attorney, would ask me the same questions. When I wouldn't answer them anything, they would take me back to jail. I was in good company in that jail, talking for long hours with older union organizers like Clarina Michelson, who had been an organizer of the women in the needle trades in the big cities. She gave me an education I could not have gotten anywhere else.

"After three days, they turned me out of jail. I think their arresting me had begun to get under the skin of some of the people who were supporting them. To arrest the Waldo Frank Committee, take them to the state line, and beat them up was one thing, but to arrest a local girl with many relatives who might not be above shooting the hell out of someone was quite another thing. The last thing they wanted was a feud, because feuds are fought along family lines and even the gun thugs had some relatives who were poor working people."

W.J. Stone's son, who is also a lawyer, now claims that his father didn't know anything about the NMU or the real concerns of the people he defended. I told Steve Stone, though, that his father knew very well what he was doing, being a workingman himself who had passed the bar examination by hard work, hook or crook, or whatever means. He called himself a "little lawyer" and would always say, when a big case came up, "They don't want me; they want a big lawyer like Jimmy Burns." And this was true. The UMW of A would take all the free help that Stone would give, but in any case that involved large sums of money, the union would always hire a high-paid lawyer.

In one instance, Tilman Cadle says, the union had made out a check for $1,000 to give to Stone for his work defending various jailed miners. Union officials asked Stone how much they owed him, thinking that he would ask for much more than their $1,000, but when Stone figured up his fee, he asked for only $50.

Harry Simms died the next day, February 11, 1932.

The day of Harry's death, my brother told me that they had taken out four warrants against me, the worst one being a peace warrant. Someone I didn't even know swore that he was afraid of me; that peace warrant could be used to keep me from union activity of any kind. Banding and confederation, criminal syndicalism, and conspiracy to overthrow the United States government, these charges, in addition to the injunction they had already sworn out against me, meant that I just about had a warrant for every foot I was tall.

We who were left of the NMU in Knoxville held a meeting at WIR headquarters there, at which time everyone decided that my usefulness in the field had come to an end. I was to go north and, with the Workers International Relief, raise funds for striking miners. I left my wife in the Pineville jail and went first to Washington, D.C., with Allan Taub and Mary Heaton Vorse.

While in Washington, I and others from Kentucky testified before a Senate subcommittee investigating the conditions in the eastern mine fields. Elizabeth Baldwin, whose husband Julius had been killed by gun thugs at a Harlan soup kitchen, testified also and received a good deal of attention from the press because she nursed her baby during the hearings. The newspapers claimed this had embarrassed the senators.

Also during my brief stay in Washington, young John Hammond, Jr., a member of the Waldo Frank Committee, paid me to visit an eye specialist. This was when I first learned how bad my eyes actually were; the effects of trichoma in childhood had left them so badly scarred that I couldn't even be fitted with glasses that could in any way truly help my vision.

I arrived in New York on the same day that Harry Simms's body arrived. I, Tilman Cadle, and ten or twelve other Kentucky miners attended the funeral service in the Bronx Coliseum. Members of the Young Communist League served as pallbearers, and we miners, as a special honor guard, marched into the funeral service with our carbide lights burning for Harry. He had never stressed his connections with the Young Communist League while in Kentucky; in fact, his politics mattered little to us. We considered Harry to be ours, a leader and friend whom we loved. As for my feelings in particular, I was sure that Harry had taken the bullet that was meant for me there on Brush Creek. Before at least 25,000 people, I spoke over Harry's body that day and attended the burying. Later I went to his home and met his folks. Though Harry Simms was ten years younger than I, he has been my idol in all the years since I first met him.

Once I returned to New York City after the funeral, I sat down in my apartment and composed "The Ballad of Harry Simms," a song which tells the story of his death and which describes the feelings belonging to a man who loved and respected him. This ballad has now been sung and honored all over the world and I include it here. May people everywhere sing it, and may no more of our working-class heroes have to be killed by gun thugs claiming to represent the law.

> Comrades, listen to my story,
> Comrades, listen to my song.
> I'll tell you of a hero
> That now — is dead and gone.
> I'll tell you of a young boy
> Whose age was just nineteen.
> He was the strongest union man
> That I have ever seen.
>
> Harry Simms was a pal of mine,
> We labored side by side,
> Expecting to be shot on sight
> Or taken for a ride
> By the dirty coal operator gun thugs
> That roam from town to town
> To shoot and kill our Comrades
> Wherever they may be found.

Harry Simms and I were parted
At five o'clock that day.
"Be careful, my dear Comrade,"
To Harry I did say.
"I must do my duty,"
Was his reply to me.
"If I get killed by gun thugs,
Please don't grieve over me."

Harry Simms was walking down the track
One bright sunshiny day.
He was a youth of courage.
His step was light and gay.
He did not know the gun thugs
Were hiding on the way
To kill our dear young Comrade
This bright sunshiny day.

Harry Simms was killed on Brush Creek
In nineteen thirty-two.
He organized the miners
Into the NMU.
He gave his life in struggle,
That was all that he could do.
He died for the union,
Also for me and you.

(final verse of the original)
Comrades, we must vow today,
This one thing we must do —
We must organize all the miners
In the good old NMU.
We'll get a million volunteers
From those who wish us well,
And sink this rotten system
In the deepest pits of hell.

(final verse which I composed later)
Comrades, we must vow today,
There's one thing we must do —
We'll organize all the miners
Into the good old NMU.
We'll get a million volunteers

From those who wish us well,
And travel over the country
And Harry's story tell.

After Harry's funeral, I began a steady schedule of speaking engagements, traveling with different groups to raise money for the miners still on strike. At some of the larger meetings, various committees spoke and solicited money, but usually I would speak to three or four smaller groups or clubs each day by myself. I would talk for about five minutes about the miners' families and then ask the group to send us any amount they wanted to donate. With the Waldo Frank Committee, I addressed many college students at schools throughout the northeast, Mount Holyoke, Yale, and Harvard among them. The committee most often used me to make the collection speech.

Hazel, meanwhile, had remained in the Pineville jail for three days until the thugs finally realized she wouldn't tell them anything. She then went to Knoxville. At one of my fund-raising meetings, I met a fine old woman who, hearing of my wife's predicament, asked me to come up to her apartment. When I got there, she gave me enough money to bring Hazel to New York to join me. Once my wife arrived, we worked as a team, speaking and raising funds.

Really, I did every kind of thing to raise money. A miner from East Ohio, where the men were also on strike, and I would go down into the subway with our miners' caps and lamps on. Standing at opposite ends of a subway car, we talked loudly about the strike; then, after one of us passed around the collection can, we would move to the next car and begin our speeches again.

Before this strike, I had never been out of the mountains, except my trip to Lexington when I took the mine foreman's exam. You can imagine what an experience this trip north was for me. I saw things that before I had only read about in books and newspapers. In New York, I saw people dispossessed because they couldn't pay their rent; I saw the mounted police ride people down with horses. I was struck by the realization that poor people everywhere had the same problems, that the struggles for a place to live and something to eat were universal. I saw employment houses offering folks jobs, taking most of their first week's pay, then letting them go and hiring someone else. I saw the workers smash some of these gyp establishments in frustration. I saw boys with college degrees waiting tables for $15 a week. After witnessing all of this, I could no longer think of our fight in Kentucky as purely local.

Perhaps best of all, I remember speaking from the rostrum at the Old South Meeting House in Boston with members of the Waldo Frank Committee. That audience, in addition to being extremely courteous, contributed $2,300 to the coal miners' strike. On this my first trip to Boston, I stayed in the home of Henry Wadsworth Longfellow as the guest of his great-grandson, Henry Wadsworth Longfellow Dana; he was a puppeteer who had trained in Russia. I might mention that the second time I addressed a group in the Old South Meeting House, the audience was not quite so responsive. We had to speak from the floor this time, maybe because no writers accompanied us. We were just a group of union people. I believe this attitude is often the case with liberal groups: if someone with a name, like Theodore Dreiser, says that miners in Kentucky are starving, the liberals will believe him, but if the miners themselves say they are starving, liberals will think they are bellyaching.

After my second trip through the northeast, I planned to attend an NMU convention in Pittsburgh. I had jumped on a bus and was heading south when outside Rye, New York, a truck skidded on the slick road and ran halfway through our vehicle. The collision killed one child and injured most of the passengers. My leg was hurt so that I couldn't continue to Pittsburgh as I'd wanted. Instead, I stopped in New York City where Hazel and I at that time were keeping a base. I was shocked at the number of ambulance chasers who offered to represent me in a suit against the bus company.

The reports I got from Kentucky were bad; by April 1932, the union had just about been beaten and shot out of the field, and the struggle looked as if it were ending. I was anxious to return home and see if any of the organization could be salvaged, so I asked the WIR leaders to send me back. They were hesitant to let me go because, they told me, I was one of their most effective fund raisers, averaging $500 per day. Another Senate subcommittee hearing on labor was to be held in Washington in early May. The WIR people asked that I stay on until that time; then, if Hazel and I felt safe from the threat of arrest, they would pay our way back to Kentucky.

As the date for the hearings approached, I managed to settle my case with the bus company, receiving about $100. Hazel was pregnant for the first time and wanted to get home. But as we traveled by car to Washington with another couple for the Senate hearings, my wife began to feel ill. As soon as we got into Washington, we got Hazel to the home of Jewish family we knew. They immediately called up a doctor to come examine her. After the doctor concluded that Hazel was about to miscarry, I ran off to the local welfare office to arrange for her admittance to Gallagher Hospital. The woman at the welfare office gave me a hard time, demanding to know why I was dragging my pregnant wife around with me all over the country. At this, being extremely nervous and frightened already, I got mad and began to cause quite a ruckus. Finally, the welfare officials decided that my wife had a right to go anywhere she damn well pleased and admitted her into the hospital. Hazel did lose this baby.

The very same day that my wife had her miscarriage, I had to testify before the Senate Subcommittee on Labor. I must have looked a holy fright and to beat it all, I noticed that a Kentucky congressman had showed up, not to testify but to harangue the miners who were there as witnesses. He asked sneering questions on the order of "Have you stopped beating your wife?" insinuating that we miners were lying. Getting madder and madder, I tried to think of some way to get back at this son of a bitch.

I remember telling the subcommittee that had it not been for my trade union, I would probably have become an anarchist. They jumped on this and asked, "Do you believe in the government?" I answered, "Let's see . . . who is the government to me? I am no big educated man. The constable, the deputy sheriff, the county and circuit judges? All these people whom I have seen call for the state militia? Now if that's my government (and those are the only government leaders I ever see), I'm against them, every damn one of them."

When I had finished testifying, La Guardia, the chairman of the committee, asked if I knew of anything else which I should say. I commented that I did have one thing to add, if I might, so La Guardia told me to go right ahead. Well, I stuck my finger right in that Kentucky congressman's face and said, "Summon that son of a bitch there. Put him under oath. He has been trying to make a liar out of me here, and so I say put him under oath just like I am. He knows that he ran for Congress in 1930 under the slogan, 'More bread and butter on the miner's table,' because he knew we were starving then. And he knows the miners are starving now. Swear him in. Make him testify. He can make you a darn good witness." The gallery roared at this, and I heard someone say, "He's not as dumb as he looks." That congressman turned red and white both. La Guardia adjourned the hearing for the day.

In the days after I gave my testimony, while Hazel recuperated in the hospital, I learned that the ex-servicemen had just been driven out of Washington. I believe that the Ex-Servicemen's League, a left-wing organization, had arranged this demonstration of veterans at the Capitol, asking for relief from unemployment. Though I didn't talk with any of these demonstrators, I did speak with some Washington natives about the trouble. They were just sick about it all and thought the state of the war veterans was a dirty shame.

You can tell when people have been taking a beating. I saw a hunger march in Washington and men selling pencils on the street just to make a few pennies. I read of jobs advertised in the newspapers and saw men lined up for blocks, hoping to be hired, men who would wait and wait, only to find that the position had been filled the night before by a relative of the boss. I heard Haywood Broun, organizer of the Writer's Guild, asking employers to "Give a Job Till June." He asked that anybody with grass to cut, anyone who needed small repairs taken care of, hire the unemployed in hopes that by June of 1932, things would be better. This country was in one hell of a mess, and the only people who seemed to give a damn were members of the left wing.

When Hazel was released from the hospital, both of us were more than ready to get back to Kentucky. What awaited us there we didn't know. At this time, in all my curiosity and apprehension about the reception we would meet, I composed the following song:

Chorus: For to welcome the traveler home,
         For to welcome the traveler home,
         The gun thugs they are waiting
         To welcome the traveler home. (*Repeat after each verse*)

There's an old judge in Bell County,
His nose is big and long,
And the son-of-a-gun is a'waiting
For to welcome the traveler home.

There's Walter B. Smith the attorney,
Why he's got Gils and Combs,
And the son-of-a-gun is a'waiting
For to welcome this traveler home.

The beans and potatoes are ready
For to feed the traveler home,
And the jailhouse cell is a'waiting
For to welcome a red-neck home.

Here's these old chinches and graybacks,
They say, "We're glad you've come,
For we know we'll have our dinner."
They'll welcome this red-neck home.

When I get back to Kentucky,
And I get my .45's on,
There'll be another Boston Tea Party
If they try to welcome this red-neck home.

19. Reading between the Lines

When Hazel and I landed back in Kentucky in May of 1932, we found that union activity had slowed almost to a standstill. Even so, there were quite a few men and women who wanted to try to hold something together; I was among them. Hazel and I had stopped in Knoxville first and met up with Clarina Michelson who asked me if I would spend a day talking with the miners around Jellico to determine the state of our organization. Even though I was not well known there, I agreed.

When I got up to Jellico, in the middle of some kind of public celebration, I looked around for the few contacts I had there but didn't see a soul I knew. I sat down on the curb in town, not knowing quite what I should do next, and after a few minutes, a Negro guy came up and asked, "You're union, aren't you?" I told him that I was.

Together we got some men gathered up by the railroad track to discuss what should be done about the union. They told me, "There ain't nothing to do. The union's been ripped." I asked what they wanted to do: Hold the union and blow the party? Drop the union and hold the party? Try to hold both? Their consensus was that if we could hold onto anything, we should hold onto the party and let the union go. Once I passed this information back to the folks in Knoxville, it was decided we should try to sustain an underground party and concentrate on unemployed councils.

Taking all kinds of steps to get food for families of men out of work, we began to organize these unemployed councils. We forced the county judge to issue a few more food vouchers and created a movement to get medical treatment for the unemployed and their families. By this time, the people were willing to fight harder for medical care than for anything else.

As for the leadership of the National Miners Union, Joe Weber had left the field and his replacement, after being beaten up, had also decided to leave Kentucky. This second organizer told me that I was to assume charge. Of course, I didn't take up the leadership quite that smoothly; I didn't think I had a right to that authority simply on the spoken word of this one man who, after all, was leaving the state. The miners, however, got disgusted and wrote a letter to the Trade Union Unity League in New York claiming that I was refusing to act. When the TUUL forwarded this letter to me, I brought it out at a meeting of miners and told them, "Now, I don't blame you for writing this, but you've got your facts a little bit backwards. Just because somebody ran out of here and said to me, 'You're in charge' doesn't put me in charge. A man's got to have more authority than that."

Soon after this confusion became evident, Harry Jackson from Pittsburgh, and Hathaway, editor of the *Daily Worker*, came down to Kentucky and told us they wanted a meeting of the remaining NMU supporters at the International Labor Defense office in Louisville. So many strikes had been lost, and since the rest were failing, we had to decide what to do. Were we going to go ahead with the plan of organizing the unemployed people, most of whom had lost their jobs because of the earlier W.B. Jones union and had nothing truly to do with the NMU, or were we going to pull out entirely?

People from all over the state attended the Louisville meeting, several carloads driving up from Wallins Creek alone. I made the trip with some folks from Knoxville. I chaired the meeting, recognizing Frank Borich, Jackson, and Hathaway, who were the principal speakers. All of their speeches amounted to requests that the Kentucky miners report honestly on the state of the NMU so that together, all of us could make the wisest decision as to what we could and could not then accomplish.

After this day-long discussion, I attended a smaller meeting over supper at the home of some Louisville people. At this time, the NMU national leadership suggested that I go to a school for organizers in New York to undergo intense training in organizing and, particularly, in political economy. Jackson and Hathaway especially believed that through my education, the NMU could be assured of one capable leader in Kentucky.

I didn't like the idea. Hazel and I had just returned from New York, had just found and moved into a house. Also, I knew how little remained of the union and feared that by the time I finished the organizers' program, nothing would be left to work with. I just believed that the unemployed councils needed me more than I needed schooling.

Harry Jackson commented, "Well, I'm all for Jim's going. He doesn't have but one fault — he wouldn't drive the workers hard enough."

I told him, "Well, if it's a matter of driving people, I won't drive anybody. I would try to lead them right, but if they didn't want to go along, that would be their business."

Hathaway agreed with my attitude but went on to ask me, "Do you think that now you'd be able to give leadership to 10,000 miners?" I told him immediately I knew damn well I couldn't. Once I'd admitted this, they asked me to reconsider the training program. I agreed, again leaving my wife behind in Kentucky.

Hazel explains that in my absence, "They allowed me five dollars a week to live on and to get around and see as many of our people as I could. I wasn't alone. I had good help from Tilman Cadle and Silus Birge in the Middlesboro section and Si Burton and Ed Garland in the Pineville section. I couldn't do much, but we figured that by the time Jim got back, we would have made a start in organizing the unemployed."

I think I learned more in those six weeks than during any other time in my life. I know that I never studied harder. I was one of about fifty-six students who had come to this school in the Bronx from all over the United States. There were more men than women, more whites than blacks, but our group was quite a mixture. I distinctly remember a group of black students from Alabama and Bill Breem from the Young Communist League.

As for the instructors, Hathaway lectured regularly, teaching us how to run local sheets and how to make leaflets. Jack Stachel, the TUUL's organizing secretary, took part in the school; William Z. Foster, one of the originators of the TUUL, lectured. But for me, Earl Browder's talks on political economy meant the most (Browder later became the secretary of the Communist party). Once you have received a really stiff dose of political economy from the working-class viewpoint, the whole face of politics changes. Generally, economics is taught from the basis of a profit system, but Browder instructed us according to the basis of use, showing what value lay in all parts of the economic system and where economic systems come from. His lectures ripped the whole system of unpaid surplus profits to pieces.

On a typical day at the school we were up early. All of us would run down to a nearby park where a big muscular guy led us all through calisthenics. Then it was back to the school for breakfast and into the classroom. We studied until noon. At first our exercises consisted of simple problems of political economy, combined with a good deal of Hathaway's Communist party propaganda. Later we worked up to more complex problems. After noon lunch, we went back to the classroom until six or seven o'clock when we broke for supper. Then we were back studying for two or three more hours. Often in the evenings we "characterized each other," meaning one student would stand up and deliver a speech on trade unionism, after which the rest of us would criticize his or her presentation.

Once I had taken all this in, I could pick up an article by a capitalist newspaper writer and read between the lines. I could draw a conclusion completely different from the journalist's once I understood why he said what he said.

When I returned to Kentucky with all of this wisdom, I did my best to educate others. The union had dried up, leaving only some unemployed councils and a few small groups in Kentucky and Tennessee, but I managed to pass along a good bit of what I had learned. For example, one afternoon I spoke to a group of small farmers on the courthouse lawn in Pineville and pointed out to them how the banks were beating them out of their small farms. One of the old thugs who knew me ran upstairs in the courthouse and, after producing one of the old warrants sworn out against me, managed to arrest me and throw me in jail. Uncle Jim Howard, better known as Cussing Jim Howard, said they couldn't do this, take out an old warrant and lock me up. He came right over and went my bond.

By this time, Hazel was pregnant again so I was trying every way I could to stay in Kentucky. I was busy organizing first one group, then another. I even went up to Louisville to try to organize the women back-up workers in the cigarette industry. The Liggett-Myers Company put the union label on their cigarettes even though a good deal of the work was done by underpaid women. The meeting we held to discuss this issue was the first integrated meeting of its kind in a Louisville hotel. Some thought we should first ask the hotel's permission, but I felt we should go ahead with our plans. The hotel management could just move us out if it disapproved. We held this meeting undisturbed, and in fact organized several others like it later, which people of both colors attended.

It was during this first meeting of the back-up cigarette company employees that I first ran into the National Workers party. They were holding a card party of some kind and entered our meeting to ask me some questions. I couldn't much answer them since I knew nothing of their party's program, but I did comment that if they wanted to lead the workers, they were certainly going about it in a strange way. "I just don't think that when the workers need leadership, they'll come find it wherever those leaders may be playing cards." They didn't have an answer to this kind of talk, for, as a matter of fact, they never did anything about the day-to-day struggles of working people.

When Roosevelt came in with his New Deal program and the Public Works Administration, which was later declared unconstitutional, many people exclaimed, "Glory be! The unemployed will not have to starve after all." Since Hazel and I were still a family unto ourselves, I could only work two days per week at the wonderful wage of $1.25 per day. I signed up and began working through this program until it was discovered that I'd been receiving $5 per week from the National Miners Union to run the unemployed councils. Once the U.S. Post Office reported the checks I'd cashed, I was cut out of the PWA program.

I got hold of an old Studebaker and cut it down to make a half-ton truck, hoping I could get by hauling coal. I dug all my own coal right out of Straight Creek and delivered it to local folks.

Early in 1933 somebody bombed UMW of A representative Peggy Dwyer's house. For some reason, the law was trying to tie me into the incident, even going to the trouble of hiring a woman to keep an eye on me in the hopes that she would give them a positive identification. Their only problem was that all my neighbors knew I had been close to home from the day before the bombing through the day afterward because Hazel had been almost three days in labor with our first child. For those three days I had alternately been caring for my wife and running to the doctor's house to ask him for help. When it was finally time for Hazel to deliver, the doctor sent over a dentist in his place. Margaret, our first child, was born December 28, the day after the bombing.

About this time we decided to send a delegation of miners and their families to the governor to ask for relief from the harassment of the law in Bell, Knox, and Harlan. Forty-six people loaded into a big truck and drove to Frankfort; and a sorry lot we were too. The press had been notified about our plans. Allan Taub, an International Labor Defense lawyer, and Joe Weber had promised at least to try to join us at the Capitol. When we arrived, we held a meeting in the parking lot to choose a committee of five. They were to go up the hill and ask to see Governor Laffoon. I was on that committee; in fact, I was chosen as its spokesman, seeing as how I was acting local organizer at the time (offices and titles changed so fast during those weeks of the union that no one truly knew who he was).

When we got to the governor's office, his secretary met us and relayed that the governor was too busy to meet our delegation. I demanded to know what business could be more important than the hundreds of miners, their wives and children, starving in the state of Kentucky. She informed us that Governor Laffoon was in conference with his advisors, seeking a solution to that very problem. I said, "Lady, we are forty-six desperate people representing ten to twenty thousand others like us. We have ridden all night to see the governor and that is just what we intend to do."

The five of us returned to the remainder of the group, reported to them what had happened, and laid out our plan: we would march up to the governor's office again, two by two, and demand to see him. If we were refused again, we planned to burst across the hall into the Senate chambers and voice our complaints as loudly as possible there. I was supposed to start the speaking, Burt Sanders and his wife would be right behind me, after them the group from the steering committee, followed by the rest. Of course, we expected that I might be arrested, that pandemonium might break out and all of us would be taken to jail, but at least, we hoped, we would get the ordinance we wanted.

In spite of our expectations, the governor decided to meet with us when we returned with the entire delegation. We thanked him very kindly for being so generous with the people's time and all moved into a large room, sitting down against all four walls. They did provide chairs for the ladies in our group, seeming quite surprised that women were taking part in a miner's delegation at all. But when our women rose to speak of what was wrong in our part of the state, the government officials well understood why the women had come.

Governor Laffoon was a large man with a very red nose. He tended to look as if he were always about the burst out weeping. While the delegates spoke one after another (each of them restricted to a limited time), the governor just sat quietly in his chair. We had not planned what each person was to say, for we knew that there were many grievances to speak of and that each one of us had experienced enough to talk convincingly about the conditions in our mountains.

Those of us in the NMU leadership, however, were to bring forth the union's point of view. To this end, Joe Weber made an excellent speech, although his accent immediately gave him away as an outsider. The governor asked Weber whom he represented. Joe answered that he represented the NMU and then proceeded to ask Governor Laffoon whom he represented.

Once I'd seen the governor was to meet with us, I deliberately arranged to speak last, hoping to be able by that time to construe the governor's response to us and sum up our arguments. Frankly, I didn't expect much. Once my turn came, I was really burned up. The governor had offered us nothing and seemingly lacked any concern for our grievances. When asked to speak, I did not address the man as "Your Honor," but simply called him "Governor Laffoon."

"I am here to express an honest opinion, not only about our conditions (of which you say you know little or nothing), but also about our local law and law enforcers and about our governor. I am just a simple coal miner and I do not claim to be smart, but I do know that the taxpayers' money was spent by your predecessor, Flem Sampson, to compile a twelve-page report on the conditions in the mine fields. That report is filed away in the governor's office. So when you tell Jim Garland that you do not know about the things that are going on in the mining fields of Kentucky, you simply tell me either that you do not give a damn about the conditions, or Governor, that you lie. I assure you that this is what I intend to tell the people who sent me here."

The governor looked as if he would cry. Rubbing his nose with his handkerchief, he said, "I can have you arrested and put in jail."

"Governor Laffoon, yes you can," I said, "but you won't get any maidenhead — I have been arrested and put in jail before, and besides, you have a lot of people who are a damn sight better men and women than me in your filthy jail for nothing."

Laffoon didn't arrest any of us. After hearing us out, the only thing he said he could or would do was to send in the militia. We knew this meant referring us right back to our local courts, courts that had proved to be hand-in-glove with the operators. Probably the only benefit that came out of our delegation's trip was that we'd gotten the chance to speak our minds.

Those of us who had been involved with the unemployed councils were becoming disgusted. Tilman Cadle, Ed Garland, Jack Smith, and I, after seeing yet another NMU official leave Kentucky, decided we wanted to know what the hell New York was planning. We simply weren't getting enough help, enough financing, or enough answers. As soon as Hazel felt healthy and strong, all of us borrowed Sam Reese's car and drove up east.

The slogan of the TUUL had been that Kentucky was the gateway to the South: organize a strong base there and then extend it. But by 1933 no one in the TUUL leadership seemed to have a real plan for how to continue working effectively in Kentucky. When we got to the offices, prepared to voice our complaints, the man who met us said, "Go ahead, shoot."

"I don't see a damn thing to shoot at," I told him. "You don't make any sense to me. I want to see Stachel, Hathaway, Browder, the people who run this damn thing and find out what they're going to do. They've been holding me down there and I don't know whether to stay or go." A meeting with the TUUL leadership was arranged for the next day.

Silus Burton, Tilman, Jack Smith, Hazel, and I laid it on the line. I told them that I couldn't run the unemployed councils by myself, that $5 wasn't enough even to pay for the gasoline we needed. I recommended that with increased funding we might set up a committee to try to extend our work. While everyone at the meeting agreed this was a good idea, once we returned to Kentucky, the money never came through.

From 1933 through the next two years, very little organizing went on. I opened up a little wagon mine on Dorton Branch and managed to sustain my family with it until 1935. That winter, Don West came in to replace me. I introduced him to members in all of our twenty-three units of the district at a meeting we held in the Middlesboro park, posing as a church group. Anyway, by this time the UMW of A had started organizing again and many miners who had been out on strike scabbed for three days in order to get back into the UMW; even Don West took a big hand in this.

As for us, by this time another child was on the way and I had no idea how I was going to support my family. My sister Aunt Molly Jackson, who had remained in New York, invited us to come up there. The day my wagon mine fell in, I came home and said we would go to New York City the next day. We had no other choice. We only had $20 to our names, and that was just the amount the doctor would charge to come out and deliver the baby, who was due any time. So we sold everything we had, including the mine pony and an old car, leaving us with $85 in cash. The bus fare to New York would be $40 for the both of us.

I told Hazel not to worry, that if she came into labor during the trip, I would have her taken off the train and admitted to a hospital. I would take our daughter on to New York, leave her with Molly, and then return to wherever Hazel was hospitalized. As it happened, we arrived in New York fifteen days before Jim, Jr., was born. We didn't have to take Hazel to the hospital in that Molly was such an experienced midwife. The umbilical cord was wrapped twice around the baby's neck, but because Molly knew what to do, Jim, Jr., was fine, just skinny as a snake because of the meager diet Hazel had been living on.

By this time, Molly was well known in New York. She had spoken all over the state for relief for striking miners and had become active on the East Side in the Workers Alliance, a relief organization. She had also led a demonstration to City Hall and demanded that a fence be erected along the East River, after a child had fallen in and drowned.

Hazel adds, "Some of Molly's friends gave us furniture enough so that we could start living in an apartment of our own. Jim got a job working for a Negro friend, helping on a moving truck. Here we were on the Lower East Side, only one block from the East River on Fourth Street. We had expected things to be better in New York than they were in Kentucky, and to a certain extent, things were better. Not as many people were starving, but the struggle for food, clothing, and shelter was having to be fought there also."

Like almost all the other folks who during the Depression went to New York where home relief and WPA work were available, I faked residence after losing my job on the moving van and got work through the WPA. I was allowed to earn $62 per month, as the head of a family of four. After paying our monthly rent of $25, we were left with about $1.50 per day to spend on food, electricity, and gas to cook with. But before long, I learned ways to supplement this income.

One friend showed me how to open and slice coconuts and pineapples to sell. Another friend of mine, a Greek, introduced me to an old Jewish man who rented two-wheeled push carts. We fixed up my cart, loaded it with coconut, pineapple, and cold drinks, and I was off working, vending mainly around Union Square. Periodically the lock-up cops would show up, round up a group of us push-cart men, and take us to the Twenty-Third Street station. There, because we had no licenses, we were fined. This happened so many times that I soon distinguished a pattern in the fines handed out: generally a woman judge would turn us loose with a reprimand, a Jewish judge would fine us $2, an Italian judge would fine $3, but the Irish judges were the worst of all. They would fine $5 and throw in a tongue-lashing besides. Then all of us would go right back to work, usually at the same spots, knowing the cops wouldn't come around again, at least not that same day. The whole darn thing just amounted to a racket.

In the wintertime, I sold hot chestnuts, having fixed up the front of a baby carriage with a charcoal burner. For awhile I ran quite a business. When the furriers, the shoemakers, and workers in the needle trades came off the job, they would line up to buy my roasted chestnuts — seven for a nickel.

After awhile the party spoke to me about working among the longshoremen. I told them, "Not on your damn life. I don't know the back end of a boat from the front; let the longshoremen organize themselves." I was beginning to get upset by all the yak-yak-yak, all feathers and no meat. I got tired of the intellectual hassles, struggles between people in the party, so I branched off into folk singing and folk music. This was something that I enjoyed, something much more my style than splitting political hairs. Just the other day, a guy asked me what I thought about the CPML, saying that this is the Trotsky Western branch. I said, "You mean there's more than one split-off from the old party?" "Oh yeah," he said, "they've already split off and split again." My question is, how can an organization like that accomplish anything? A man may retain his political beliefs, but in my view, it is better to be independent of these kinds of squabbles.

By 1936 I was spending much more of my time singing and picking on the guitar. I was scheduled by the International Workers Order and the Cafe Society to sing before numerous groups, one of them being the Workers Alliance, an organization of the unemployed. With that group we went on demonstrations to the relief office, marched in the May Day parades, and attended mass meetings at Madison Square Garden.

I also began to take part in Elizabeth Barnicle's classes at New York University. Though hers was officially an English class, she concentrated her course on the culture of the Appalachian Mountains. Miss Barnicle had spent many of her vacations in the mountains, had in fact met my sister Molly a number of years back, though Molly had not introduced us (I guess my sister was a little bit jealous). On several occasions, at Miss Barnicle's request, I lectured on Kentucky folklife and culture at NYU. Later I went back to Kentucky with Elizabeth Barnicle to record songs for the Library of Congress. Alan Lomax also recorded several of my songs for the national library.

I was becoming more and more involved with music. In 1938 I had a weekly radio program for about four months on New York University's own station NYC — "Jim Garland and his Kentucky Mountain Folk Singers," who were Sarah Garland Ogan, Mamie Quackenbush, Dorothy Burton, and Hazel Garland.

Each week the show was set in a different location, for example in a miner's house, in jail, or out on a fox hunt. A Jewish boy would write up the original script, which we would then cut down to thirty minutes. We didn't exactly talk politics on the air, since the show was meant to be musical, but I sang all kinds of songs, IWW songs, even "The White Slave," which was pretty raw back then. Even so, I got by with singing songs like these and heard that people wanted more like them. I also brought on some guest stars, among them Miss Barnicle, Cisco Houston, Huddy Ledbetter, and Woody Guthrie.

I first met Woody early in 1937 at the headquarters of the Almanac Singers in Greenwich Village. I had heard of him and he'd heard of me; in fact, he said he'd been planning to look up Sarah, Aunt Molly, and me since we were all living in New York by then. The first thing that struck me about him was his long mass of wild hair. Having quite a head of hair myself at the time, I thought we looked a little bit alike; later many people commented on this similarity.

After getting acquainted with him, I found that Woody and I were also alike in our outlooks on life, politics, music, and religion. Though he was from Texas and I was a hill man raised in Kentucky, we had had very similar up-bringings. Woody confided in me many of the thoughts that he kept quiet about around others: his interest at one time in fortune-telling and soothsaying, his belief that he could talk people out of their illnesses.

Obviously Woody was homesick for the children he'd left down in Texas because he would come over to Hazel's and my house so often to play with our three children. I would want to practice playing and singing for the next radio broadcast, but he was far more interested in romping with the children. He would have all three of them on his back, riding through the apartment until they'd make so much noise, the janitor would ask us to quiet down.

Woody had all the confidence in the world in himself and got peeved at me when I showed signs of nervousness. I recall one time when we were both scheduled to sing at a big affair, I got so worried that my guitar picking wouldn't sound good enough that I asked him to play guitar for me while I sang. He flatly refused, making clear his disappointment with me.

Another time when Woody returned from a trip, I told him I was writing a work song to the tune of "The Wabash Cannon Ball" and calling it "The Union Cannon Ball." Giving a funny little smile, he said, "All great minds work in grooves; I'm working on the same kind of song in that tune." I turned what I had worked out over to Woody, who did go on to write a labor song called "The Union Cannon Ball."

My children and I would go over to the Almanac Singers' headquarters every Sunday to participate in the program they held in the basement. My youngest child Betty, only three years old, would sing some of the songs Aunt Molly had taught her, and of course, as kids always are, she was the hit of the show. When she got on stage, Woody would tease her, pulling the microphone up too high for her to reach. When Betty bawled him out, he would lower the microphone right down to the floor, until she turned to the audience and said, "He's crazy. He knows I can't sing 'I Have a Little Pussy' way down there." Here is her little song:

I have a little pussy, her hair is silver grey.
She lives down in the meadow, she never runs away.
She will always be a pussy, she will never be a cat.
She is just a pussy-willow, and what do you think of that?

Woody would sing anyone's songs if he thought they were good, but he especially liked songs he felt had messages in them. For example, he liked my sister Sarah's "I Am Going to Organize, Baby Mine" so much that he just went ahead and recorded it without her permission. When Sarah next saw him, she pretended to be angry, grabbing him by his long hair and saying, "Woody, you curly-headed son of a sea cook! I am going to beat the tar out of you. Why did you record my song without asking me?"

Woody answered her, "Oh hell, Sarie, that is a good song that needed recording, and you never would have done nothing with it."

I learned a lot from Woody and believe that he considered me and my sisters loyal friends. When the Second World War came, me being a 4F man, I went to Washington state to work in the shipyards, and Woody, as I remember, went into the Merchant Marines. Our paths separated and I never saw him again. To this day, though, I think that Woody was 100 percent with me. He has been a great influence for the good in this country, and I feel privileged to have been able to call him a friend. His songs will live forever alongside Stephen Foster's and Joe Hill's, and the world will be a better place because he passed this way and lingered long enough, as he would say, to "knock out a few tunes."

I quit my radio show eventually. After having Woody and Houston on a couple of times as guests, the woman who produced the show decided that we should leave the script and give most of the program over to Woody's music. I could understand this, because Woody's music was good, better than the rest of our group's, I guess, but I told her, "This is it. If you want to put Woody on, well ok. The man's a friend of mine and I like him, but nobody comes in and takes my show and me stay with it." She tried using Woody by himself; that didn't work. She then tried Woody and Houston together, but that was no good either. Eventually she got Leadbelly onto the program, one fine musician (but he was a dangerous man; I was afraid of him).

Due to the radio program, our Kentucky Mountain group was invited to play at the 1939 World's Fair at the American Commons during Farm Week. We also got passes to the square dancing held every Thursday night; I was the alternate caller.

In 1938 my wife came down with a sickness that lasted two years, pneumonia. At the time we all thought it was tuberculosis since so many people that year came down with TB. As Hazel remembers, "Jim's sister

Sarah also came down with it. One of her little boys died with TB of the spine. They tried to operate on him, but he died on the operating table. Every one of us was having to go through the examinations for TB when it turned out that I had it, what they called quick TB. Nothing but bed rest could cure it. When I was sent to the hospital, I thought I would die from grief. I loved my children so much, and now there was no one but Jim to take care of them, while he was already working so hard to make a living. I thought this was the end.

"Jim managed to get the two youngest ones in a nursery. He would take them in and pick them up as he went to and from work. He was doing a passable job of taking care of the children, but we feared the church would try to have the children taken away from us and put in an orphanage. The church people did come and offer to take the children, saying that we could have them back once I got well. But getting cured of TB was not very likely back then. Jim was upset and talked about going back to Kentucky with the children. Then the doctor at Bellevue claimed that Jim, too, had TB, though Jim never did have a positive sputum test. Finally, after he had been in the hospital for six months, they decided that he had coal dust in his lungs, what they now call black lung. When he had to go to the hospital, we rented an apartment next door to Jim's sister Molly on Broom Street, and I came home. I was diagnosed as negative by that point, but I still had bad-looking X-rays. I was on my way back to health for eighteen months, taking bed rest while Molly and her husband took care of the children."

Once I left the hospital, I took two jobs: I was the janitor at the Gospel Tabernacle Church of God, a big church on Thirty-Third Street just across from Penn Station, and I was also working for the New York Association for the Blind in their broom and mop factory on First Avenue and Twenty-First Street. This was my situation when the war broke out. The very day that Pearl Harbor was bombed, I was on stage at the Almanac Singers' party singing "Old Sheep." When Millard Lampell came in and said that the Japs had bombed Pearl Harbor, I switched over and began to sing:

The war it is raging and Johnny you must fight.
May I go with you, Johnny, from morning to night?
No, my love, no. No, no, my love, no.
May I go with you, Johnny? Oh no, my love, no.

Hazel: "Jim came out to Washington state in February 1943 and the children and I followed two months later. By the time Jim met us in Portland, he had managed to find a house and have it furnished. He had taken a job at the Kaiser shipyard in Vancouver, Washington. That company was begging for women to work, so I decided to try working. When I went down, they gave me a job as an electrician's helper at 95 cents an hour. Jim worked on the day shift and I worked on the swing shift. When I got home from work, he and the children were in bed asleep, and he had to leave before I woke up in the morning. The children had to make out by themselves from the time I left for work to the time Jim got home. Since we were both working, we could save my paycheck and soon had enough to put a down payment on a house. We began to look around for a place where the children could go to school all day; they were doubling up on the school sessions in Vancouver. We finally found a house through a lady who worked on Jim's same shift, moved out of Vancouver, and have lived in Washougal ever since. I left the shipyard when they no longer needed me so much. I was really afraid I might come down with TB again.

"Jim couldn't stay out of music. He soon started singing and playing for various groups. We also started giving the children music lessons. By 1947, all three of them were able to play instruments; they had always been able to sing. People's Songs was organized in Portland, Oregon, and Jim was elected vice-president of the chapter there.

"When the Progressive party was organized to run Wallace for president, we joined up and began helping out with that campaign. By the time the war was over, Jim had established a broom and mop factory in Washougal, hiring blind and handicapped people to work in it. He had learned the trade himself in New York working for the School for the Blind. We also used this shop to silkscreen billboards for local candidates.

"After the election was over, Jim and the children and I, along with a man named Mike Peters who played the fiddle, began playing every Saturday night for a club in Vancouver. We joined the Grange and started making music for them to dance to. Soon Jim had organized a group of musicians that called themselves the 50/50 club, because the musicians would get 50 percent of the gate and the Grange or the union would get 50 percent. The people who paid for admission were members of the club so no tax had to be paid to the state. The group was also known as the Garland Orchestra, playing for Grange and union dances for quite a number of years, until our children began to marry and move away or get busy with schoolwork.

"We ran the broom factory for twenty-one years. On the side (Jim said it was recreation), we built six houses. We still own two of these, in addition to the first one we bought for ourselves.

"In 1963 Jim was invited back to Newport, Rhode Island, to a folk festival, and he got interested in folk singing again. Folkways Records wanted him to work for them down in Kentucky, collecting songs and stories. At this time, we closed the broom shop, sold the machinery, sold the building, and joined the so-called retired. During 1966 we worked for Folkways.

"In 1968 we built a house down at the ocean where we lived part of the time. Jim returned to Washington, D.C., in 1971 and 1974 for the Folklife Festival.

"I am now sixty-seven years old. Jim asked me to include this as part of his book, so here is my share. Many more things happened; it has been a long life with ups and downs. But when I think about Jim and me back in the '30s, I believe that we accepted the challenge and we worked hard. No one said it would be easy. No one said we would win the sun, moon, and stars. We only wanted to live and work and raise our family as we saw fit. We know now that we were up against great odds to win. We had all the powers of county and state government against us, but we fought, and in fighting we shined the light of day on an unbearable condition. And who is to say we did not win?"

20. I Don't Want Your Millions, Mister

I have written about how two classes grew out of the mountains after a few people gained ownership of the land. These same people sold themselves to the big corporations and, after receiving coal royalties, weakened, succumbing further and further to the exploitative demands of the operators. Coming to live solely off coal revenues, many of them lost any reason for working and began to deteriorate, becoming drunkards and whoremongers, dying of sexual diseases. Many of these wealthier families completely died out in the mountains.

But beyond this split between landowner and landless, there is another division in the mountain people. Let us take two families of working people, both sprung from the same grandmother and grandfather, both raised in the same location, the fathers of both families being coal miners. During the Roosevelt regime, both families experienced the rebirth of the UMW of A and both saw the decline of deep mining. They saw the mine industry turn to strip mining, the mountains torn apart, streams contaminated and destroyed. Both have seen the mining camps torn down and government commodities handed out. They have lived with the home relief system, the Supplemental Security Income programs, the Heads of Families program under Johnson. But though their circumstances have been the same, their reactions have been quite different.

One family deteriorated, beginning during those same years when deterioration of people began all over this country — when in the late '20s machines replaced workers and men in large numbers began to lose their jobs. Instead of jobs and free transportation being offered to workers, the freight trains began to load down with unemployed men, hoboing from one place to another. Hoovervilles sprang up all over the country, tar paper shacks, hobo jungle camps, until by 1930, the average wage had been cut so low that working men were no longer able to support their families.

Many men gave up, choosing to leave their families rather than see them starve. Trade unions had been ruthlessly destroyed, perhaps more so in coal mining than in any other trade. The farmers, unable to pay their taxes or pay back loans, lost their property at bank auctions. These farmers fought back as best they could by stopping sales in mass, but federal judges were also issuing restraining orders against all who protested. Judges also issued injunctions against workers who dared to strike against wage cuts. In the cities, carpenters and painters were bound to a kick-back system, unless they wanted to lose their jobs.

These conditions, from which the Depression sprang, worsened until by 1932 employers were openly fighting against any and all plans to keep people from starving. They put unemployed miners out of company shacks, put the sharecroppers off the land, and branded those who tried to gain some foothold as Communists or subversives.

Out of these massive injustices came one family, half-starving and home-broken. Like all people after such a disaster (which was exactly what these conditions amounted to), they were weak, but they did not have to go on to give up their birthright and manhood. They lost faith in everything — their trade unions, their churches, their government, themselves. They had tried and failed at the only trade they knew; many of their wives were sick from overwork and worry. They prayed for something to happen, addressing a God they thought had forsaken them. Mothers, searching for any way to get food, took their little girls into the towns to sell their bodies. And the fathers, knowing this, sank deeper and deeper into themselves.

With the election of Roosevelt and the instigation of his WPA program, many disheartened miners perked up and rushed to sign up for work at $1.25 per day. Of course, since the courthouse gang decided which men would work and how much each man could work, many people weren't even allowed jobs at this pittance, especially if they were known "troublemakers."

Then came the program that gained the name "The Henry Wallace Pigs." The same people who had called the miners union advocates "reds" claimed that the government's buying and dressing out surplus hogs constituted a Communist plot. This program was a good thing; it gave good-sized hogs to people who had gone without meat for many a day.

Once the Wagner Act passed, the miners believed the right to organize would bring them jobs once again, meaning a resurgence of the UMW of A. But the UMW, as it bargained with the companies for union representation, found itself in the same old struggle. The UMW officers had laughed when the NMU, accused of Communist intentions, was shot out of the mine field, but they found themselves branded soon enough with the same charge. Many miners joined yellow-dog or company unions rather than the UMW for this very reason. But the worst part was that, in spite of the Wagner Act, thousands of blacklisted miners could not get back to work in the mines and chose, once they had gotten into the WPA or on home relief, to stay on the dole rather than trying to return to mining or some other occupation.

The older mines being more expensive to run, small operators gave up, selling the mining camps to more mechanized companies. Of course, because of this mechanization, the newer mine operation did not require so many company houses since it employed fewer men; to escape paying taxes, large mine companies simply bulldozed entire coal camps, leaving blacklisted families with no place to live.

The younger and better-educated people left the mountains by the thousands. All who could went into the Civilian Conservation Corps, many serving one term under their own names and then returning to serve again using the name of a relative who already had a job. In the cities and the CCC camps, these mountain boys soon found that moonshine whiskey was old hat and began for the first time to experiment with marijuana and other drugs. Mountain people had rarely practiced drug use of this kind before the Depression in 1929 (except for the old women who drank cordial). Most of the middle-aged miners, in addition to those who were uneducated or handicapped, remained in the mountains on WPA or home relief.

Then came the war, and the mountains were scoured for war industry work to employ both men and women. Many mountain boys joined up, as mountain men have always done, but quite a number of others were turned down for military service, some because they could not read or write, others because of injuries sustained from mining. No efforts were made toward building war-oriented factories in the mountains though, so those who could not serve, including most older mountaineers, all had to go elsewhere for work. With the onset of war came another breakdown of morals, in and out of the mountains. I believe this kind of damage always occurs during wartime.

When the ex-servicemen returned to the mountains after the peace was signed, again they found no work; even the CCC camps no longer existed. I would say that more young men were killed after they came back home from the war than were killed during the fighting itself. My sister's son, who came back from combat with a Purple Heart, simply could not adjust. He was killed by one of his own buddies as they were wrestling over a pistol. It is hard, once young men have been trained to kill, to rehabilitate them, especially if they have no occupation, nothing to do except drink, smoke pot, and take nerve pills.

What effect did all of this have on the mountain women? The mechanization of the mines meant little directly to them since women during these years were not employed as coal miners. But once the boys went off to the CCC camps or to war, there were no young men left in the mountains to marry. Too, the starvation diets of the Depression sent many girls into the streets to sell their bodies. This is absolutely true.

Out of this horrible situation grew a third generation of people dependent on home relief, a prospect so demeaning that many men felt the best they could do was to leave their wives and children so their spouses could receive Aid to Dependent Children. Many later became part of what was known as the beat generation, drowning their troubles in drugs until they couldn't put in a day's work, even if they could manage to find jobs. They were afraid to accept part-time work, for if such a job were lost, there was no telling how long it would take to get back on the relief rolls. They dodged work and fell lower and lower in self-esteem under the guise that they were indeed protecting their families. They had become victims of the No-Job Syndrome, a fatal disease.

I asked the head of a family like this why he didn't move from his family's little shack into one of the government apartments. And he said, "Ah, buddy, I would rather live in a shack than have some of those big shots coming every month to see if I have a little dog or cat around the place." This man's wife is a drug addict on the needle. When he got his miner's pension, $1,300 of back pay, he found a doctor's bill against him for $1,100.

They have become so demoralized that they no longer understand how to handle money. In spite of the $800-per-month pension and black lung benefits, he receives and despite his daughter's getting SSI and home relief for her children, they are living worse than when he was working in the Heads of Families program.

I include here an interview I held with his daughter, a young widow: "I was raised at Arjay, Kentucky, in a coal mining camp. My daddy worked in the coal mines to raise me and my three sisters. I went to school every day that I wasn't sick during the school months. I did not have the best clothes, but I went clean and we always had shoes to wear.

"I married young, at age sixteen, and I now have two children. I lived with my husband six years. It was a very disappointing marriage. My husband and I didn't get along too well. He was on drugs, and I couldn't see that. He wouldn't make any effort to take care of me and the two children. He left me twice. The first time he came back, and the second time I divorced him.

"I love to sing. I have always sung ever since I was a little girl, at school and at church. I even got to attend a folk festival in Cumberland, Kentucky, when I was thirteen, and they liked my singing there. My uncle thought I had a future in the field of music and wanted me to move in with him and his wife. I did not want to leave my family, so I guess I passed up my big chance at getting an education. Who knows what I might have become?

"My hardest times had to do with my married life. It is hard to try to live

with a man who is mentally retarded and a dope addict too. He took me to Detroit where he had a job, and I got a job there also. We could have made out, but he quit his job and wouldn't even watch the little boy while I worked. He would take my pay and spend it for drugs, leaving the baby and me without food. After his unemployment compensation ran out, he claimed he got jealous of the foreman at the factory where I worked and he made me quit my job and go back to Kentucky. When we got there, we had to go on home relief. He didn't try to get work, claimed that he was unable to work.

"I have been on some kind of government program all my married life, except the few months when I was working. Before I was married, my daddy worked in the Heads of Family program.

"After my husband left me and the two children, I had to do something. I didn't have enough money to go to my father's home, but I asked a neighbor to take me and he did. I have been living in the house with my father and mother ever since I got the divorce. Now I get help from the SSI and home relief for me and the children.

"I am twenty-three years old now. I only weigh about one hundred pounds. My father and mother are both sick and I have to do the housework for us all and take care of my chidren. We live way up in a hollow with only a very rough dirt road leading to our house. The road is full of rocks, and the stream runs right in the road. Our house is a little four-roomed house, and we get our water from an outside well. We have no hot water and we cook on an old wood stove. The house sets right against a steep hill. If my little girl falls down, she could very well fall right into the road. We use an outside toilet. I have to do all the washing by hand.

"You ask why I don't get out of a situation like this? Well, it is easier said than done. I feel a great obligation to my parents who are old and sick, and in this place a young widow like me can hardly live alone; she is always meeting men who want to make time with her. I don't know how to drive a car, even if I had one to drive. That is another thing my former husband did — he refused to let me learn to drive. And now I have no one to teach me.

"I realize that I'm a slave to my parents and to my two children. There is very little chance of finding a man here who's worth marrying, who would take me and my two children to raise. I may find someone just like the one I got rid of. All the men my age around here are on dope or already married, and most of the married ones are on dope also. I never get to go out anyplace, not even to church. My folks say they can't take care of the children, and no one would ask me out even if my parents could. So I do the best I can and hope against hope that I can stay well and raise my children. Some say I should give my children up for adoption, but as long as I live, I will keep my children."

Garland: "Did you have parties or games when you were growing up?"

"No, I never knew what a girl party like a slumber party was until after I was married, but we did make up some games ourselves: watching lightning bugs and June bugs and playing with them, running and playing along the sand bar in the creek, going to church. I liked to go to church and Sunday school and hear them sing. I guess this is what led me to singing. My father taught me many songs, like "Pretty Polly" and "Barbara Ellen" and others. I used to sit on his lap and he would sing for me and I would sing for him. After I got married, my husband didn't want me to sing and discouraged me every way he could. I loved going to the folk festival with my aunt and uncle. This had a great impression on me. This was the first time anyone except my own family had shown any interest in me or my singing. I was well received there, and it felt good to hear people applauding me."

Garland: "How does a young girl in the mining camps act if she is stuck on a boy and wants to go out with him?"

"Oh, I guess it is up to the individual girl. The boy I married was the first and only boy I really courted. We went together about seven months, what we called going steady, and then we got married. After about two months, we started in having trouble. I should have quit him then but stayed on and became pregnant; then I thought I had to stay on with him.

"The little boy was born, and I thought we might get along better, but it got worse, if anything. He even started to beat me up, but I fought back as well as I could, and like a fool I stayed on until I was pregnant again. This time, I had a little girl, and when she was born, he insisted that I have myself made sterile so that I couldn't have any more children. So I did this. But even the fact that I can never have any more children would turn some mountain men against me, especially if they didn't have some children of their own already."

Garland: "Are there any jobs for girls here?"

"No, there are no jobs here for a girl like me. By the time I paid a babysitter, I would not have anything left. I finished grade school, which I liked very much, and I started to high school, but I didn't like high school and I dropped out. But even if I had gotten a high school education, there would have been no jobs here in Kentucky for me."

Garland: "What was the real reason for your marriage breaking up?"

"Well, the biggest thing, I guess, was that my husband just did not want to work and support his family. I was brought up that a man was supposed to support his wife and kids, because my daddy always worked for us. We had clothes and shoes to wear, maybe not the best, but we had them. And my husband got hooked on drugs. After he made me come back to Kentucky to live on food stamps, I would have to go to my neighbors and bum a quart of milk for my baby to eat.

"I would like to have a better life for my children and myself, but there is *no better life here. So I have to live in this old shack with all these sick people and work, and even then I have very little to say about how things are run. This is my mother's house and I am staying with her. I am just here and having to live on welfare, and it looks like my children will have to be raised on welfare."*

Garland: *"Do you think it would be better if the government or some other agency would start something for women like you to work at?"*

"Yes, I do. I would love to have a job, and I would work for my children. I don't like to be on welfare. I would much rather work if I could."

Garland: *"How much do you get in all to live on?"*

"We get $62 SSI and $119 home relief each month. If I wasn't living here with my mother and had to pay house rent and electric bills, I just couldn't make it."

What an end to a good family. There is nothing more pitiful than the fact that they will probably spend the rest of their days among filth and dirt and drugs and raise another generation who will never know the satisfaction of having a worthwhile job.

We can take up another family to see how they met with this challenging situation, without the benefits of formal education and in subjection to all of the same circumstances as the first family I have just described. In this second family there were eleven children, five girls and six boys, none of whom have ever been on home relief. Their father died before the youngest child had finished common school, so the rest drew on his social security. Before they had finished high school, their mother died. The oldest girl, who by this time had six children of her own, took her younger brothers and sisters under her protection. Because of social security, the younger children were able to get all the way through high school. The older six children, however, did not study further than common school; some did not even finish those eight grades. One of the boys refused to go to school at all and so received no formal education. These older children, who lacked the benefit of education, especially interest me in this comparison.

The son with no education took a good long look at the situation and sensibly decided that he didn't stand much of a chance in the contest for good jobs around the mines. He worked as a miner long enough, however, to save money for the down payment on a coal truck. Next he hired someone who could read road signs to ride with him as he hauled six to eight ton loads of coal from Kentucky into North Carolina. By watching the roads carefully and noting landmarks, he soon could make the trip alone. He built up a good number of regular customers in North Carolina and has been hauling coal to them ever since. Now, with a fine wife (who luckily did receive a high school eduation), a home of his own, two coal trucks, and money in the bank, he asks no one to be his benefactor. I must say that he can figure faster in his head than most college-educated men can with a pencil. No one can beat him out of a dime.

The second son of the family tried working in the mines, but decided he didn't care for it. Though he had little eduction, he managed to move to another state and find a job working on state roads, a job he held for over twenty years. This man is now dead, after a long sickness, but he never had to ask for welfare. He spent his life as a substantial workingman, true to his union and his family. While he wasn't well educated, he preserved his self-respect and never sank into the dark morass of self-pity.

The family's third son, with less than eight years of schooling, started working in the coal mines with his father. Soon he had performed most of the jobs involved in mining but, too, found he wasn't satisfied. Even though he had no other trade, he didn't want to remain in the hills and compete for the fewer and fewer jobs left in deep mining. Like so many other young men, he left the mountains and moved to Ohio where he learned how to make large trailer bodies. Once his employers realized what a fine worker he was, they suggested he encourage one of his brothers also to move to Ohio and come to work for them. A bit later, a nephew moved up too and started to work for the same company. Meanwhile, this third son became very interested in heavy machinery, teaching himself to operate and repair most of the company's equipment. When an opening became available, the company moved him to this line of work. They paid to train him to install and assemble such machinery, work so precise that some of it has to be done with a laser beam. These machines are valued at a half-million dollars apiece, and only a few men have the training to work with them. Now this mountain boy, without the benefit of a formal education, travels all over the United States, installing equipment, fixing machinery, and teaching local employees how to use the equipment. By his own intelligence, he has been able to pull himself up and become a useful cog in our industrial society. He is proof that willingness to work is a man's greatest advantage, a willingness that is bred into many and most mountain people.

The fourth child in the family, a woman who never attended high school, held down many jobs. She is a shrewd businesswoman who has married, raised three children, and put them all through college. One of her children now leads a very successful musical group. She owns her own home in Indiana, as well as property in Kentucky. One may say, "Yes, but her husband was educated." Not so, her husband was also raised in the coal mining camps and, in fact, has less education than she does.

The fifth member of the family, a man who didn't get much formal education, had the added disadvantage of a childhood injury. As a boy, he was caught up in electric wire and burned very badly. Did he give up and sink into self-pity? Not on your life. He now works for the Ford Motor Company, owns a fine home in a large city, and is married to a kind and pretty woman. Although he is bothered by a bad heart, he asks no man to be his master. He wears no man's collar. He is a strong union man, active in his church and an asset to his community.

The sixth child, the eldest, had the least chance of any to get ahead. After her parents died, she raised the four smallest brothers and sisters and six children of her own. She had five years of schooling, and her husband, a coal miner until his retirement, also had very little education. Her husband has black lung and total disability as the result of a mining accident, yet he is one of the handiest men I have ever met. While he cannot do the work himself, he can instruct anyone in repairing any machine, from the smallest motor or household appliance to the largest coal mining equipment. He also built his own house. What a waste of a good brain; he should be teaching his skills to young people, but no, he does not have a sheepskin.

His wife has worked as a cook in the public schools for the last eighteen years, is an election officer in her precinct, and was recently elected to an important position on the school board. She worked in a federal program, signing elderly people up for government commodities and has helped many old miners arrange for their black lung benefits. I call her the Queen of Arjay. She works as an answering service for all her neighbors. If they're sick, they all call on her to take them to the doctor (though she also makes her own cough syrup out of a mixture of whiskey, honey, rock candy, and glycerin). Her door is always open so that hungry neighbors can come in and help themselves. She also watches out for the school children, making sure each one of them has enough clothes to wear.

Even though she is good to everyone, she has her breaking point, and when pushed too far, she will fight a circle saw, as the saying goes. I saw this happen once when an alcoholic to whom she and her husband had given an old Studebaker was about to be beaten out of the car by a bunch of no-goods. They promised this man a few dollars and some whiskey for the car. At this, the Queen of Arjay blew her lid. She walked into the house, picked up a .38 special, came back outside, and gave these no-goods just one minute to get out of her yard. They went.

You may claim that I have given only one example of a family that made good with little or no formal education. May I say, there are many more such cases but not enough time to portray them all. Too, I wish to point out that my purpose is not to denegrate formal education, not at all. I only want to show that a lack of education has been used to justify failure by many people who simply will not try, and that a program which substitutes welfare for an honest job does not work.

I have used these two families to point up a further division among the mountain people, a division which has occurred not just because some are weak and others are strong, but because our present policies serve only to weaken the weak. Don't worry about the strong ones; be proud of them. But before it's too late, something must be done to give back to those who have weakened a reason to live. They must have work. They must be made to realize that they, and they alone, will have to support themselves. The sick should be placed in hospitals, and the healthy must be made to earn their food, clothing, and lodging. They must be made to understand that food stamps and dope and a doctor's card are not the answers.

At some time, we have to discuss trade unions in terms of communities. Is a union good or bad? Legal or illegal? Why would people choose to form a union? Who does a union truly serve? All of these questions have been disputed over for at least the past one hundred years; in fact, this country as a whole has not yet decided, in spite of the Wagner Act, whether unions should be legal. Many in the ruling class believe that unions are bad for a community and should even be outlawed.

Harvey Valentine: "The people who came into Kentucky to organize the National Miners Union did a lot of good. They at least were trying to get food for starving people. They didn't come as any kind of political organization; if they were Communist, they tried to hide it. The National Miners Union was not a political party, for it took in miners regardless of their politics. Maybe some were Communists, but to offset this, many of the local leaders were ministers of the gospel and pastors of churches. No, the NMU leaders were treated badly when they should have been praised for what they were doing for the miners and their children."

Tilman Cadle: "Instead of believing the stories being told in the press and by the WIR, many CP members, through the National Miners Union, thought they would come down to Kentucky with food and see for themselves. Well, they came all right, and the law tried to keep them from entering Pineville. The Waldo Frank Committee came down with the food on the same day that Harry Simms was murdered on Brush Creek. Well, there was getting to be quite a crowd, several people trying to speak, when Harold Hickerson stood up. He told how he had been away to fight in a war to make the world safe for democracy, but he'd found there was no democracy at all in Kentucky. As soon as he finished speaking, they arrested him and took him to jail."

The Communist party made the big mistake of denying its existence in Kentucky and its support of the blacklisted miners. The party did yeoman service in helping people who had been left with no jobs, who had been left to starve. These outsiders should have accepted the honor due them for this help. They should have worked out their authority on the basis of being a legal political party. Instead, the forces opposed to the union were able to lump the IWW, the NMU, the WIR, the ILD, and the Communist party together as Russian agencies determined to overthrow the American form of government. Subsequently, the union's opponents claimed that all union men were under Russian control.

Later, largely in response to red-baiting like this, the NMU began to weaken, pull out organizers, while counseling patience. The natural militancy of the miners was quieted. Personally, I believe that a good, first-class rout by the mountain people at that time would have done wonders for everybody. I believe that a true confrontation would have forced the government to recognize that here were people who refused to be starved to death. Sometimes it seems the meek will never inherit the earth.

The NMU was shot out of the mine fields by the combined forces of the coal operators and the state and federal governments. Every civil right was denied the mountain people, and every promise made to these people was broken. But the very fact that the issue was forced this far was the beginning of a birth of unionism, a fact which I believe led to the Wagner Act, to minimum wage, to the portal-to-portal pay system. I realize, though, that at the same time, this disturbance led to the formation of yellow-dog unions on a much larger scale and meant the death of many smaller, older mines. Many good coal-producing mines were just abandoned and allowed to fill with water. Some have never been opened again, and may never be.

But the working people, without a union we would still be in wage slavery. We would still be under the thumbs of those who operate industries: people who have the money to insure that the proper men are elected to office; people who finance the elections of judges and others in political power; people who hold enough money to hire murderers as deputy sheriffs.

In most cases, the natural resources of this planet benefit no one until labor is applied to them. Once labor is applied to any resource, it becomes valuable, and as more labor is applied, the resource increases in value. Therefore, labor truly creates the wealth of this country, labor from the strength of the worker's arms and the power of the laboring man's or woman's brain. In this country alone, working people have created at least 10 billion dollars of new wealth every year — new wealth, remember. But this wealth is never dispersed. Instead, it becomes a kind of fog that rises up into the existing umbrella of power, to the international corporations which know no national or geographic boundaries. One can no longer point out John D. Rockefeller or Henry Ford as the enemy, for those who have absorbed the newly created wealth hire managers to maintain the existing corporate umbrella, paying them with surplus profit that has been withheld from underpaid laborers.

Since nothing can be done in this country without paying loans, no one will ever have enough money under the existing system to buck these corporations. The institutions that loan money, forming a large part of this umbrella, pay the little man up to 7.5 percent on his savings; then his money is loaned to others for 10 and 12 percent. But don't think that is all the banks get. For each single dollar deposited in savings at 7.5 percent, the bank can loan more dollars at 10 or 12 percent; thus its percentage of gain constitutes far more than 5 or 6 percent. Even so, the small man with his savings account contributes to the existing system. With his few thousand dollars, he too has become an exploiter.

I say, let the corporations take their wealth and go to hell with it.

Chorus: I don't want your millions, Mister.
    I don't want your diamond ring.
    All I want is the right to live, Mister.
    Give me back my job again.

    I don't want your Rolls Royce, Mister.
    I don't want your pleasure yacht.
    All I want is food for my babies.
    Now give to me my old job back.
    (Chorus)

    We worked hard to build this country, Mister,
    While you enjoyed a life of ease.
    You've stolen all that we've built, Mister.
    Now our children starve and freeze.
    (Chorus)

    Yes, you have a land deed, Mister.
    The money all is in your name.
    But where's the work that you did, Mister.
    Demanding back my job again.
    (Chorus)

    Think me dumb if you wish, Mister,
    Call me green or blue or red.
    There's just one thing that I know, Mister,
    Our hungry babies must be fed.
    (Chorus)

    We'll organize together, Mister,
    In one big united band,

And with the Farmer-Labor Party
We will win our just demands.
(Chorus)

Take the two old parties, Mister,
No difference in them can I see,
But with the Farmer-Labor Party
We will set the workers free.
(Chorus)

Woody Guthrie told me he didn't like my song "I Don't Want Your Millions, Mister," saying that indeed he did want that money. But we can make money out of rattails. If the corporations could just be satisfied with the wealth they have thus far accumulated, I would let them keep it. I just ask that they don't take what working people will create from here on out in new wealth. If they wanted to take their billions of dollars and invest them in stocks, we wouldn't be hurt. We wouldn't borrow their money but print our own.

Wealth would not be allowed to take over again if people were permitted to use up what they produced. As the Aztec Indians knew, there should be some surplus kept aside for times of famine or sickness, but aside from this, surpluses are unnecessary. Instead of people's working eight hours per day simply to keep the existing society in motion by producing a surplus, why not cut the work day back to six hours or set aside another day each week for pleasure? We should cut back to the number of work hours that, guaranteeing every man and woman a job, would produce what we need.

As conditions now stand, the institutions of wealth are frantically building new banks. In a little bitty town of 3,000, three or four banks will all be rushing to get people using credit cards to encourage people to borrow. Why? Because there's damn good money in that kind of borrowing. They can talk us into buying automobiles that run 100 miles per hour when we have a 55-mile-per-hour speed limit and ask us to pay more for the faster car. We may have a little left over if we're not coaxed into buying everything in the world.

Since working people have been permitted legally to organize, some conditions have improved. Over the last forty years, the blacks in particular have advanced economically. Just as Harry Simms told me, "Jim, everything has a material base," the blacks have not made a better living by prayer or petition. They have done it through militant demonstrations, by saying, "You can throw me in jail or you can put your dogs on me, but you cannot deny me my rights."

Forty years ago people were so afraid of breaking the law that they would allow their children to starve first. Now many people have learned that the laws, because they're made by the rich, can become instruments of oppression. Our laws are oriented to protect private property rather than to protect civil liberties. You can beat a man up and only receive a fine for assault and battery, but if you break a window and steal from a man's house, you've committed an offense that could very well send you to the penitentiary. People are beginning to realize that breaking the law in some cases proves beneficial.

The United Mine Workers today is in big trouble. Why? Because time and time again folks have not stuck by the union. They have been disillusioned by leadership which has again and again let the rank-and-file miner down. Still, if that union goes out of business, I will guarantee that the working people will construct something to take its place, some organization to maintain their standard of living. We're not going back to corn bread and bulldog gravy.

Bibliography

Basically, this bibliography brings to the surface important materials concerning Garland and his peers: miners, unionists, and musicians. Readers interested in Appalachian folklore may turn to the *Kentucky Folklore Record* for valuable articles too numerous to mention here. The Dreiser Committee's *Harlan Miners Speak* presents a collection of testimonies given by striking miners and their families in Bell and Harlan counties, November 1931; Aunt Molly Jackson's testimony is included. James Hevener's book and Theodore Draper's article offer two accounts of the National Miners Union's activities in Kentucky; additionally, the Appalachian Movement Press's *Harlan & Bell, Ky., 1931-32, The National Miners Union* contains articles from *Labor Defender* and *Labor Age* written during the strike. Readers should also note Dunaway's and Klein's respective biographies of Pete Seeger and Woody Guthrie, both of which recount the folksong revival. Garland took part in this movement as an enthusiastic performer and, perhaps unwittingly, served as an exemplar to its generation of mostly urban, mostly middle class activists.

Aaron, Daniel. *Writers on the Left: Episodes in American Literary Communism.* New York: Harcourt, Brace, 1961.

American Civil Liberties Union. *Kentucky Miners Struggle.* New York: American Civil Liberties Union, 1932.

Auerbach, Jerold S. *Labor and Liberty: The La Follette Committee and the New Deal.* Indianapolis and New York: Bobbs-Merrill, 1966.

Barnicle, Mary Elizabeth. "Harry Simms: The Story behind This American Ballad." In brochure accompanying *Songs of Struggle & Protest, 1930-1950,* Folkways FH 5233, pp. 3-4.

Barnum, Darold. *The Negro in the Bituminous Coal Industry.* Philadelphia: University of Pennsylvania Press, 1970.

Bernstein, Irving. *The Lean Years: A History of the American Worker, 1920-1933.* Boston: Houghton Mifflin, 1960.

Bimba, Anthony. *History of the American Working Class.* New York: International Publishers, 1927.

Bishop, Bill. "Death Takes Jim Garland, Early Union Advocate." *Mountain Eagle* (Sept. 14, 1978): 2-3.

———. "1931: The Battle of Evarts." *Southern Exposure* 4, nos. 1 and 2, pp. 92-101.

Bishop, Bill. "Radical Revisits the '30's." *Courier Journal & Louisville Times Magazine,* Jan. 15, 1978, pp. 29 ff.

Bubka, Tony. "The Harlan County Coal Strike of 1931." *Labor History* 11 (Winter 1970): 41-57.

Byars, J.C., Jr. "Harlan County: Act of God?" *Nation,* June 15, 1932, pp. 672-74.

Campbell, John C. *The Southern Highlander and His Homeland.* Lexington: University Press of Kentucky, 1969.

Caudill, Harry M. *Night Comes to the Cumberlands: A Biography of a Depressed Area.* Boston: Atlantic Monthly Press; Little, Brown, 1963.

Christenson, Carroll L. *Economic Redevelopment in Bituminous Coal: The Special Case of Technological Advance in United States Coal Mines, 1930-1960.* Cambridge: Harvard University Press, 1962.

"Class War in Kentucky." *New Masses* 7 (Sept. 1931): 23.

Costello, E.J. *The Shame That Is Kentucky's!* Chicago: General Defense Committee, n.d.

Cowley, Malcolm. *The Dream of the Golden Mountains: Remembering the 1930's.* New York: Viking Press, 1980.

———. "Kentucky Coal Town." New Republic, Mar. 2, 1932, pp. 67-70.

Cressey, Paul Frederick. "Social Disorganization and Reorganization in Harlan County, Kentucky." *American Sociological Review* 14 (June 1949): 389-94.

Crowell, Suzanne. *Appalachian People's History Book.* Mountain Education Associates & Southern Conference Education Fund, 1971.

Day, John F. *Bloody Ground.* 1941. Rpt. Lexington: University Press of Kentucky, 1981.

Denisoff, R. Serge. *Great Day Coming: Folk Music and the American Left.* Urbana: University of Illinois Press, 1971.

Dix, Keith. *Work Relations in the Coal Industry: The Hand-Loading Era, 1880-1930.* Morgantown: West Virginia University Press, 1977.

Dos Passos, John. *The Theme Is Freedom.* New York: Dodd, Mead, 1956.

———."Working under the Gun." *New Republic,* Dec. 2, 1931, pp. 62-67.

Draper, Theodore. "Communists and Miners 1928-1933." *Dissent* 19 (Spring 1972): 371-92.

Dubofsky, Melvyn, and Van Tine, Warren. *John L. Lewis: A Biography.* New York: Quadrangle/New York Times Co., 1977.

Dunaway, David King. *How Can I Keep from Singing: Pete Seeger.* New York: McGraw-Hill, 1981.

———."Pete Seeger and Modern American Political Song." Ph.D. dissertation, University of California, 1981.

Eaton, Allen. *Handicrafts of the Southern Highlands.* New York: Russell Sage Foundation, 1937.

Evans, Herndon J. "Kentucky Hits Communism." *Kentucky Progress Magazine* 4 (April 1932): 12-15, 21, 28.

Fowke, Edith and Glazer, Joe. *Songs of Work and Freedom: Famous Labor Songs from Appalachia, Part Two.* Chicago: Roosevelt University, 1960.

Gannes, Harry. *Kentucky Miners Fight.* N.p.: Workers International Relief, 1932.
Garland, Jim. "Harry Simms." In brochure accompanying *Songs of Struggle & Protest, 1930-1950,* Folkways FH 5233, p. 7.
Glusman, Preval. "Harry Simms — A Young Revolutionist." *Daily Worker,* May 8, 1934, p. 5.
Grauman, Lawrence, Jr., "'That Little Ugly Running Sore': Some Observations on the Participation of American Writers in the Investigations of Conditions in the Harlan and Bell County, Kentucky, Coal Fields, 1931-32." *Filson Club History Quarterly* 36 (Oct. 1962): 340-54.
Green, Archie. "Aunt Molly Jackson Memorial Issue," *Kentucky Folklore Record* 7 (Oct. 1961).
―――. Brochure notes to *Girl of Constant Sorrow* (Folk-Legacy FSA 26).
―――. Brochure notes to *Tipple, Loom & Rail* (Folkways FH 5273).
―――. "A Discography of American Coal Miners' Songs." *Labor History* 2 (1961): 101.
―――. "A Discography (LP) of American Labor Union Songs." *New York Folklore Quarterly* 17 (1961): 186.
―――. "A Folklorist's Creed and Folksinger's Gift." *Appalachian Journal* 7, no. 1-2 (1979-80): 37-45.
―――. *Only a Miner: Studies in Recorded Coal-Mining Songs.* Urbana: University of Illinois Press, 1972.
―――. "Record Review: *Songs and Ballads of the Bituminous Miners* and *Songs and Ballads of the Anthracite Miners,*" *Ethnomusicology* 10 (1966): 361.
Greenway, John. *American Folksongs of Protest.* Philadelphia: University of Pennsylvania Press, 1953.
Harlan & Bell Kentucky, 1931-2: The National Miners Union. Huntington, W.Va.: Appalachian Movement Press.
Hays, Arthur Garfield. "The Right to Get Shot." *Nation,* June 1, 1932, p. 619.
Hays-Bablitz Commission. *Report to the Governor of Kentucky on Hearings Held in Bell County, Kentucky, 1932.* Unpublished, located in the files of the Kentucky National Guard, Lexington.
Hevener, John W. *Which Side Are You On?: The Harlan County Coal Miners, 1931-39.* Urbana: University of Illinois Press, 1978.
Hille, Waldemar. *The People's Song Book.* New York: Boni & Gaer, 1948.
Israel, Boris. "I Get Shot." *New Republic,* Oct. 21, 1931, pp. 256-58.
Jillson, Willard Rouse. "A History of the Coal Industry in Kentucky." *Register of the Kentucky State Historical Society* 20, no. 58 (1922): 21-45.
Johnson, Oakley, "Starvation and the Reds in Kentucky." *Nation,* Feb. 3, 1932, pp. 141-43.
Kahn, Kathy. *Hillbilly Women.* New York: Avon Books, 1974.
Keedy, Allen. "A Preacher in Jail." *Christian Century,* Aug. 26, 1931, pp. 1068-70.
Kentucky. *Commonwealth of Kentucky v. William Hightower.* Transcript of trial. 17 vols. U.S. National Archives, Record Group 60. Justice Department, General Records. Central Files. Classified Subject Files. Enclosures.

Kentucky. Montgomery County Circuit Court. *Commonwealth of Kentucky v. W.B. Jones.* Transcript of trial. 18 vols. U.S. National Archives. Record Group 60. Justice Department, General Records. Central Files. Classified Subject Files. Enclosures.

Kentucky State Reformatory. Prison files of W.B. Jones, 1932-41. La Grange, Kentucky.

Klein, Joe. *Woody Guthrie: A Life.* New York: Alfred A. Knopf, 1980.

Korson, George. *Coal Dust on the Fiddle: Songs and Stories of the Bituminous Industry.* Hatboro, Pa.: Folklore Associates, 1965.

Landsberg, Melvin. *Dos Passos' Path to U.S.A.* Boulder: Colorado Associated University Press, 1972.

Lewis, Helen M. "Occupational Roles and Family Roles: A Study of Coal Miners." Thesis, University of Kentucky, 1970.

Lomax, Alan, et al. *Hard Hitting Songs for Hard Hit People.* New York: Oak Publications, 1967.

McGoldrick, Joseph Daniel. "College Students and Kentucky Miners." *American Scholar* 1 (July 1932): 363-65.

Meyers, Frederic. "The Knights of Labor in the South." *Southern Economic Journal* 6 (1940): 479.

Miles, Emma Bell. *The Spirit of the Mountains.* New York: J. Pott, 1905; rpt. Knoxville: University of Tennessee Press. 1975.

Montell, William Lynwood. *The Saga of Coe Ridge.* Knoxville: University of Tennessee Press, 1970.

Morris, Homer Lawrence. *Plight of the Bituminous Coal Miner.* Philadelphia: University of Pennsylvania Press, 1934.

National Committee for the Defense of Political Prisoners. *Harlan Miners Speak: Report on Terrorism in the Kentucky Coal Fields.* Edited by Theodore Dreiser. New York: Harcourt, Brace, 1932.

Ornitz, Sam. "Bleeding Bowels in Kentucky." *New Masses* 7 (Oct. 1931): 3-4.

Primitive Baptist Hymn and Tune Book. Available from Old School Hymnal Co., Inc., Box 17032, Cincinnati, Ohio 45217.

Rinzler, K. Brochure notes to *Old Mother Hippletoe: Rural and Urban Children's Songs* (New World Records, NW 291) 1978.

Roberts, Leonard. *South from Hell-fer-Sartin: Kentucky Mountain Folklore Tales.* Berea, Ky.: Council of Southern Mountains, 1964.

Ross, Malcolm H. *Machine Age in the Hills.* New York: Macmillan, 1933.

Sherburne, James. *Stand Like Men.* Boston: Houghton, Mifflin, 1973.

Slone, Verna Mae. *What My Heart Wants to Tell.* Washington, D.C.: New Republic Books, 1979.

Spero, Sterling D., and Arnoff, Jacob Broches. "War in the Kentucky Mountains." *American Mercury* 25 (Feb. 1932): 226-33.

Stachel, Jack. "Lessons of Two Recent Strikes." *Communist* (June 1932): 527-36.

Swanberg, W. A. *Dreiser.* New York: Charles Scribners Sons, 1965.

Taylor, Paul Floyd. "Coal and Conflict: The UMWA in Harlan County, 1931-1939." Ph.D. dissertation, University of Kentucky, 1969.

Thomas, Daniel L., and Thomas, Lucy. *Kentucky Superstitions.* Princeton, N.J.: Princeton University Press, 1920.
Thrush, Paul W. *A Dictionary of Mining, Mineral, and Related Terms.* Washington, D.C.: Department of Interior, Bureau of Mines. 1968.
Titler, George J. *Hell in Harlan.* Beckley, W.Va.: BJW Printers, n.d.
"Toothpicks." *New Republic,* Nov. 25, 1931, pp. 32-33.
United Mine Workers of America. *Correspondence, District 19 to National Office, 1929-1932.* Washington, D.C.: UMWA National Headquarters.
U.S. Congress, Senate. Committee on Education and Labor. *Violations of Free Speech and Rights of Labor.* Hearings before a Subcommittee of the Committee on Education and Labor on S.R. 266, 75th Cong., 1st sess. (1937), pts. 9-13.
———. Committee on Manufactures. *Conditions in the Coal Fields in Harlan and Bell Counties, Kentucky.* Hearings before a Subcommittee of the Committee on Manufactures on S.R. 178, 72nd Cong., 1st sess. (1932).
U.S. Department of Labor. Bureau of Labor Statistics. *Hours and Earnings in Bituminous Coal Mining: 1922, 1924 and 1926.* Bulletin no. 454. Washington, D.C.: Government Printing Office, 1927.
———. *Hours and Earnings in Bituminous Coal Mining: 1929.* Bulletin no. 516. Washington, D.C.: Government Printing Office, 1930.
———. "Wages and Hours of Labor." *Monthly Labor Review* 29 (Sept. 1929): 630-79.
———. "Wages and Hours of Labor." *Monthly Labor Review* 33 (Oct. 1931: 910-47.
Walker, Charles Rumford, "'Red' Blood in Kentucky." *Forum* 87 (Jan. 1932): 18-23.
"Which Side Are You On? An Interview with Florence Reece." *Mountain Life and Work* 48 (Mar. 1972): 22-24.
Williams, Cratis. "The Southern Mountaineer in Fact and Fiction." Ph.D. dissertation, New York University, 1961.
Wilson, Edmund. *The Thirties.* New York: Farrar, Strauss, Giroux, 1980.
Workers Music League. *Red Song Book.* New York: Workers Library Publishers, 1932.

Discography

This discography includes recordings of three general types: field recordings Jim Garland, Sarah Ogan Gunning, and Aunt Molly Jackson made for the Archive of American Folk Song (since 1955, the Archive of Folk Song) from 1935 to 1940; their commercially available records; and recordings other singers have made of the Garlands' songs, both for the national archive and for record companies.

Nearly all the AFS recordings can be found in *Check List of Recorded Songs in the English Language in the Archive of American Folk Song to July, 1940* (Washington, D.C., 1942) and *Supplementary Listing of Recorded Songs in the English Language in the Library of Congress Archive of Folk Song Through Recording No. AFS 4332 (October 1940)*, (Washington, D.C., 1977). In the AFS geographical listing, Aunt Molly Jackson's songs appear under Clay County, Kentucky, while Jim's and Sarah's songs are divided, some listed under Pineville, Kentucky, others under New York, New York. A few of Aunt Molly Jackson's songs omitted from the Library of Congress checklists appear in Archie Green's discography of Aunt Molly's material, *Kentucky Folklore Record* 7 (Oct. 1961): 162. These oversights may mean that a few of Jim's and Sarah's pre-1940 recordings too have been omitted from the checklists and therefore from this compilation. I have adopted for this discography the AFS abbreviations of the collectors' names — Alan Lomax, John A. Lomax, and Mary Elizabeth Barnicle — and I have marked with an asterisk those songs preceded on the recordings by spoken, introductory material. Because no reference work has catalogued AFS materials recorded since 1940, this discography does not document such recordings.

For locating the Garlands' songs as recorded by other singers, I have three generous experts to thank: Richard Reuss, whose labor song discography is forthcoming from the Institute of Labor and Industrial Relations at the University of Michigan; Joseph Hickerson, head of the Archive of Folk Songs; and Archie Green, particularly for his "Discography of Coal Miners' Songs," *Labor History* 2 (1961): 101.

One final problem arose in assigning songs to songwriters. For example, in the liner notes of John Greenway's *Songs and Stories of Aunt Molly Jackson*, Aunt Molly claims to have written both "Dreadful Memories" and "Hard Times in Coleman's Mines." Archie Green and others feel certain that Sarah Gunning is responsible for "Dreadful Memories"; Jim takes credit for "Hard Times in Coleman's Mines" in his book. This being an appendix to Jim Garland's work, I have given him credit for all the songs he claims; indeed I have found no evidence that Aunt Molly did write "Hard Times." To ascertain the authorship of other songs, I have trusted in Archie Green, a meticulous scholar and militant friend. Song titles marked with double asterisks are the compositions of the singer under whose name they appear. Other songs (with a few exceptions, as Florence Reese's "Which Side Are You On?") are either traditional or of unknown composition.

I especially thank Mark Wilson of the University of California at San Diego for getting Jim Garland on record and for helping me so readily.

In the course of assembling this list, I have heard many tributes to the Garlands' music. But to my mind, none is more vivid than the present-day story of musician and activist Tom Juravich. With gratitude, I quote from his letter of April 15, 1982.

> I am happy to report that Jim Garland's music is quite alive up here in New England. I've been involved with the U.A.W. with a strike up here in Westfield, Massachusetts which is now in its 14th month. It's very much a classic case of union busting, where the old timers who built the company were forced out on strike, only to be replaced by young scabs at minimum wage. Very early on, I started singing "I Don't Want Your Millions, Mister" (which tells their story better than any song I know) and before long, they adopted it as *their* song about the struggle. It became almost as popular as "Solidarity Forever."
>
> As the strike continued with no end in sight (and the failure of most traditional tactics), we formed something called the entertainment committee. Its purpose was to follow the owner of the mill, and at every opportunity sing for him "Millions, Mister." We even just "happened" to be in the same restaurant as him for lunch and even serenaded him there. So, much more than just being sung, Jim's music is part of the ongoing struggle of members of Local 430 to get the justice they deserve.

JIM GARLAND

Field Recordings in the Archive of Folk Song

"Ask That Sinner to the Mourner's Bench" (sung with Arthur Williams)
    Pineville, MEB, 1938, 1968 Bl
"Canaan Land Where the Soul of Man Never Dies" (sung with Sarah Garland)
    Pineville, MEB, 1938, 2022 B
"Death of Two Lovers"
    Pineville, AL, 2008 B1
"Forsake Not the Way"
    NY, AL, 1937, 1953 A2
"Give Me Back My Job Again"**
    NY, AL, 1937, 1946 B
"God Gave Noah the Rainbow Sign" (sung with Sarah Garland)
    Pineville, MEB, 1938, 2024 A
"Had a Little Dog, Its Name Was Rain"
    Pineville, MEB, 1938, 2008 A4

"Hard Times in Foxridge Mines "**
  NY, AL, 1937, 1950 A2
"How about You?"**
  NY, AL, 1937, 1038 B2
"I'll Be Satisfied" (sung with Sarah Garland)
  Pineville, MEB, 1938, 2020 B
"It Is Love" (sung with Sarah Garland)
  Pineville, MEB, 1938, 2024 B
"Look for Me I'll Be There"
  NY, AL, 1937, 1949 B
"Mother's Good-Bye" (sung with Sarah Garland)
  Pineville, MEB, 1938, 2023 B
"Nobody Works but Father"
  Pineville, MEB, 1938, 2007 A2
"One More Trip, Said the Sleepy-Headed Driver"
  NY, AL, 1937, 1950 A1
"Preacher Went A'Huntin'"
  Pineville, MEB, 1938, 2007 A1
"Rock of Ages" (sung with Sarah Garland and Huddie Ledbetter)
  Pineville, MEB, 1938, 2023 A
"Shake Hands with Mother Again" (sung with Sarah Garland)
  Pineville, MEB, 1938, 2022A
"Silver Daggers"
  Pineville, MEB, 1938, 2008 A3
"Sugar in the Gourd"
  Pineville, MEB, 1938, 2008 A2
"Telephone to Glory" (JG and Mamie Garland sing background to John Hensley, with guitar) Pineville, MEB, 1938, 1977 B
"Welcome the Traveler Home"**
  NY, AL, 1937, 1947 A
"What a Wonderful Thought"
  NY, AL, 1937, 1951 B2
"Which Side Are You On?"
  NY, AL, 1937, 1951 B1
"White Slave, The"
  NY, AL, 1937, 1953 A1
"Wild Bill Jones"
  Pineville, MEB, 1939, 2008 A1

Commercial Recordings

"Ballad of Harry Simms, The"**
"I Don't Want Your Millions, Mister"**
  on *Newport Broadside: Topical Songs at the Newport Folk Festival, 1963,* Vanguard VRS 9144

"Down in the Valley to Pray"
"God Moves in a Windstorm"
   JG sings with Sarah Ogan Gunning on her LP *Silver Dagger,* Rounder 0051
"One-Eyed Riley"
"Crawling and Creeping"
"Granny Hare"
"Little Girl from Arkansas"
"Ryestraw"
"She Went around the Huckleberry Bush"
"Blackeyed Susie"
"Old Granny Cripplecunt"
"God Damn Her Old Soul"
"I Sent a Rabbit for a Bucket of Beer"
"A Conversation between President Buchanan and Queen Victoria"
   on *Just Something My Uncle Told Me: Blaggardy Folk Songs from the Southern United States,* Rounder 0141. Edited by Mark Wilson.

His Songs Recorded by Other Artists

"Death of Harry Simms"
— on John Greenway, *American Industrial Folk Songs,* Riverside RLP 12-607, 1955.
— on John Greenway, *The Songs and Stories of Aunt Molly Jackson,* Folkways FH 5457, 1961
— on Pete Seeger, Charter 25 and Charter C-45-B
— on Pete Seeger, *American Industrial Ballads,* Folkways FH 5251
— on Pete Seeger, *American History in Ballad and Song–Vols. 1,2,* Folkways FH 5801, 5802
— on Pete Seeger, *Essential Pete Seeger,* Vanguard (S)VSD-97/98, 1978

"Harry Simms"
— on Pete Seeger, *Songs of Struggle and Protest, 1930-1950,* Folkways FH 5233
— on Pete Seeger, *Dangerous Songs!?,* Columbia CL 2503/CS 9303
— on Pete Seeger, *Canto Obrero,* Americanito A 1004

"Ballad of Harry Simms"
   on Pete Seeger, *Circles and Seasons,* Warner Brothers WBR (S) K-3329, 1979

"Hard Times in Coleman's Mines"
— on John Greenway, *American Industrial Folksongs,* Riverside RLP 12-607, 1955
— on Aunt Molly Jackson, *Aunt Molly Jackson,* Library of Congress Recordings, Rounder 1002
— on Mike Seeger, *Tipple, Loom & Rail,* Folkways FH 5273

"How about You?"
   sung by Pete Seeger on *What Now People, No. 1,* Paredon Records, P-2001

"I Don't Want Your Millions, Mister"
— on Pete Seeger, *Songs of Struggle and Protest, 1930-50,* Folkways FH 5233
— on Barbara Dane, *I Hate the Capitalist System,* Paredon Records P-1024, 1973

— sung by the Almanac Singers on *Brother, Can You Spare a Dime*, New World Records, NW 270, 1977
— sung by Pete Seeger on *Hootenanny*, Prestige/Folklore 14020
— on Almanac Singers, *Talking Union*, Folkways FH 5273
— on Tom Juravich, B Side of 45 rpm *Trying to Break My Union*, U.A.W. Records, 1981
— on Tom Juravich, *Rising Again: Union Songs for the 80's*, U.A.W. Records, 1982
— sung by Tilman Cadle, AFS 1401

"That 25 Cents That You Paid" ("Sad the Day")
as sung by Sarah Gunning on *Come All You Coal Miners*, a collection of coal mining songs, Rounder 4005

SARAH OGAN GUNNING

Field Recordings in the Archive of Folk Song

"Come All You Coal Miners"**
NY, AL, 1937, 1944 A
"Come on, Friends, and Let's Go Down"
NY, AL, 1937, 1944 B1
"I Am a Girl of Constant Sorrow"**
NY, AL, 1937, 1945 A
"I Hate the Capitalist System"**
NY, AL, 1937, 1943 A
"I'm Goin' to Organize, Baby Mine"**
NY, AL, 1937, 1952 A2 & B1
"The Love Bug"
NY, AL, 1937, 1945 B1
"Old Faithful Alarm Clock, The"
NY, AL, 1937, 1952 B2
"Old Time Religion" (sung with Huddie Ledbetter)
Pineville, MEB, 1938, 2020 A
"That Old Feeling"
NY, AL, 1937, 1945 B2
"Thinking Tonight on an Old Southern Town"**
NY, AL, 1937, 1943 B
"This Good Union Spirit Let It Fall on You"
NY, AL, 1937, 1952 A1

(see also AFS recordings listed under "Jim Garland")

Commercial Recordings

"I Am a Girl of Constant Sorrow"**
"Loving Nancy"
"Old Jack Frost"
"May I Go with You Johnny"
"The Hand of God on the Wall"
"Down on the Picket Line"**

"I Hate the Company Bosses"** "Captain Devin"
"I'm Going to Organize"** "Gee Whiz, What They Done to Me"
"Christ Was a Wayworn Traveler" "Davy Crockett"
"Why Do You Stand There in the Rain" "Battle of Mill Spring"
"Dreadful Memories"** "Just the Same Today"
"Old Southern Town"** "Sally"
"I Have a Letter from My Father" "Oh Death"
    Girl of Constant Sorrow, Folk-Legacy FSA 26, 1965

"I Am a Traveling Creature" "The Miller's Will"
"Mister Bartender" "Papa's Billy Goat"
"I Love Little Willie" "The Drunkard's Dream"
"The Silver Dagger" "The House Carpenter"
"I Hear the Low Winds Sweeping" "'Indian' Songs"
"Davy Crockett" "Ring Dang Rantigan"
"The Lonesome Dove" "The Downward Road"
"I Hate the Capitalist System"** "God Moves in a Windstorm"
"Down in the Valley to Pray"
    The Silver Dagger, Rounder 0051

"Come All You Coal Miners"**
"Dreadful Memories"**
"That 25 Cents That You Paid"
    on *Come All You Coal Miners,* an LP of coal mining songs, Rounder 4005

"Come All You Coal Miners" (reissue of Library of Congress recording)
    on *Oh, My Little Darling,* New World Records, NW 245, 1977

"Captain Devin"
    on *Traditional Music on Rounder: A Sampler,* Rounder 0145. Edited by Mark Wilson

Her Songs Recorded by Other Artists

"Babe of Mine"
    on Woody Guthrie, Keynote Records, 1941

"Come All You Coal Miners"
    on Mike Seeger, *Tipple, Loom & Rail,* Folkways FH 5273

"Dreadful Memories"
— on John Greenway, *American Industrial Folk Songs,* Riverside RLP 12-607, 1955
— on John Greenway, *The Songs and Stories of Aunt Molly Jackson,* Folkways FH 5457, 1961
— on Kathy Kahn, *The Working Girl: Women's Songs from Mountains, Mines and Mills,* Voyager VRLP 3055, 1972

"Girl of Constant Sorrow"
— on Bonnie Dobson, *Dear Companion,* Prestige PRS 7801
— on Barbara Dane, *Anthology of American Folk Song,* Tradition TRS 2072

"I Hate the Capitalist System"
— on Barbara Dane, *I Hate the Capitalist System,* Paredon Records, P-1024, 1973
— on Kathy Kahn, *The Working Girl: Women's Songs from Mountains, Mines and Mills,* Voyager VRLP 3055, 1972

AUNT MOLLY JACKSON

Field Recordings in the Archive of Folk Song

"Ain't Nobody's Business but My Own"
  NY, AL & MEB, 1935, 828 A1
"Amazing Grace"
  NY, AL & MEB, 1935, 821 B2
"Archie D."
  NY, AL, 1939, 3337 A&B
"Autobiography of Aunt Molly Jackson" (sung and spoken)
  NY, AL, 1939, 2534 A, 2588
"Baker and White Feud Song"
  NY, AL, 1939, 2588 A1
"Ballad of Lazarus, The"
  NY, AL, 1939, 2583 A & B1
"Barbara Allen"
  NY, AL & MEB, 1935, 824A
"Beauty Bride, The"
  NY, AL, 1935, 825 A4
"Beauty Bride, The"
  NY, AL, 1939, 2541 A
"Black-Eyed Nancy"
  NY, AL, 1939, 2546 B
"Blind Girl, The"
  NY, AL & MEB, 1938, 825 A1
"Boston Burglar, The"
  NY, AL & MEB, 1935, 826 A1
"Brisk Young Farmer, The"
  NY, AL, 1939, 2551 B
"Brisk Young Soldier, The"
  NY, AL, 1939, 2570 A
"Brown Girl, The"
  NY, AL & MEB, 1935, 825 B2
"Buck Creek Gals"
  NY, AL, 1939, 2547 B2
"Butcher Boy, The"
  NY, AL & MEB, 1935, 827 B1
"Casey Jones"
  NY, AL, 1939, 2573 A3 & B1

"Charming Betsy"
   NY, AL, 1939, 2554 A2
"Charming Billy"
   NY, AL, 1939, 2547 B1
"CIO Union Song"**
   NY, AL, 1939, 2534 B
"Christmas Eve in the East Side"**
   NY, AL, 1939, 2537 A2 & B
"Coal Creek Disaster"
   NY, AL, 1939, 2539 A
"Coal Miner's Child"
   NY, AL, 1939, 2575 A & B
"Come All You Fair and Tender Ladies"
   NY, AL, 1939, 2552 A, B1 & 2, 2553 A
"Come with Me to the Old Churchyard"
   NY, AL, 1939, 2579 B
"Crossbones Skully"**
   NY, AL, 1939, 2556A
"Cuckoo, The"
   NY, AL & MEB, 1935, 823 B1 & 2
"Cumberland Gap"
   NY, AL & MEB, 1935, 826 A3
"Darling Cory"
   NY, AL & MEB, 1936, 828 B1
"Day Is Past, the Shade of Night Draws Near"
   NY, AL, 1939, 3340 A2 & B1
"Dear Friends, Farewell"
   NY, AL, 1939, 2562 B, 2563 A1
"Death of Edward Hawkins, The"*
   NY, AL, 1939, 2559 B
"Death of Harry Simms, The"
   NY, AL, 1939, 2536 A & B
"Devil and the Farmer, The"
   NY, AL, 1939, 2569 B
"Dishonest Miller, The"
   NY, AL, 1939, 2553 B
"Dog and Gun, The"
   NY, AL, 1939, 2574 A & B
"Dog and Gun"
   MEB, 1939, AFS 18, 963, LWO 9417, A9
"Don't Believe in a Woman, You're Lost if You Do"
   NY, AL, 1939, 2568 A
"Don't Let Your Woman Have Her Way"
   NY, AL & MEB, 1935, 824 B1
"Down in Karo"
   NY, AL, 1939, 2554 A1

"Dry Bones"
    NY, AL & MEB, 1935, 828 A4
"Easter Ballad, The"
    NY, AL, 1939, 2582 B
"East Ohio Miners' Strike"
    NY, AL, 1937, 1940 B
"Ellen Smith"
    NY, AL & MEB, 1935, 822 B2
"Farewell, Sweet Jane"
    NY, AL & MEB, 1935, 825 B1
"Fare Ye Well, Old Elie Branch"**
    NY, AL, 1937, 1939 B
"Flora Dean"
    NY, AL, 1939, 2555 A
"Frankie and Albert"
    Wilton, Conn., JAL, 1935, 73 A2
"Frog Went A'Courting"
    Wilton, Conn., JAL, 1935, 73 B2
"Gambling Man, The "
    NY, AL & MEB, 1935, 826 B1
Ghost Stories (spoken)
    NY, AL, 1939, 2567 A & B
"God's Getting Weary with Your Wicked Ways"
    NY, AL & MEB, 1935, 821 B1
"Goose Chewed Tobacco"
    NY, AL, 1939, 2572 A3
"Green Corn"*
    NY, AL, 1939, 2549 B, 2550 A1
"Happy Chandler"
    MEB, AFS 18,963, LWO 9417, A6
" 'Happy' Chandler Song"
    NY, AL, 1939, 2545 A
"Hard Times in Coleman's Mines"*
    NY, AL, 1939, 2534, 2535 A
"Hark the Voice of Jesus Crying"
    NY, AL, 1939, 3339 B, 3340 Al
"Homesick Blues"
    MEB, 1939, AFS 18,963, LWO 9417, A12
"Honey, Take a Whiff on Me"
    NY, AL & MEB, 1935, 820 B2
"House Carpenter, The"
    NY, AL & MEB, 1935, 821 A2
"How Firm a Foundation"
    NY, AL & MEB, 1935, 821 B3
"How Tedious and Tasteless the Hours"
    NY, AL & MEB, 1935, 820 A1

218 DISCOGRAPHY

"How Uncle Wilts Lost His Pants When He Went A'Courtin'" (spoken)
    NY, AL, 1939, 2564 A
"How Uncle Wilts Was Churned Up for the Devil"
    NY, AL, 1939, 2564 B
"Hungry Disgusted Blues"**
    NY, AL, 1939, 2538 A
"Hymn"
    NY, AL & MEB, 1935, 820 A4
"Ida Red"
    NY, AL & MEB, 1935, 820 B1
"I Don't Know What You Stay Here For"
    NY, AL & MEB, 1935, 821 B4
"I Got up This Morning, Put My Clothes on Wrong"*
    NY, AL, 1939, 2558 A & B
"I Love Coal Miners, I Do"**
    NY, AL, 1937, 1942 A
"I Love Coal Miners, I Do"**
    NY, AL, 1939, 2538 B
"I Married Me a Wife"
    NY, AL, 1939, 2573 A2
"I Want to See My Mother When She Enters In"
    NY, AL, 1939, 3338 B2, 3339 A
"I Was Born about Four Thousand Years Ago"
    NY, AL & MEB, 1935, 827 B4
"Jesse James"
    Wilton, Conn., JAL, 1935, 73 A3
"Jim Douglas"
    MEB, 1939, AFS 18,963, LWO 9417, A10
"Joe Bowers"
    NY, AL & MEB, 1935, 827 A3
"John Garland's Member Lesson"*
    NY, AL, 1939, 2572 B2 & 2573 A1
"John Henry"
    NY, AL & MEB, 1935, 828 B3
"John Henry"*
    NY, AL, 1939, 2551 A1
"Johnny Randall"
    NY, AL, 1939, 2545 B1, 2546 A
"Join the CIO"**
    NY, AL, 1937, 1939 A1
"Joseph and Mary"
    NY, AL, 1939, 2582 A
"Katy Dorsey"
    NY, AL, 1939, 3334 B
"Katy Dory"
    NY, AL & MEB, 1935, 828 A2

"Kentucky Miners' Dreadful Fate"
    NY, AL, 1937, 1940 A, 1941 B
"Kentucky Soldier, The"
    NY, AL, 1939, 2555 B, 2557 A
"Lady Claire"
    NY, AL, 1939, 2554 A & B
"Lady Gay, A"
    NY, AL, 1939, 2581 A & B
"Lady Marg'et and Sweet Willie"
    NY, AL, 1939, 2568 B, 2569 A
"Lady Nancy"
    NY, AL, 1939, 2588 B
"Land of the Yeahoes" (spoken)
    NY, AL, 1939, 2565, B
"Let Me Be Your Teddy"
    NY, AL, 1939, 2537 A1
"Little Dove, The"*
    NY, AL, 1939, 2579 A
"Little Mohee, The"
    NY, AL & MEB, 1935, 827 A2
"Little Scotchee, The"
    NY, AL & MEB, 1935, 825 B3
"Little Talk with Jesus, A"
    NY, AL, 1939, 2583 B2
"Liza Jane"
    NY, AL, 1939, 2551, A2
"Lonesome Jailhouse Blues"**
    NY, AL, 1939, 2535 B
"Lonesome Road"
    NY, AL & MEB, 1935, 820 B3
"Lord Bateman"
    NY, AL & MEB, 1935, 822 A1 & B1
"Lord Bateman"
    MEB, 1939, AFS 18,963, LWO 9417, A11
"Lordy, Lordy"
    NY, AL, 1939, 2549 A
"Merchant's Son and the Parson's Daughter, The"
    NY, AL, 1939, 3336 B
"Miller, The"
    NY, AL & MEB, 1935, 823 A1
"Monologue on Dancing after Marriage"
    NY, AL, 1939, 3338 A2 & B 1
"Monologue on Dulcimers and Tongue Bows"
    NY, AL, 1939, 2559 A
"Monologue on Feuds and on Their Causes"
    NY, AL, 1939, 2586 A & B, 2587 A & B, 2588 A

"Monologue on Her Early Life"
   NY, AL, 1939, 2541 B1
"Monologue on Holiness Church"
   NY, AL, 1939, 2576 B2, 2577 A & B, 2578 A1, 2 & B
"Monologue on Little Funny Songs"
   NY, AL, 1939, 2572 A1
"Monologue on Square Dancing"
   NY, AL, 1939, 2565 A
"Monlogue on Violence"
   NY, AL, 1939, 2385 B
"Moonshine Bill"
   NY, AL, 1939, 2543 B1
"Mr. Cundiff"**
   NY, AL, 1939, 2541 B2, 2542 A & B, 2543 A
"Murder of Harry Simms, The"
   NY, AL & MEB, 1935, 821 A2
"My Lovely Bright-Eyed Jane"
   NY, AL & MEB, 1935, 827 A4
"My Warfare Will Soon Be Ended"
   NY, AL, 1939, 2563 A2
"New River Train, The"
   Wilton, Conn., JAL, 1935, 73 B3
"Nothing Goes Hard with Me"
   NY, AL, 1939, 2537 B
"Old Joe Clark"
   NY, AL, MEB, 1935, 823 B4
"Oma Wise"
   NY, AL & MEB, 1935, 824 B2
"Oma Wise"
   NY, AL, 1939, 3340, 3341 A
"One Morning in May"
   Wilton, Conn., JAL, 1935, 73 B1
"Orphan Girl, The"
   NY, AL & MEB, 1935, 825 B4
"Outshine the Glittering Sun"
   NY, AL & MEB, 1935, 821 A3
"Poor Stranger"
   Wilton, Conn., JAL, 1935, 73 A1
"Pretty Polly"*
   NY, AL & MEB, 1935, 823 A2
"Pretty Polly"
   NY, AL, 1939, 2550 A2 & B
"Prisoners' Call, The"
   NY, AL, 1937, 1942 B
"Rich Irish Lady, The"
   NY, AL, 1939, 2584 A & B1

"River Is Chilly and Cold, The"
  NY, AL & MEB, 1935, 820 A3
"Roll on, Buddy"
  NY, AL, 1939, 2548 A & B
"Roving Gambler, The"
  NY, AL & MEB, 1935, 827 B2
"Rye Whiskey"
  NY, AL & MEB, 1935, 828 A3
"Shooting of His Dear, The"
  NY, AL, 1939, 2576 A & B1
"Silver Dagger, The"
  NY, AL, 1939, 2540 A & B
"Skip to My Lou"
  NY, AL & MEB, 1935 826 B2
"Skip to My Lou"
  NY, AL, 1939, 3335 B
"Skip to My Lou, My Darling"
  NY, AL, 1939, 2563 B
"Soldier and the Lady, The"*
  NY, AL, 1939, 2560 A & B
"Some Mother's Boy Tonight"
  NY, AL, 1939, 2571 B2
"State of Arkansas, The"
  NY, AL & MEB, 1935, 827 A1
"Sugar Babe"
  NY, AL & MEB, 1935, 827 B5
"Sweet Irene"
  NY, AL, 1939, 2571 A & B1
"Sweet Willie"
  NY, AL & MEB, 1935, 828 B4
"Taggy Jackson's Story"*
  NY, AL, 1939, 2584 B2, 2585 A
"Take Me Home, Boys, Take Me Home"
  MEB, 1939, AFS 18,963, LWO 9414, A8
"Ta-Ra-Ra-Boom-De-Aye"
  NY, AL & MEB, 1935, 823 B3
"Tee-Dup, Tee-Dup"
  NY, AL, 1939, 2572 A2
"Ten Thousand Miles"
  Wilton, Conn., JAL, 1935, 73 A4
"Ten Thousand Miles."
  NY, AL & MEB, 1935, 825 A3
"Ten Thousand Miles."*
  NY, AL, 1939, 2570 B
"Texas Rangers, The"
  NY, AL, 1939, 2556 B, 2562 AL

"Toasts"*
  NY, AL, 1939, 2572 B1
"Way Down in Karo"
  NY, AL, 1939, 2562 A2
"Weavily Wheat"
  NY, AL, & MEB, 1935, 826 A2
"We Have Game Today"
  NY, AL & MEB, 1935, 826 B3
"We'll Be Happy in the Kingdom"
  NY, AL & MEB, 1935, 820 A2
"When You Hear My Bulldog Barking"
  NY, AL, 1939, 3338 A1
"White Pilgrim, The"
  NY, AL 1939, 2580 B
"Wicked Polly"
  NY, AL & MEB, 1935, 825 A2
"Wild Bill Jones"
  NY, AL & MEB, 1935, 828 B2
"Wild Bill Jones"
  NY, AL, 1939, 2554 B
"William and Nancy"
  NY, AL, 1939, 3335 A
"William Hall"
  NY, AL, 1939, 3336 A
Witch Stories (spoken)
  NY, AL, 1939, 2556 A & B
"With His Old Shoe Boots and His Leggings"
  MEB, 1939, AFS 18,963, LWO 9414, A7
"With His Old Shoe Boots and Leggins"
  NY, AL, 1939, 2547 A

Commercial Recordings

"Hard Times in Coleman's Mines" "Crossbones Skully"**
"Lonesome Jailhouse Blues"** "Fare Thee Well Old Ely Branch"**
"I Love Coal Miners, I Do"** "Join the CIO"**
"Let Me Be Your Teddy" "Prisoner's Call"
"Christmas Eve in the East Side"** "The Lone Pilgrim"
"Witch Stories" "Holiness Church Monologue"
"Hungry Disgusted Blues"** "Just A Little Talk With Jesus"
  Aunt Molly Jackson, Rounder 1002, n.d., Library of Congress Recordings.

"The Little Dove"
"Ten Thousand Miles"
  on *Anglo-American Shanties, Lyric Songs, Dance Tunes and Spirituals,* AFS L2, recorded by Alan Lomax, Herbert Halpert, and others, 1937-41.

"Lord Bateman"
"Lazarus"
>on *Child Ballads Traditional in the United States (I),* AFS L57, recorded in various parts of the United States by several collectors, 1935-46. Edited by Bertrand H. Bronson.

"Barbara Allen"
>on *Versions and Variants of "Barbara Allen,"* AFS L54, recorded in various parts of the United States by several collectors, 1933-54. Edited by Charles Seeger.

"Roll on, Buddy"
>on *Railroad Songs and Ballads,* AFS L61, recorded in various parts of the United States by several collectors. Edited by Archie Green.

"I Am a Union Woman"**
"Poor Miner's Farewell"**
"Dishonest Miller"
"The Birth of Robin Hood"
"Hunger"
"Mr. Cundiff, Won't You Turn Me Loose?"**
"Death of Harry Simms"
"Dreadful Memories"
"Pistol-Packin' Woman"**
"Hungry Ragged Blues"**
"Hard Times in Coleman's Mines"

>*The Songs and Stories of Aunt Molly Jackson,* stories told by Aunt Molly Jackson, songs sung by John Greenway, Folkways FH 5457, 1961.

Her Songs Recorded by Other Artists

"Ely Branch"
>on Fleming Brown, *Fleming Brown,* Folk-Legacy, FSI 4

"Fare Ye Well, Old Ely Branch"
>on Pete Seeger, *American Industrial Ballads,* Folkways FH 5251, 1956

"Hard Working Miner"
>— on Mike Seeger, *Tipple, Loom and Rail,* Folkways FH 5273
>— sung by G.C. Gartin on *Songs and Ballads of the Bituminous Miners,* AFS 160, 1965. Edited by George Korson.

"I Am a Union Woman" ("Join the CIO")
>on John Greenway, *American Industrial Folk Songs,* Riverside RLP 12-607, 1955.

"Join the CIO"
>as sung by Mike Seeger on New Lost City Ramblers, *Songs from the Depression,* Folkways FH 5264, 1959.

"Join the NMU"
>on Robin Flower, *More Than Friends,* Spaniel Records 1916114, 1979.

"Poor Miner's Farewell"
>on Hedy West, *Hedy West,* Vanguard VRS 9124

Index

Aid to Dependent Children, 192
Almanac Singers, xvi, 184, 186
"Amazing Grace," 84
American Federation of Labor (AF of L), xxvi, 132
American Red Cross, 136
Appalachian Coal Operators Association, 40
Arjay, Ky., 118, 120, 144, 145, 151-52, 197

Bailey, Custer, 127
Baldwin, Elizabeth, 168, 145-46
"Ballad of Harry Simms, The," xvi, xvii, xviii, 169-71
banjo, 13-14
Baptist church, 5, 80, 81, 83-84, 86, 131. See also Missionary Baptist church; Primitive Baptist church
"Barbara Ellen," 194
Barbourville, Ky., 77, 167
Barnicle, Mary Elizabeth, 183, 184
bartering, 74, 76-77, 78
"Battle above the Clouds," 21
Bell County, Ky., 39, 81, 123, 137, 140, 142, 150, 165
Berea College, 52
Bible, 29, 30, 81, 82
Birge, Silus, 177
blacklist, xxii, 94, 139, 142, 148, 156
black lung, 105, 107, 186
black miners, 113, 114-15, 136
Black Mountain, xxiv, 133, 134, 140, 141. See also Peabody Coal Company
Blair, John Henry, xxii, xxiv-xxv, 137, 141, 142

Blanche, Ky., 123, 127
bloody flux, 88, 119, 146-47
booms, 137
Boone, Daniel, 3
Boonesboro, Ky., 3
Borich, Frank, 148, 166, 176
Boston, Mass., 171-72
Bracket, Tom, 45, 97
Breem, Bill, 177
Bronx Coliseum, 169
Brophy, John, 131, 132
Broun, Haywood, 173
Browder, Earl, 177, 181
Brush Creek, Ky., 155, 162, 163-64, 165, 166
"Buddy, Won't You Line That Track," 23
Bundy, Ford, 152
Burns, Jimmy, 168
Burton, Dorothy, 183
Burton, Joe, 139
Burton, Si, 177

Cadle, Tilman, 37, 111-12, 135-37, 140, 141, 168, 169, 177; and the National Miners Union, 144, 150, 151, 156, 181, 198; and the United Mine Workers, 112-13, 149
Cafe Society, 183
captive mines, xix-xx, 135-36
carnivals, 14, 45, 74-75
Cary, Ky., 49, 113, 114-15, 127, 146, 148, 154, 155
Castro mines, 99, 142, 144-45
checkweighman, 140, 146
Chenoa Hollow, Ky., 46
Cherokee Indians, 3, 4, 32

Chevrolet mines, 109
Childers, Bob, 133, 134, 137, 149
child labor, 89, 106, 127
children's games, 53-56, 193-94
Civilian Conservation Corps (CCC), 191
Civil rights movement, 201
Civil War, 18, 21, 22, 34, 74
Clark, Ollie, 99
clean-up system, 136
coal, xix, 105, 139
Coal Creek, Tenn., 37-38
coal mining:
—camps, xxii-xxiii, 14-15, 34, 61, 78-79, 102-3; entertainment in, 52-56, 58-60; food in, 64-65, 66; funerals in, 89, 128-29; housing in, 50, 191; race relations in, 114-15; women's work, 64-66, 120, 126. *See also* children's games; company stores; housing; marriage
—hazards, 97-98, 100-101, 103, 119-20; machine-related, 105, 106, 138; slate falls, 93, 100-101, 107; windies, 91. *See also* Workman's Compensation
—industry, ix, xi, xvii-xix, xx, 22, 24, 102, 111; employment in, xx, xxi, 88; markets, xiii, ix, xx, 40, 135; production, xxii, 36, 110
—mechanization, 103-4, 136; effects of, xi-xii, xxi, 99-100, 103, 191; machinery, 92, 93, 104-5, 106, 107-8; miners' equipment, xxiii, 90, 106
—methods, 35, 36, 90-92, 95; faulty, 96-97; shooting coal, 35-36, 90-92, 106-7; ventilation, 89, 94-95
—occupations, 28-29, 89, 98, 109, 138; entry driving, 92-93, 97; foremen, 101, 126-28, 134; gobbing slate, 94; hostling, 105; laying track, 104, 108; machine men, 104-5, 109; mucking crew, 46; mule driving, 36, 95-96, 98-100, 103; steel driving, 92-93; timbering, 96, 128, 134; trapping, 89, 103
—operators: early, 25-26, 35; large,

xiii, xviii, 40, 89, 103, 110, 123, 135 (*see also* Peabody Coal Company); small, 26, 35, 36-37, 40, 40-41, 109-10, 135, 139, 191 (*see also* Coleman, C.R.)
—wages, 88, 108, 112-13, 127, 134, 136, 142, 144, 199; cuts in, xii, xxiii, 115, 137, 140, 146
Coleman, C.R., 25-26, 109-10, 112, 123, 126-27, 155
Collett, Silus, 49
Communist party, xxviii, 177, 198, 199; Jim Garland and, xvi, 153, 183, 198-99; and the National Miners Union, xiv, xxvi, 154, 164; red-baiting, 149, 152, 154, 158, 164, 165, 190, 199
company stores, xxiii, 25-26, 40-41, 64, 88, 89, 119, 136, 144, 145, 156
Congress of Industrial Organizations (CIO), xxviii-xxix
contract mining, 100, 109
Corbin, Ky., 125
corn, 9, 11
Curtz, Tom, 151

Daily Worker, 149, 150, 155
Dana, Henry Wadsworth Longfellow, 171-72
dancing, 85-87
Daniels, Jim, 138, 141
"Darling Cory," 14
Debs, Eugene V., 34, 111
Depression, xiii, 135, 171, 173-74, 182, 189, 190, 191-92
Detroit-Edison Company, xix-xx
doctors, 5, 32, 33, 120; in coal camps, xxiii, 38, 89, 119
Dorton Branch, Ky., 181
Dos Passos, John, xxvii
Dreiser, Theodore, xxvii, 149-50, 172
Dwyer, Lawrence "Peggy," 137, 139, 149, 179-80

East Bernstadt, Ky., 26-27, 38
education, xxiii, 11-12, 34, 52, 67, 124, 197-98
Elliot, Jim (uncle), 139-40
Evans, Herndon, 154, 155, 158

Evarts, Ky., 133, 136; Battle of, xxiv-xxv, 141
Ex-Servicemen's League, 173

"Fare Thee Well, Old Ely Branch," 64
Farmer-Labor party, 111, 201
farmers, 88-89, 115-16, 148, 152, 178, 190
farming, 9, 18-19, 26, 124. *See also* sharecropping; tobacco
Federal Coal Corporation, 146-47
feuds, 19-20, 22, 167
50/50 Club, 187
First Baptist Church of Pineville, 165
Fisher, Martha (aunt), 32, 33
Folkways Records, xvii, 87, 187
"Foolish Jack and Wise Peter," 58-59
Ford Motor Company, xix, 40, 140
Foster, Stephen, 185
Foster, William Z., 177
Fourmile, Ky., viii, 43, 70, 155, 157
Fox Ridge, Ky., 52
Frank, Waldo: committee of, xxvii, 165, 166, 169, 171, 198
Frankfort, Ky., 137, 179-81

Garland, Betty (daughter), 184-85
Garland, Bill (brother), 31, 80, 84, 89, 91, 130, 147, 152
Garland, Bob (brother), x, 27, 46, 52, 89, 93
Garland, Deborah Robinson (father's first wife), 26-27
Garland, Ed (nephew), 177, 181
Garland, Elizabeth Lucas (mother), 27, 34, 44, 52, 56, 57, 62, 126
Garland, Hazel (wife), 137, 138-39, 182, 183, 185-86, 186-87: family life, 123-24, 124-26, 172, 178, 179, 181-82; involvement in 1931-32 strike, 138, 146, 147, 152, 157, 163, 166, 167, 171, 177, 188; religion, 85, 130-31
Garland, Jess (cousin), 117-18
Garland, Jim: fund-raising, 158, 171, 172; mining, 52, 89-90, 91, 97, 105, 108, 113, 126-27, 134, 140, 142, 178; and music, 81, 84-85, 169, 183-84, 185, 187-88; and the National Miners Union, 143-44, 145, 146-48, 150-52, 155-58, 162-69, 181; in New York City, 182-86; organizing in Kentucky after the strike, 175-81, 183, 198-99; and race relations, 114-15; religion, 130, 152-53; at Senate hearings, 136, 173; and the United Mine Workers, xxiv, 112, 123, 128, 131-32, 134, 139; in Washington state, xvii, 186-87; youth, 52, 66, 71-72, 111, 123-26
Garland, Jim, & His Kentucky Mountain Folk Singers, 183, 185
Garland, John (half brother), 26, 45-49, 62-63, 69-72
Garland, Lonie (sister), 27
Garland, Myrtle (cousin), 117-20
Garland, Oliver Perry "Peoria" (father), 26-27, 32, 34, 44-46, 52, 56, 62-63, 75-76; mining, x, 28-29, 37-38, 41, 94; preaching, 29-31, 41, 46-47, 57, 114
Garland, Richard (brother), x, 27, 34, 89, 91, 93, 97, 99, 100, 101, 130
Garland, Robert "Popeye" (nephew), 133
Garland, Sarah. *See* Gunning, Sarah Ogan
Garland family: genealogy, ix
Garland Orchestra, xvii, 187
General Motors, xix
ghosts, 42-45
ginseng, 67
Glendon, Ky., 145-48
Grace, Jim, 145-46
Grange, the, 187
Greasy Creek, Ky., 162, 166
Gunning, Sarah Ogan, xvi, 126, 130-31, 137, 159, 183, 185-86
gun thugs, xxii, xxix, 41, 98, 141, 161, 162; in Bell County, 130, 138, 148, 150, 163, 164-66; in Harlan County, 138, 145-46
Guthrie, Woody, xvi, 159, 184-85, 201

Hammond, John, Jr., 169
"Hard Times at Coleman's Mines," 122

Harlan, Ky., 137, 163
Harlan County, 118, 123, 133, 136, 141-42; development of coalfields in, xx, 40, 102; National Miners Union in, 145-46, 148, 149
Harlan County Coal Operators Association, 40, 135
Harvey, John, 150, 156
Hathaway, Clarence, 176, 177, 181
Hays, John, 52
Hays, Lee, xvi
Heads of Families program, 189, 192, 193
Hensley, Alfred, 120
Herd, John (cousin), 33
Hickerson, Harold, 198
Hill, Joe, 185
Hindrickson, John, 43-45
Hindrickson, Press, 43-45
"Hold the Fort," 161
Holiness church, 80, 85-87, 145; tenets of, 81, 83-84, 86. *See also* Snakehandlers church
Hoover administration, xiv, 189
horses. *See* livestock
hounds, 71-74
housing, 39, 50-51, 89, 133-34, 135, 191
Houston, Cisco, xvi, 184, 185
Howard, Jim, 178
Hughes, Roy, xxix-xxv
"Hungry Ragged Blues," 149-50
hunting, 4, 56, 71-74. *See also* hounds

"I Am Going around This World," 158-59
"I Am Going to Organize, Baby Mine," 159, 185
"I Don't Want Your Millions, Mister," xvi, 200-201
"I Have a Letter from My Father," 87
"I Have a Letter from Your Sire, Baby Mine," 87, 158
"I Have a Little Pussy," 184-85
immigrants, 25, 119, 123, 131
Industrial Workers of the World (IWW), 140, 161, 183-84, 199
injunctions, 147, 168
Inman, Pauline (niece), 106-9

In New Kentucky, 158
International Labor Defense (ILD), xxvi, 148, 176, 179, 199
International Workers Order, 183

Jackson, Aunt Molly (half sister), 26, 34, 44-45, 62-63, 129, 130; and marriage, 63, 64; and midwifery, 33, 182; in New York City, 64, 181, 183, 186; singer/songwriter, xvi, 61-63, 100, 149-50, 184
Jackson, Bill, 64
Jackson, Harry, 150, 151, 162, 176
"Jack Straw Fannigan," 77-78
Jellico, Tenn., 137, 175
Jesus Only church, 81
"Jim Bolin," 57-58
Jones, W.B.: organizing effort, 136-37, 140-42, 145, 148

Kaiser shipyard, 186-87
Kemenovitch, Vince, 150, 156
Kentucky rifle, 74, 75
Kettle Island, Ky., 155
Kitts, Ky., 105, 134, 137-38
Knox County, Ky. *See* Brush Creek, Ky.
Knoxville, Tenn., 148, 167-68, 171
Ku Klux Klan, 28, 131

Laffoon, Ruby, 179-80
LaFollette, Robert, 111
LaGuardia, Fiorello, 136, 173
Lampell, Millard, 186
Lawson, Green, xxvii-xxviii
Ledbetter, Huddie, xvi, 184, 185
Lee Hollow, Ky., 155, 157
Lewis, John L., xiii, xxii, xxviii, 112, 113, 130; opposition to, xxi, xxv, 131-32, 139
Liberty Coal Company, 113
Library of Congress, xvi, 183
Liggett-Myers Company, 178
livestock: chickens, 69-70, 78; horses, 75-77; mules, 77, 98-99; oxen, 15-16
logging, 13, 37
Log Mountain, 157
Lomax, Alan, 183

Louisville, Ky., 176, 178
"Loving Nancy," 14
Lucas, Bob (uncle), 26
Lucas, Wilson (grandfather), 13, 17-18, 20-22, 43
Lynch, Ky., 123, 135-36

McFarland, Alfred, 92-93, 115
March of Tears, 17
marriage, 31, 63, 65, 74, 78
May Day, 183
"May I Go with You, Johnny," 186
Meeks, Bill, 157
Methodist church, 5, 80, 81, 86
Michelson, Clarina, 156, 157, 167, 175
Middlesboro, Ky., 77, 151
midwifery, 33, 120, 182
mills, 9-11, 15
Mills, John, 44-45, 63, 75
Missionary Baptist church, 27, 29, 31, 130, 145; tenets of, 5, 31, 80, 118
Monhollen, Boxknocker, 32, 49
moonshiners, 113, 116
"Mr. Condiff," 62
Murray, Phil, xxiii, 139-40
"My Old Kentucky Home," 74

National Committee for the Defense of Political Prisoners. *See* Dreiser, Theodore
National Guard, 121
National Industrial Recovery Act, xxviii
National Labor Relations Act, xxviii
National Miners Union, xiv, xv, xxv-xxvii, 143-44, 158, 161, 164, 168, 198; and Communist Party, 155, 164, 190, 199; meetings, 147, 151; membership, 145-49; 1931-32 strike, 147-48, 150-51, 155, 156-58, 168; after 1931-32 strike, xv, 172, 175-78, 180-81. *See also* Garland, Jim
National Workers party, 178
New Deal, xv, 178
Newport Folk Festival, xvii, 187
New York City, 169, 171, 181, 183
New York University, 183
Night Riders, 28
1977 coal strike, 113

Ogan, Andrew, 137
"Old Kentucky Cradle Me," 74
"Old Sheep," 186
"Old Ship of Zion," 23-24, 159-60
"Old Zeb Coon," 14

pack peddlers, 11
Parks, Doris, 152, 156, 158
"Parting Hand, The," 7-8
Peabody Coal Company, xxiv-xxv, xix, 40, 109, 127, 133, 141
"Peg and Awl," 12-13
People's Songs, 187
Perry, Ky., 146
Peters, Mike, 187
Pineville, Ky., 67-68, 77, 115; National Miners Union in, 150-51, 156, 165-67; United Mine Workers in, 137, 139-40
Pineville Sun, 154, 155, 158
poor farms, 38-39
"Poor Old Coal Miner Left out in the Cold," 51
portal-to-portal pay system, 108-9, 199
preachers, 4-5, 29-31, 60, 80, 85; and 1931-32 strike, 146, 165
Presbyterian church, 80
"Pretty Polly," 194
Primitive Baptist church, 5-8
Progressive Miners Union, 144
Progressive party, 187
prostitution, 13, 47-48, 113, 115
Public Works Administration (PWA), 178

Quackenbush, Mamie, 183
quilting bees, 61

"Rack Fa Diddle I Day," 10
railroads, 23-24, 37, 38, 89; Louisville and Nashville (L&N), xii-xiii, xix
Red Bird Settlement School, 52
Reed, Charley, 143-44, 145, 150
Reese, Sam, 181
Roark, Girt, 114
Robinson, Earl, xvi
Roosevelt, Franklin D., xv, 178
Ross, Ky., 130, 146
Roth, Ky., 84

"Sad the Day," 24-25
Sampson, Flem, 141, 180
Scotia mines, 114
scrip, 40, 89
Seeger, Peter, xvi
Set Back, 70-71
Shahn, Ben, 149
sharecropping, 27, 29, 31, 39
"She'll Be Coming around the Mountain When She Comes," 160
shoemakers, 12-13
Simms, Harry, xviii, xxvii-xxviii, 151, 153, 156, 165-69, 201; and Jim Garland, 150, 158, 162. *See also* "Ballad of Harry Simms, The"
slavery, 20-22
Slick Lizard, Ky., 100
Slinger, Dan (Dan Brooks), xxvi
Smith, Bolter, 136
Smith, Jack, 181
Smith, Walter B., 167, 174
Smithsonian Folklife Festival, xvii-xviii, 188
Snakehandlers church, 81-85. *See also* Holiness church
Socialist party, 34
songs, 11, 14, 57, 61, 73, 159, 160-61; lining out, 7, 23-24. *See also individual songs by title*
soup kitchens, 145, 152
Spivey, Serina, 121
Spivey, Wilson, 127-28
Stachel, Jack, 177, 181
state militia, 41, 43, 112, 120, 141, 152, 180-81
Stewart, Jim, 15, 64
stir-offs, 53
Stone, W.J., 167, 168
Straight Creek, Ky., 33, 70-71, 81, 114-15, 131, 140, 142, 146, 152, 155; Straight Creek strike, 113, 117, 118-19, 120
strikebreakers, 116-17, 130, 135, 147
superstitions, 32, 42-45, 66
Supplemental Security Income (SSI), 189, 192, 193, 195

Taub, Allan, 179
Tennessee Valley Authority (TVA), 105
"They Sell Us the Same Colored Hat," xvii
Thomas Hymn Book, 6, 8
tobacco, 27-28
Tobacco Wars, 28
Trade Union Unity League (TUUL), 149, 176, 177, 181
Turnblazer, Bill, xxii, xxiv, 132, 137, 139, 141, 149

unemployed councils, 175, 178, 181
"Union Cannon Ball, The," 184
United Mines Workers (UMW), 37, 40-41, 189; contracts, 112, 123: development of, xi, xx, xxi, 38, 40, 102, 108-9, 112, 131-32, 142, 146, 202; District 19, xxii, xxiv, 112, 131, 137; District 23, 112; in Harlan County, xxv, xxix, 118; membership, x, 38, 106, 109, 112-13, 116; and the National Miners Union, xxviii, 149, 164, 190; in Pineville, xxiii-xxiv, 139-40; practices of, 114, 128, 129, 131, 161, 168; strikes, xi, xiii, xxi-xxii, 37-38, 113, 116, 121; after 1931-32 strike, xv, 179, 181. *See also* Lewis, John L.; Jones, W.B.
U.S. Department of Labor, 164
U.S. Senate Subcommittee on Labor, 136, 168, 173
U.S. Steel, xix, 40, 109, 135-36

Valentine, Harvey, 81-84, 145, 198

"Wabash Cannon Ball," 184
Wagner Act, 190, 199
Wakefield, Jessie, xxvi
Wallace, Henry, 187, 190
Wallins Creek, Ky., 140, 145, 152, 155, 176
Walsend, Ky., 24
"We Are the Heroes of Kentucky," 14
Weber, Joe, 162, 167, 175, 179-80
"Welcome the Traveler Home," 174
"We'll Join that Picket Line, One and All," 161
West, Don, 181
White, Ardill, 17, 21, 27-29

"White Slave, The," 183-84
Whitfield Coal Company, 134. See also Kitts, Ky.
Wilson, Al "High Pockets," 70-71
Wilson, Boyd, 52
Wilson, R.E., 151
Wisconsin Steel (International Harvester), xix
"Woa Back Buck," 15
Workers Alliance, 182, 183
Workers International Relief (WIR), 145, 147-48, 156, 168, 172, 198, 199
Workman's Compensation, 93, 94, 103, 120
Works Progress Administration (WPA), xvi, 109, 182, 190
World's Fair, 1939, xvi, 185
Writers' Guild, 173-74

Young Communist League (YCL), 150, 165, 169, 177